Ecuador's Environmental |

Ecuador's Environmental Revolutions

Ecoimperialists, Ecodependents, and Ecoresisters

Tammy L. Lewis

The MIT Press
Cambridge, Massachusetts
London, England

This book was set in Stone Sans and Stone Serif by Toppan Best-set Premedia Limited. Printed and bound in the United States of America.

Library of Congress Cataloging-in-Publication

Names: Lewis, Tammy L., author.
Title: Ecuador's environmental revolutions : ecoimperialists, ecodependents, and ecoresisters / Tammy L. Lewis.
Description: Cambridge, MA : MIT Press, [2016] | Includes bibliographical references and index.
Identifiers: LCCN 2015039697| ISBN 9780262034296 (hardcover : alk. paper) | ISBN 9780262528771 (pbk. : alk. paper)
Subjects: LCSH: Environmentalism—Ecuador—History. | Environmental policy—Ecuador—History. | Sustainable development—Ecuador—History.
Classification: LCC GE199.E2 L49 2015 | DDC 333.709866—dc23 LC record available at http://lccn.loc.gov/2015039697

10 9 8 7 6 5 4 3 2 1

Contents

Acknowledgments

In small and large and sometimes unknown ways, many people have helped me bring this book to fruition.

The National Science Foundation, the Institute for Global Conflict and Cooperation, Muhlenberg College's Class of '32, the Fulbright Commission, and the Leonard and Claire Tow Foundation provided the financial support.

For sharing copies of their organizational surveys, I thank JoAnn Carmin, Bob Edwards, Patrick Gillham, Russ Dalton, and Robert Rohrschneider. A special thanks is due to JoAnn for walking me through the process of conducting an online survey and for bouncing around ideas with me. I miss her.

For helping me with the lay of the land in Quito and for accompanying me and my daughters on our mini-adventures, I thank my fellow Fulbrighters and their families: Susan Webster and Hernán Navarrete, Agnez Czeblakow, and Chuck "Carlito" Bergman. Karen Aguiler and Suzana Cabeza de Vaca, both of the Fulbright Commission, educated me in Ecuadorian customs and Susana reviewed and corrected my Spanish on the 2007 Ecuadorian Environmental Organization Survey. Also in Quito, Montse Rios kept me smiling with her witty humor and helpful suggestions; Diego Quiroga provided me with an intellectual connection at the Universidad San Francisco de Quito; Tania Ledgerberger and Susan Poats provided me with useful links and insightful feedback. Carlos Zorrilla inspired me and my students at Brooklyn College.

Thanks to Erika Sutherland for translating my important documents. Jennifer Jarson from the Muhlenberg College library tracked down indexes of environmental organizations. My colleagues from the Sociology and Anthropology Department at Muhlenberg took on additional duties so that I could be on leave in 2006 to 2007. Special thanks to Janine Chi and Sue Jansen. Tracy Kline went out of her way to help transcribe interviews. At

Brooklyn College, Isabel Rodriguez transcribed interviews in Spanish. Rebecca Boger compiled the map of Ecuador.

My honest, smart colleague and friend Craig Humphrey took time away from his retirement to read and comment on the entire manuscript. He and I and the ghost of Allan Schnaiberg have had some interesting interactions.

Beth Clevenger at the MIT Press has been clear, gracious, and professional in shepherding me through the process of moving this project from manuscript to book. I especially thank her for choosing three insightful reviewers whose useful comments are evident in these pages: Steven R. Brechin, Pamela L. Martin, and David Naguib Pellow. Thank you reviewers. Thanks, too, to Miranda Martin and Dana Andrus at the MIT Press.

Without my family, I could not do this work. Thank you Mom and Enoch for taking care of Anna and Isabel when I traveled. Mom, thanks, too, for transcription assistance. Thanks Dad for managing the house when I was away. Thank you Anna and Isabel for enduring my absences and for being good sports in our Ecuadorian adventures. Finally, for listening to my anecdotes, talking through conceptual issues, reading and re-reading my work, enduring the trials of lost luggage, and being a steady source of support, my endearing gratitude to Ken Gould.

The individuals who participated in this research have dozens of projects competing for their time. Thank you for talking to me and completing a long survey. It is my hope and intention that your successes, frustrations, and hopes for Ecuador are accurately portrayed herein and that this book assists you and your organizations in creating a more sustainable Ecuador. I am humbled by the pride you have in your nation and your commitment to your work. I dedicate this to the individuals and institutions working for *buen vivir*.

Brooklyn, New York, August 2015

Acronyms

AE	Acción Ecológica (Ecological Action)
ANA	Asamblea Nacional Ambiente (National Environmental Assembly)
C-CONDEM	Coordinadora para la Defensa del Ecosistema Manglar (Coordinator for the Defense of the Mangrove Ecosystem)
CAAM	Comisión Ambiental de la Presidencia de la República (President's Environmental Advisory Commission)
CEDENMA	Comité Ecuatoriano para la Defensa de la Naturaleza y el Medio Ambiente (Ecuadorian Committee for the Defense of Nature and the Environment)
CORDAVI	Corporacíon de la Defensa de la Vida (Corporation for the Defense of Life)
CI	Conservation International
DECOIN	Defensa y Conservación Ecológica de Intag (Defense and Ecological Conservation of Intag)
GTZ	German Technical Cooperation Agency
IMF	International Monetary Fund
INGO	International nongovernmental organization
IUCN	International Union for the Conservation of Nature
Natura	Fundación Natura (Nature Foundation)
NGO	Nongovernmental organization
SMA	Social movement actor
TOP	Treadmill of production
UNCED	United Nations' Conference on Environment and Development
UNESCO	United Nations Educational, Scientific and Cultural Organization
USAID	United State Agency for International Development
WWF	World Wide Fund for Nature

1   Key Players and Conflicting Goals in the Development Trajectory

Our interest in history is not owing to any view that the future is inevitable .... We study history to discern the alternatives within which human reason and human freedom can now make history. We study historical social structures, in brief, in order to find within them the ways in which they are and can be controlled. For only in this way can we come to know the limits and the meaning of human freedom.

—C. Wright Mills, *The Sociological Imagination*, 1959: 174

Keep the Oil in the Soil?

In 2007 Ecuador's newly inaugurated President stood before the United Nations to propose an initiative to address global climate change. Ecuador, a small nation in South America, is biologically diverse, petroleum rich, and economically poor, about a third of its population living below the poverty level.[1] President Rafael Correa presented a plan to keep a large portion of Ecuador's untapped oil reserves "in the soil," if the international community would contribute 50 percent of the revenues that Ecuador could have earned from twenty years of extraction into a trust fund for the country. The initiative would slow climate change, preserve biodiversity, and protect two indigenous groups in the Amazon.[2] According to the United Nations, "The Initiative is based on a paradigm change towards a post-fossil fuel model of development and builds on the internationally agreed [upon] Millennium Development Goals."[3] The proposal is called the Yasuní-ITT Initiative: Yasuní for the name of the national park where the oilfields are located, and ITT for the name of the oilfields that would be preserved, Ishpingo-Tambococha-Tiputini. It was a bold and innovative plan for a new development model, but it failed.

The Ecuadorian government brokered similar proposals in the past, leveraging the country's high biodiversity against foreign commitments to funding, with the goal of protecting its environment for the good of humanity. In the late 1980s and early 1990s Ecuador agreed to protect its flora and fauna by creating and managing national parks in exchange for having a portion of its foreign debt reduced. International conservationists supported these "debt-for-nature swaps" for the same reasons that climate change activists hail the Yasuní-ITT Initiative: the mechanisms solve two problems at once. They protect the "global" environment and they provide economic resources for the nation foregoing natural resource extraction. These "win-win" situations, providing both environmental protection and economic development, are the hallmarks of "sustainable development." At the time of the debt-for-nature swaps, the state was weak, and the ideology was such that private groups—environmental nongovernmental organizations (NGOs)—within Ecuador managed the funds. Times have changed and a stronger, greener state now proposes to operate such projects.

The Yasuní-ITT Initiative emerged in the context of other national-level support for environmental protection in Ecuador, highlighted by the inclusion of the rights for nature in the new 2008 Constitution. It also came at a time when Ecuador's people had just chosen a new path with President Correa's election. His party, Alianza PAIS (Country Alliance/Proud and Sovereign Fatherland), promises a "citizen's revolution," which among other key features, vows to provide state-funded health and education, and other social and economic benefits to the people.[*] Figuring out how to finance and deliver these benefits is the primary task of Correa's administration. If the Yasuní-ITT Initiative had been funded, the contributions would be available for projects related to the state's environmental goals, such as transitions to renewable energies, not necessarily for across the board social development. In Correa's appeals to the international community, he reminded the world that if they would not fund the proposal, Ecuador had limited options and immediate needs. "Plan B" was to drill. State revenues from drilling could be used for the social and economic goals of the citizen's revolution.

Like most nations, Ecuador's economy has been built on its natural resources. Petroleum extraction is the nation's leading source of revenue, accounting for more than half of its export earnings. However, oil drilling is a major cause of environmental destruction. Other forms of extraction, such as timber and mining, also serve economic interests and threaten biodiversity. Like many "developing" nations, Ecuador faces high debt in addition to its poverty. In 2012 its public external debt amounted to 21 percent of its GDP.[5] Thus its citizens are not the only ones expecting economic growth, so are its creditors. Ecuador is embedded in a global system concerned with environmental protection, dependent on petroleum, and expecting loan repayment. Ecuador must balance these competing concerns at the same time the administration tries to deliver its promise to address its citizens' needs.

Despite President Correa's leadership in the Yasuní-ITT proposal and Ecuador's new constitutional rights for nature, the state's multiple goals are frequently at odds with each other. The challenges are evident in the government's sometimes contradictory actions. For instance, on the one hand, the state's Yasuní-ITT Initiative would relinquish drilling for oil in order to protect one of the most biodiverse places on the planet and the indigenous peoples living there, thus supporting Ecuador's environmental agenda. On the other hand, the government has changed laws to make it easier for the state to profit from mining, contributing to its economic growth and social welfare agenda. The Ministry of the Environment and the Ministry of Mines do not have equal power. Typically resource extraction wins.

Private Ecuadorian environmental groups pressure the state to prioritize its environmental goals. Most of Ecuador's leading environmental organizations are embedded in transnational environmental networks that link them financially to transnational organizations, such as the World Wide Fund for Nature (WWF) and Conservation International (CI). Because of these connections and the Ecuadorian state's commitments to international financial institutions, there are significant "outside" influences that enter into national-level policy making.

In August 2013 President Correa ended the Yasuní-ITT Initiative declaring that "the world has failed us ... in our fight against climate change" by not providing enough funding for the project. At the time only $13 million had been deposited in the trust (the goal was $3.6 billion). The state announced it would drill for oil. Immediately environmentalists and indigenous groups protested in the streets of Quito, Ecuador's capital of approximately 2.5 million people. YouTube videos showed impassioned musicians singing of Yasuní's beauty and demonstrators being shot with rubber bullets. Online petitions were distributed around the world. Ecuadorians, global environmentalists, and human rights activists were not ready to give up on the promise of a post-fossil fuel future.[6] A social movement coalition called YASunidos (a creative combination of YAS from Yasuní and *unidos*, which can be translated as joined or united) collected signatures to require a referendum for the people to vote on the issue. As I write (2015), the issue is unresolved though development for drilling is proceeding. A transnational campaign to prevent drilling has been launched and the updates from across the globe arrive daily.

A complex set of actors—the Correa administration, indigenous groups, potential international funders, and YASunidos—are entangled in this struggle over the future use of Ecuador's natural resources.[7] In this instance, it appears that the state will have the final say in deciding the outcome. However, in earlier times, other actors with different ideologies have been the final arbiters. In the 1990s, international conservationists favoring sustainable development protected national parks; in 2013, a state with a populist agenda chose to drill for oil in those parks.

Issues and the Case

I examine the main players, forces, and mechanisms that have shaped the public and private efforts to shift Ecuador's development model toward a sustainable path, some form of a post-fossil fuel model of development, and assess the conditions affecting whether Ecuador will develop along sustainable or extractivist lines, or something in between or completely different. I pay particular attention to the role of the environmental movement industry, including national and transnational actors, in affecting Ecuador's development path.

The Ecuadorian story is a common one in the Global South: a national government's environmental protection goals are at odds with its economic growth goals. Members of the government are split based on their roles. The nation's citizens and its international creditors push for growth. Some citizens and nongovernmental organizations press for environmental protection. Additionally players from abroad, namely transnational environmentalists, present an external set of actors with financial resources to the conversation. The question is, Which side will win (or at least have influence) and which side will lose? What are the conditions that determine which side shapes history?

However, the case of Ecuador is unique in two ways that are less common in the storyline, and are reasons to consider it "most likely to succeed in sustainability" among nations in the Global South. First, Ecuador is a high biodiversity country and therefore of particular interest to transnational environmentalists with resources. Second, a result of the persistent work of activists, its 2008 Constitution elevates the rights of nature to a level that, to that moment, no other constitution anywhere had granted nature. Given these favorable international and national circumstances,

Ecuador's chances appear good for developing along sustainable lines. However, if Ecuador is unable to proceed sustainably, it raises the question, why not? What does it take for nations to alter their development trajectory toward a more sustainable path? Bad news from Ecuador would be bad news for the rest of the Global South in terms of sustainability. As goes Ecuador, so goes the earth.

Sustainable Development or Extractive Development or an Alternative to Development?

In considering the pressures to simultaneously protect the environment and develop economically, I use the broad lens of "sustainability" that has been advanced since the concept was popularized in Rio de Janeiro at the 1992 United Nations Conference on Environment and Development (UNCED, also referred to as the Earth Summit).[8] At that time the concept of "sustainable development"—the idea that environmental protection and economic growth are not incompatible—amounted to a paradigm shift.[9] It reflects a transition in environmental ideologies from one of simple nature protection, what in the United States was conceptualized by the conservationism of John Muir and the Sierra Club, to a more utilitarian view, what in the United States can be understood as the Chief US Forester Gifford Pinchot's and the progressives' preservationism: "for the greatest good of the greatest number for the longest time."[10] In Rio, poorer nations asked richer nations to support them in their efforts to achieve sustainable development.

Sustainable development was later articulated as having three pillars, illustrated as three legs of a stool: (1) environmental protection, (2) economic development, and (3) social justice. The addition of a "social" leg acknowledged the importance of power and decision-making roles regarding the choices of development. The social aspect has been interpreted in a number of ways, including at least two facets. The first, which focuses on process, is meaningful social participation in the choices that are made about the uses of natural resources. The second, focused on outcome, is the equitable distribution of environmental goods and bads. To label an activity "sustainable," it must combine these additional elements. Numerous definitions and critiques of the concept exist, but that is not the purpose of this discussion.[11] For this analysis I use the following definition: *sustainable development protects the environment, facilitates economic well-being, and enables people to have the capacity to make their own choices about resource use.* There will always be trade-offs among these elements of sustainability. Sustainable development seems utopic, if not elusive, but certainly desirable. Who could be against it!? One of the main tasks of this book is to understand if some approximation of sustainable development is possible, and under what conditions it could be achieved.

Given the historical record, it is more likely that traditional extractive development that leads to negative social and environmental outcomes will prevail in Ecuador.[12] There is ample evidence of a "resource curse" also known as the "paradox of plenty" for oil-rich nations. To "develop," nations exploit their oil. However, extractive development in resource-rich nations is ironically associated with slow economic and social development, internal conflict, corruption, volatility, and environmental degradation, thus the curse.[13] Similarly projects to "modernize" the "third world," even those not focused on oil, have not led to their desired outcomes, and have left many behind to redefine "development" and "progress."[14] Neoliberal policies have curtailed investments in social welfare and the environment. In the late twentieth and early twenty-first centuries, Latin America, in particular, has tried to move away from these schemes, which have left most of the region poor, indebted, and environmentally distraught. Nevertheless, in resource-rich countries, the fall back option is extraction. Indeed Ecuador's, Plan B, to drill, looms, though it is not inevitable. If and how to drill remains a choice, but oil extraction is the path of least resistance.[15]

While Ecuador's continued extractive practices provide sufficient evidence that the state is continuing along traditional development paths, alternative, "post development" challenges are also evident, even at the state level. In addition to the Yasuní-ITT Initiative, Ecuador has proposed an alternative to traditional development in the state's Plan Nacional para el Buen Vivir, 2009–2013 (National Plan for Good Living). This plan was developed during President Rafael Correa's first term as part of the "citizen's revolution" platform that brought him to power. The Plan does two things. First, it rejects the traditional development paradigm, which has not succeeded. Second, it presents an alternative vision for the country's future: *buen vivir* (in Spanish) and *sumak kawsay* (in Quechua, an indigenous language spoken in the Andes), generally translated into English as "good living."[16] The Plan merits quoting and some analysis.

Much of the Plan is a refutation of the traditional development paradigm. It critiques the Global North's definition of development due to its evident failure to improve the quality of life for the majority of citizens;

and then because of its focus on extraction, its unequal power relationships, and its lack of environmental sustainability:

The prevalent concept of "development" is undergoing a profound crisis. In part this is only due to the colonial perspective from which the concept is derived. But it is also a result of its failure throughout the world. The present global crisis has demonstrated that it is impossible to maintain the current patterns of accumulation. For the South, it has meant an extractivist and devastating path to development, with unequal relations of power and trade with the North. Moreover the unlimited consumption patterns derived from this model are leading the entire planet to collapse, given that the biosphere is unable to ensure its capacity for regeneration. It is essential, therefore, to promote new modes of production, consumption, and organization of life and coexistence.[17]

The Plan then summarizes the alternative vision, which does not focus on traditional development measures, such as increasing gross domestic product (GDP) per capita. Good living is defined as:

... [c]overing needs, achieving a dignified quality of life and death; loving and being loved; the healthy flourishing of all individuals in peace and harmony with nature; and achieving an indefinite reproduction perpetuation of human cultures. Good Living implies having free time for contemplation and personal emancipation; enabling the expansion and flourishing of people's liberties, opportunities, capabilities and potentialities so as to simultaneously allow society, specific territories, different collective identities, and each individual, understood both in universal and relative terms, to achieve their objectives in life (without causing any kind of material or subjective dominance over any other individual). Our concept of Good Living compels us to re-build the public sphere in order to recognize, understand and value ourselves as diverse but equal individuals, and in order to advance reciprocity and mutual recognition, enable self-advancement, and build a shared social future. ...[18]

Sumak kawsay is an indigenous concept that precedes the idea of Western "development" and does not use it as a referent. The concept includes aspects of what we would consider sustainable development, but it goes well beyond sustainable development to deeply consider quality of life. This is a clear alternative to the traditional development perspective that values economic growth above all else.

Countries like Ecuador have choices regarding their development trajectory and they are grappling with them. They can continue down the path of least resistance, which leads to extraction. Or they can walk along a greener and more just "sustainable" path. Or they can use their machetes to clear a path through their dense jungle, creating a new way toward *buen vivir/sumak kawsay*.

The Treadmill of Production and Key Actors in the Development Trajectory

The specific questions about Ecuador's development trajectory connect to environmental sociologists' concerns about the institutions that shape sustainability decisions for society. The treadmill of production (TOP) theory provides a logic for understanding the reasons that major social actors favor economic growth and production, which go hand in hand with environmental disruptions and social dislocations, rather than creating some sort of steady state of economic growth along with environmental and social protections.[19] The theory was developed to explain the acceleration of resource withdrawals (extraction) and additions (pollution) in the industrialized world in the period following World World II. In short, the theory argues that powerful social actors (political and economic elites) benefit when there is increased production and economic growth, despite the fact that growth causes environmental degradation and social dislocation. The key actors in the treadmill model are corporations, the state, and citizen-workers (see figure 1.1).[20]

Corporations favor.economic growth because their main goal is profit. Increased production increases profit. Corporations will resist actions, such as environmental regulations, that limit profit. The drive for profit leads them to replace labor with energy in production, which results in both increasing ecological harm and decreasing social benefits. The state prefers growth so that it can accumulate tax revenues from corporations and workers, which provide it with its base of power. The state also needs economic growth to provide jobs for those displaced by corporations' investments in labor-saving technologies. The state has a dual role, however. Accumulation is one of its roles, and legitimation is its other. The state legitimates its role by providing protections for citizens. These protections come in a

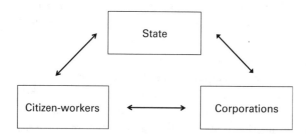

Figure 1.1
Three players in the treadmill of production (TOP) schema

number of forms, such as protection from unhealthy drinking water (environmental regulations) and protection from unsafe working conditions (labor regulations). Thus, unlike the corporations, the state must answer to citizen-workers, which can be a counterweight to the state's interests in unregulated growth.[21] Citizen-workers, like the state, have a dual perspective with regard to economic growth. On the one hand, citizen-workers need jobs for material well-being. However, they also want clean water and healthy workplaces. Citizen-workers, thought of as "civil society," have the potential to be the change-makers that force the state to take regulatory actions to slow the treadmill of production and prevent environmental degradation and social dislocation. When the treadmill does not benefit citizen-workers, they can collectively apply pressure on the state to alter the trajectory.

This analysis fleshes out the roles of the "citizen-worker" by looking at the actors in Ecuador that are seeking to alter the state's role in accelerating or decelerating the treadmill of production, and how they set their agendas. I assess two main categories: nongovernmental organizations (NGOs) and social movement actors (SMAs) (see figure 1.2). NGOs are private organizations that are officially recognized by the state to act on behalf of a sector (e.g., the environment). In the United States, they are what we call nonprofit organizations. They are bound by state rules and tend to be professionalized because they need to provide formal documentation of what they do and whether they in fact act as nonprofits for tax purposes. They have paid staff. They tend to work within the system and are reform oriented in promoting change. Social movement actors are

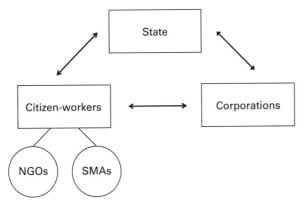

Figure 1.2
NGOs and SMAs as subsets of citizen-workers in the TOP theory

individuals or groups of actors bound together in their work for a common end (e.g., protecting the environment or ensuring labor protections). Their work is often precipitated by local challenges that mobilize a geographically bound community. They are mission driven. They may or may not be officially recognized by the state as an NGO, though typically they are not. Their resource base tends to be volunteers. SMAs are often critical of the existing system, looking for alternatives to it, and are thus considered radical.[22]

In a globalized world, transnational funders can have considerable effect on citizen-actors' decisions (see figure 1.3). Transnational funders affect what types of groups exist, which thrive, the content of their agendas, and the tactics and strategies they employ. Transnational actors include public and private organizations operating in more than one nation. They include bilateral public funders, such as the United States Agency for International Development (USAID), multilateral public funders, such as the Global Environment Facility (GEF), and private funders, such as Conservation International (CI). Transnational funders are a subset of what Margaret Keck and Kathryn Sikkink call "transnational advocacy networks" in their influential book *Activists beyond Borders*.[23] "A transnational advocacy network includes those relevant actors working internationally on an issue, who are bound together by shared values, a common discourse, and dense exchanges of information and services." Keck and Sikkink emphasize information sharing, but this analysis focuses on the distribution of material resources from outside of a country into a country (outside of Ecuador into Ecuador) to affect national civil society and potentially the state. By conceptualizing

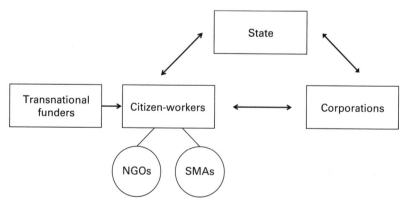

Figure 1.3
Placing the TOP in a transnational social movement context

the TOP model globally, we can better understand how transnational forces affect states' choices, and the linkage between global processes and treadmill acceleration or deceleration.

Schnaiberg's (1980) original formulation of the TOP model described the relationship between production expansion and ecological limits as the "socioenvironmental dialectic." He outlined three types of syntheses that could resolve the tension between the two. The syntheses were contingent on the choices of the actors engaged in the treadmill of production, with an emphasis on the extent to which the state would limit access to the environment for production, and in effect, ecological impact. The first is *economic synthesis* in which there are barely any state impediments to accessing the environment, and thus there is unregulated and unlimited expanding production, which causes expanding environmental problems. A second synthesis is *managed scarcity*, which involves the state creating and enforcing regulations, and as such reduces access and impact to the environment for production in order to protect the environment.[24] The third outcome is *ecological synthesis* in which the state limits producers' access to the environment based on scientifically determined biophysical limits of what is environmentally sustainable. He states, "These models [ecological syntheses] largely focus on ecosystem protection, especially on sustaining biodiversity in all ecosystems"[25] and "would entail the state's substantial control over ecosystems, without regard to issues of profitability and of wages/employment."[26]

The economic synthesis requires the fewest changes to models of development that have dominated much of the traditional extractivist development in the Global South to date; the ecological synthesis requires the most. The economic synthesis assumes that resources are infinite; managed scarcity recognizes natural limits and focuses on recycling and reuse; "the ecological syntheses involve far greater reuse and non-use of goods."[27] To put this in parallel with the discussion about Ecuador's development trajectory, extractive development aligns with the economic synthesis; sustainable development with managed scarcity; and aspects of *buen vivir/sumak kawsay* with the ecological synthesis. In a later formulation of the syntheses, Schnaiberg (2007) argued that in the ecological synthesis, the environment is valued for its use value rather than its exchange value; this parallels the ideology of the proponents of *buen vivir*. To relate these syntheses to the concrete choices of the Ecuadorian state, unrestrained oil drilling represents an economic synthesis, oil drilling with environmental rules limiting where, in what manner, and how much oil can be drilled is a form of managed scarcity, and keeping the oil in the soil through the Yasuní-ITT typifies an ecological synthesis. (See table 1.1.)

Schnaiberg's analysis of the treadmill of production suggests that the most fruitful path toward ecological synthesis is in the formation of coalitions between social groups. He concludes *The Environment: From Surplus to Scarcity* arguing, "The treadmill of political capitalism was not built overnight, nor will it disappear in the short term. Sustained efforts at consciousness-raising, commitment to political conflict and the development of

Table 1.1

Development trajectories and Schnaiberg's syntheses

Schnaiberg's terms →	Economic synthesis	Managed scarcity	Ecological synthesis
Associated development path	Extractive development	Sustainable development	*Buen vivir/sumak kawsay*/good living
Related terms	traditional development model; dominant development paradigm; modernization; free markets	limits to growth; regulated markets	Alternative development; post-development; steady-state economics; de-growth
Importance of environmental protection	Not important	A range of policies	Central
State imposed constraints on market forces	None	Minor to substantial	Major limits
Pressure from citizen-workers for environmental protection	None	A range	Significant
Measures of success for synthesis	GNP	GNP & habitat protection & social choices & regulatory compliance	Human well-being & habitat protection & sovereignty/social choices
Ecuadorian examples	Unrestrained oil drilling (Chevron in the 1980s)	Oil drilling with environmental & social protections (current status)	Yasuní-ITT Initiative—keep the oil in the soil (future?)

Source: Adapted from Schnaiberg (2007)

coordination between environmentalist and social equity movements may serve to take it apart, strut by strut."[28] Concerted actions of citizen-workers have the potential to push the state toward managed scarcity and ecological syntheses.[29]

However, writing in 2004, Schnaiberg and his collaborators argued, "In the past 25 years, there have indeed been local, national, and multinational contests challenging the treadmill. Yet it is our assessment that the empirical history of the period from 1976 to 2004 is one in which the treadmill has only occasionally been slowed."[30] Globalization, they argue, has only made the situation worse inasmuch as *more of human activities all throughout the world fall under the influence of the treadmill institutions and logic* than was true in 1980" (their italics).[31] Globalization and the neoliberal project that went hand in hand with it arguably homogenized political economic systems.[32] In later work, they argued that because the treadmill of production had become global, transnational social movements and transnational social movement organizations were key actors in potentially slowing or dismantling the treadmill process.[33]

Frederick H. Buttel, another important thinker in environmental sociology, arrives at a similar conclusion in laying out alternative environmental futures. In one of his last publications (2003), he assessed mechanisms for environmental reform to understand which mechanism was the most promising way forward for a "more socially secure and environmentally friendly arrangement."[34] He argues, "When all is said and done, the pressures for an environmentally problematic business as usual ... have become so strong that citizen environmental mobilization is now the ultimate guarantor that public responsibility is taken to ensure environmental protection."[35] Both Schnaiberg and his colleagues and Buttel argue that social movement actors will be essential in creating some form of a sustainable future.

This book advances the treadmill of production theory and environmental sociology by illustrating how power shifts in the global economy interact with Ecuadorian environmental activism to alter development trajectories (Schnaiberg's syntheses). The ultimate goals are to understand how and why syntheses change over time and under what conditions ecological synthesis is most possible.

To understanding the changes in first, the environmental movement, and second, the development trajectory, I examine the motivations and actions of the main actors who have and are attempting to shift the course: the state, national environmental organizations, social movement activists, and transnational actors focused on sustainability. Over the period of history being examined (1978 to 2015), the power and influence of these actors has shifted, thus their roles are variable, not static. Below I explain key aspects of the lead actors that guide the analysis.

The State

The state is central to understanding national pursuits toward or away from sustainability. I examine three dimensions of the state's role in the development trajectory over time: (1) the strength of the state, (2) the ideology of the state, and (3) the openness of the state. State strength matters in terms of whether or not it can accomplish goals. In Ecuador, the state has varied from weak to strong. As a weak state, it did not have the capacity to accomplish goals, while under President Correa, it has been strengthened and gained capacity. Strong states can move their ideological goals forward, whether they are pro-sustainability or pro-extraction. Strong states favoring a sustainability program can do a lot to create and fund programs that contribute to social, economic, and environmental goals. If, however, strong states are focused on economic development and have natural resources to be extracted, they can also do a lot of harm to both the environmental and social bases of society. Weak states can be pliable to civil society (and by extension, transnational actors and others' ideologies), enabling changes to laws and regulations, even though they typically cannot be enforced. But not all states are "open" to civil society. Strong states can crush it or extort from it or work with it. Weak states can be so incapacitated that the organizations of civil society, such as health NGOs, education NGOs, and environmental NGOs, essentially fill the void left by the state to carry out projects that serve the public (or sometimes just private actors). The state and its dimensions—strength, ideology, and openness—are critical to understanding the development trajectory. These dimensions are also linked to the international political economy.

Nongovernmental Organizations (NGOs), and more specifically, national environmental organizations

Nongovernmental, civil society organizations have played a role in generating sustainable development in Latin America.[36] The organizations that have been most effective at advancing sustainable development have focused on environmental issues, and have defined themselves primarily as environmental organizations. By the threefold nature of the idea of sustainable development, economic development groups or social justice groups could have logically been its promoters, but it was primarily environmental organizations that embraced the concept and used it as justification to press governments to enact policies, primarily environmental ones.[37] While the environment was the initial foray into sustainable development, environmentalists later sought to build the social and economic legs of the stool, but the environment was the point of entry.[38] Many of the organizations that succeeded in moving nations closer to a sustainable development ideal were aided by allies from abroad: international bilateral aid organizations, such as the US Agency for International Development, and by transnational nongovernmental/transnational social movement organizations, such as Conservation International and Greenpeace. Like the state, national environmental organizations vary in terms of their strength (which is often a function of their resources) and their agenda. Unlike most states, they vary in terms of their staying power (i.e., how long can they survive), which is also a function of their resources. Three key dimensions of environmental organizations that I analyze over time are their resources, agenda, and survival. As with the state, these dimensions are linked to the international political economy.

Social Movement Activists (SMAs)

Social movement activists in Ecuador have also shaped the development trajectory. For instance, activists' concerns were incorporated into the 2008 Constitution. The social movement activists relevant to this discussion differ from national environmental organizations in three ways. First, social movement activists are sometimes organized into NGOs, and sometimes not; thus they are sometimes recognized as formal organizations by the government, but not as a rule. If they are organized into a group, but not formally registered, these are social movement organizations (SMOs). For simplicity, I lump SMOs within the SMA category. Second, social movement activists have a broader environmental agenda that includes social issues. Third, SMAs differ from environmental NGOs in their resource base. Both NGOs and SMAs need resources to be maintained, be they human resources, material resources, or financial resources. Typically Ecuadorian SMAs do not receive transnational funding. Their strength is not derived from foreign resources as much as it is from their volunteer power, activists' commitment to the mission, and their willingness to act. Volunteer power is directly driven by the degree to which SMAs are immediately impacted by grievances, such as oil spills, illnesses, and threats of extraction. Like the state and NGOs, social movement activists vary in terms of strength. The rise and fall of social activism is a function of the intersection of the rise and fall of social grievances and the openness/closure of the state. In the Ecuadorian context, social movement activists have been relatively independent from international influences and perhaps best express the concerns and desires of the Ecuadorian people. This is not to say that the international political economy does not have an effect on this category of actor, but the international influence has been less obviously pronounced than it is for the state or for national environmental organizations.

Transnational Organizations—Public and Private

State-led transnational organizations, such as bilateral aid agencies like the US Agency for International Development, and private transnational organizations, such as international conservation organizations like the World Wide Fund for Nature, have had significant influence on the public and private environmental sectors in Ecuador. For the most part their participation has moved the development trajectory toward environmental sustainability. For instance, transnational assistance has had strong positive effects on the creation of laws to protect the environment.[39] Many of the national park systems in Latin America and the Caribbean were created with such aid and closely resemble the National Park System in the United States. The goals of such systems are to conserve and protect large tracts of land. National environmental actors have told me that without foreign intervention, many of the parks and protected areas, which protect important ecosystems, such as the Amazon rainforest and the Galápagos islands, would have been lost due to development efforts. These actors provide transnational environmental aid, the type requested in Rio. However, the influence of foreign actors in national affairs also raised questions related to sustainable development, namely in the social pillar: Who decides what should be prioritized and how lands should be preserved or developed? Whose interests do these groups serve? The key dimensions in understanding the roles of transnational actors are (1) which groups they fund (including state versus private organizations), (2) the types of projects they fund, and (3) what agendas they promote, especially with regard to development.

The four key actors vary in strength/resources, ideology/agenda, and their capacity to influence the direction of "development" from 1978 to 2015.

The Research Strategy

I use the case of Ecuador to tell a story about the interwoven connections among international power, state power, national and transnational social movements, and development trajectories. I look at Ecuador historically, from the founding of its first environmental NGO, Fundación Natura, in 1978 under a military government, through neoliberalism, to 2015, two years after Fundación Natura folded, USAID announced its withdrawal, and Rafael Correa, Ecuador's longest serving president, founder of the party that created the "Citizen's Revolution" was re-elected for a second time. I construct the analysis around four key periods delineated by changes in transnational funding for environmental organizations. Each period serves as a case history for understanding the interactions among key actors and how their relationships affected the development trajectory: (1) movement origins (1978 to 1987), (2) neoliberal boom (1987 to 2000), (3) neoliberal bust (2000 to 2006), and (4) citizens' revolution (2006 to 2015).

I compiled data for this analysis over a long period of time using multiple methods. The manuscript is based on three types of data: (1) documents produced by transnational funders, the Ecuadorian government, NGOs, social movement activists and the media; (2) field work and interviews conducted in Ecuador in 1994–95, 2006–07 and 2013; and (3) an organizational survey of environmental NGOs conducted in 2007. I conducted seventy-one formal semi-structured interviews with transnational funders, government ministers, directors of NGOs, and social movement activists. Interview questions clustered around the themes of the environmental movement's history, organizations' histories, relations to transnational actors, and relations to the state. I conducted scores of informal interviews with environmentalists working at field sites, ecotourism entrepreneurs and others. I also attended NGO and SMA meetings, presentations by bilateral donors and state agencies, and visited contested sites. I toured sites and met with environmentalists in all four regions of the country (Amazon, Andes, Costa, and Galapágos) in three of the four time periods analyzed. Given the contested nature of the research, I have chosen to preserve my informants' anonymity by referencing them by the type of organization they represent and by a number rather than by name. When actors' names are used in the text, it is when I quote information from already published materials. When the numbering would make the interviewee identifiable by matching it up with other statements, I omitted the number of the interviewee and simply put the date of the interview. The research has been supported by the National Science Foundation, the Institute for Global Conflict and Cooperation, Muhlenberg College's Class of '32, the Fulbright Commission, and the Leonard and Claire Tow Foundation.

The influence of foreign actors from the Global North on Ecuador, especially from the United States, has risen and fallen during the period, peaking sometime during the 1990s, at the height of the Washington Consensus, and plunging after 9/11/01, when the United States focused its resources on the Middle East, and the consensus was weakened. The power of many national environmental groups rose and fell with international influence, as noted by the periodization. The power of the social movement activists, however, proved more independent from international influence. Coinciding with the Global North's shift of attention away from Latin America, regional allies from within Latin America began shifting to the left. Rafael Correa's citizen's revolution was in line with the Bolivarian Revolution, called for and led by Venezuelan President Hugo Chávez. Bolivarianism refers to the anticolonial movement led by Simón Bolivar in the nineteenth century. A number of Latin American nations invoke Bolivar in their search for independence from the forces of international neoliberal economics. One way they are attempting this is by de-linking from the global economic system. In 2007 the Union of South American Nations (UNASUR) was formed to create independence from some of those forces. These changing international tides created a context in which Rafael Correa was elected.

The key questions I address in the book are Ecuador specific and contribute to the growing number of studies that focus on environmentalism in the Global South:[40] (1) What role has transnational funding played in the Ecuadorian environmental movement? (2) How has the Ecuadorian environmental movement changed over time and why? and (3) How has the Ecuadorian environmental movement's relationship to transnational funders ultimately affected the state's environment and development policies? In the end, I will show what the various configurations of power mean for Ecuador's development. The recent trend has been away from international political-economic influence toward regional political-economic control. The state has grown from a weak, decentralized state, limited by demands imposed by a global neoliberal order, to a strong state with a vision supported by regional allies. Environmental organizations have risen and fallen in power and have shifted their focus from global to national concerns. At the beginning of the history, the country was on an economic growth path focused on raising the gross domestic product; today the stated goals are *buen vivir/sumak kawsay*.

Beyond Ecuador

The Ecuador-specific questions and their answers are designed to contribute to theoretical debates in sociology at the intersections of social movements, the sociology of development, and environmental sociology. By analyzing how the Ecuadorian environmental movement has changed over time, I contribute to the debates around the consequences of elite sponsorship of homegrown/local movement organizations and social movement sectors.[41] In an era of globalization, when national social movements are sponsored transnationally, I show how questions about the consequences of sponsorship extend to a global level.[42] In assessing these relationships, power differentials between the Global North and the Global South are central, and in delineating the sources of power, I expand the literature on transnational social movements, development, and green imperialism[43] in Latin America.[44] A focus for development scholars is on understanding the consequences of the interventions of actors from the Global North on issues in the Global South.[45] I see this as analogous to issues raised by social movement theorists: understanding the consequences of elite intervention for homegrown/local organizations. Both question whether powerful groups are able to co-opt weaker groups to promote the powerful groups' interests. These analyses come together with environmental sociology's analysis of the intersection of social and natural systems and the relationships—national and transnational—described above, among key social institutions resulting in accelerating or decelerating the treadmill of production. Ultimately this nested analysis links global social structures to social movements and national policies to show how they interact and affect the quality of the environment and social life.

We are arguably at a moment in humanity's existence when we are aware that our current path of economic growth and "development" is not leading most people or most nations in an environmentally desirable direction. High levels of inequality—in both of wealth and power—dominate decisions made around the globe. As C. Wright Mills wrote, "We study historical social structures, in brief, in order to find within them the ways in which they are and can be controlled." In Ecuador, since 1978 numerous actors have tried to chart alternative environmental courses and have attempted to put the choices about the future in the hands of the many rather than the few. My hope is that by uncovering the historical social structures—particularly how the international context and the strength of the state affect and interact with the desired outcomes of NGOs and SMAs—that social movement actors will be increasingly empowered to affect the aspects of this equation that they can control to achieve the outcomes they desire for the good of both the people and the earth.

Overview of Book

Chapter 2 provides an overview of social, political, geographic, and environmental aspects of Ecuador from the 1970s until 2015. Chapter 3 presents a typology of environmental organizations in Ecuador. Four types are described: *ecoimperialists*, *ecodependents*, *ecoresisters*, and *ecoentrepreneur organizations*. In the following four chapters, I chronicle the four eras of the Ecuadorian environmental movement, from its origins in 1978 (chapter 4), to the neoliberal boom (chapter 5) in the late 1980s and 1990s, to the neoliberal bust (chapter 6) beginning in 2000, through to the citizens' revolution (chapter 7), which started in 2006. The final chapter (chapter 8) concludes with a summary of changes that have occurred in Ecuador and answers the main research questions specific to Ecuador. Based on the empirical findings, I also generate a series of hypotheses about social movements, the environment, and development that can be explored through analyses of other nations in the Global South, and Latin America, in particular.

2 The Ecuadorian Context

Destroying rainforest for economic gain is like burning a Renaissance painting to cook a meal.

—E. O. Wilson

This chapter provides an overview of Ecuador socioeconomically, politically, geographically, and environmentally within the global context from the late 1970s until 2015. The discussion examines biodiversity and petroleum in some depth, as they are two of its natural resources that link the country to the international financial community via aid relationships and exports, respectively. This chapter also lays out some key events in Ecuador's history that I use to create periods for the comparative analysis.

Why Ecuador?

Why choose Ecuador as a case? First, I chose Ecuador primarily because of its representativeness. Second, is the factor of its uniqueness. Third is the transnational funding for its environment, which has varied over time, allows me to assess the effects of that funding on the environmental movement.

Representativeness—Socioeconomics

Ecuador is a useful country to study in relation to socioenvironmental issues because it is similar to other Latin American and Caribbean (LAC) countries, and thus provides a glimpse into the region, in general. Over the historical period under examination (1978 to 2015), Ecuador has been fairly typical of Latin American nations in terms of its socioeconomic place in the world and in relation to global powers. World Bank data over the period show Ecuador's trends in key statistics such as gross domestic product per capita, population growth, poverty levels, and debt ratios to be similar to those of other nations in Latin America and the Caribbean. For instance, in 2004 Ecuador's gross national income per capita was $2,210; the same figure for LAC countries was $3,576.[1] Life expectancy in Ecuador was 74.5 years; in the region it was 72.2 years. In terms of environmental development, in the same year, the percentage of the population with access to improved water sources was 94 percent in Ecuador and 91percent in the region.[2] These are just single data points. Looking at trends, for instance, the percentage of the population in poverty, Ecuador is also representative of the region, with its percentage in poverty declining over the period.[3]

Ecuador's representativeness of the LAC region can also be viewed through its ranking on the Human Development Index (HDI). The HDI uses life expectancy, years of schooling, and gross national income per capita to construct the index. It has a range from zero to one, with one representing the highest human development. Ecuador's 2012 value on this scale was 0.724, ranking it toward the bottom of the "high" human development group; the average value for LAC nations was 0.741. Overall Ecuador ranked 89 out of 186 nations. Relatively speaking Ecuador was behind the "very high" human development of Chile, and the "high" ranking of nations including Cuba, Panama, Mexico, Costa Rica, and Venezuela. It was very close in rank to its nearest neighbors—Peru (ranked 77th), Brazil (ranked 85), and Colombia (ranked 91). Falling behind Ecuador, and classified as "medium" in terms of human development, included El Salvador, Bolivia, Paraguay, Honduras, Nicaragua, and Guatemala.[4] In terms of the distribution of income, Ecuador's GINI index score, a measure of inequality in which 0 is equivalent to perfect equality and 100 represents perfect inequality, has been declining, and was 49 in 2010 and 47 in 2012. It is slightly more equal than its Colombian and Brazilian neighbors, with respective scores of 56 and 54 (in 2010/2012) and 53 (in both 2011 and 2012), and slightly less equal than its neighbor to the south, Peru, scoring 45 (in both 2010 and 2012).[5]

I compile some key statistics on Ecuador covering four decades in table 2.1 from World Bank data. In the most recent period (2012) Ecuador's GDP per capita was $5,425, ranking it as a "middle income" country. Slightly more than a quarter of the population lives below the nation's poverty line, having declined significantly under the Correa administration (in 2005, it was 42 percent).[6]

Some ways that Ecuador differs from others, is that a high percentage of its export economy is dependent on petroleum (58 percent in 2011), and a significant portion of the state's revenues come from oil exports—two-fifths

Table 2.1
Socioeconomic indicators over time for Ecuador

	1982 Origins	1992 Boom	2002 Bust	2012 Revolution
Population (in millions)[a]	8.3	10.6	13.0	15.5
% Urban population[b]	49%	56%	62%	68%
GDP per capita (in current US$)[c]	$2,396	$1,707	$2,191	$5,425
% Below poverty line[d]	NA	NA	55.2%*	27.3%
Fuel exports (% of merchandise exports)[e]	64%	44%	40%	58%**
GDP (in current US million$)[f]	19,929	18,093	28,548	84,039

Source: World Bank. http://data.worldbank.org/indicator/NY.GDP.PCAP.CD/countri
es?page=6&display=default. Accessed January 22, 2014.
Notes: *Data from 2001; **data from 2011.

a. Population, total refers to the total population. (1) UN Population Division. World Population Prospects, (2) UN Statistical Division. Population and Vital Statistics Report (various years), (3) Census reports and other statistical publications from national statistical offices, (4) Eurostat: Demographic Statistics, (5) Secretariat of the Pacific Community: Statistics and Demography Programme, and (6) US Census Bureau: International Database.
b. Urban population (percent of total). Urban population refers to people living in urban areas as defined by national statistical offices. It is calculated using World Bank population estimates and urban ratios from the UN World Urbanization Prospects.
c. GDP per capita is gross domestic product divided by midyear population. GDP is the sum of gross value added by all resident producers in the economy plus any product taxes and minus any subsidies not included in the value of the products. It is calculated without making deductions for depreciation of fabricated assets or for depletion and degradation of natural resources. Data are in current US dollars.
d. National poverty rate is the percentage of the population living below the national poverty line. National estimates are based on population-weighted sub-group estimates from household surveys.
e. Fuels comprise SITC section 3 (mineral fuels). World Bank staff estimates from the Comtrade database maintained by the UN Statistics Division.
f. GDP at purchaser's prices is the sum of gross value added by all resident producers in the economy plus any product taxes and minus any subsidies not included in the value of the products. It is calculated without making deductions for depreciation of fabricated assets or for depletion and degradation of natural resources. Data are in current US dollars. Dollar figures for GDP are converted from domestic currencies using single year official exchange rates. [For Ecuador, this applies to the years prior to dollarization in 2000.]

Table 2.1 (continued)

	1982 Origins	1992 Boom	2002 Bust	2012 Revolution
Total external debt[g] (in current US million$)	2,598	12,263	16,222	16,931
Public debt as % of GDP	13%	68%	57%	20%
Debt service to IMF as % of exports of goods, services, and income[h]	78.7	26.2	34.6	9.8
Foreign direct investment (in current US million$)[i]	40	178	783	591
Official development assistance and official aid received (in current US million$)[j]	45.8	239.8	220.0	162.6**

g. External debt stocks, total (DOD, current US$). Total external debt is the sum of public, publicly guaranteed, and private nonguaranteed long-term debt, use of IMF credit, and short-term debt. Short-term debt includes all debt having an original maturity of one year or less and interest in arrears on long-term debt. Data are in current US dollars.

h. Total debt service (percent of exports of goods, services and primary income). Total debt service is the sum of principal repayments and interest actually paid in currency, goods, or services on long-term debt, interest paid on short-term debt, and repayments (repurchases and charges) to the IMF.

i. Foreign direct investment, net inflows (BoP, current US$). Foreign direct investment are the net inflows of investment to acquire a lasting management interest (10 percent or more of voting stock) in an enterprise operating in an economy other than that of the investor. It is the sum of equity capital, reinvestment of earnings, other long-term capital, and short-term capital as shown in the balance of payments. This series shows net inflows (new investment inflows less disinvestment) in the reporting economy from foreign investors. Data are in current US dollars.

j. Net official development assistance and official aid received (current US$). Net official development assistance (ODA) consists of disbursements of loans made on concessional terms (net of repayments of principal) and grants by official agencies of the members of the Development Assistance Committee (DAC), by multilateral institutions, and by non-DAC countries to promote economic development and welfare in countries and territories in the DAC list of ODA recipients. It includes loans with a grant element of at least 25 percent (calculated at a rate of discount of 10 percent). Net official aid refers to aid flows (net of repayments) from official donors to countries and territories in part II of the DAC list of recipients: more advanced countries of Central and Eastern Europe, the countries of the former Soviet Union, and certain advanced developing countries and territories. Official aid is provided under terms and conditions similar to those for ODA. Part II of the DAC List was abolished in 2005. The collection of data on official aid and other resource flows to Part II countries ended with 2004 data. Data are in current US dollars.

according to the Central Intelligence Agency's *World Factbook*. Four countries in LAC produce more crude oil exports than Ecuador (Venezuela, Mexico, Colombia, and Brazil).[7] Other leading Ecuadorian exports are bananas, shrimp, cut flowers, cacao, coffee, wood, and fish. The United States is its main trading partner for both exports (37 percent) and imports (28 percent). Ecuador's percentage of public debt has declined significantly over the last few years, for a number of reasons to be discussed later, and is now at 20 percent of the GDP (dropping from 38 percent in 2006).[8] This is another one of the ways that just recently and discussed below, Ecuador differs from some of its Latin American neighbors. For comparison, in 2012, Brazil's percentage of public debt was 59 percent of its GDP and Colombia's was 40 percent.[9] One quarter of Ecuador's people are Amerindian.[10] Sixty-eight percent of Ecuador's over 15 million people are urban dwellers, living in three major cities: Quito (in the Andes), Guayaquil (coast), and Cuenca (Andes).

Politically, Ecuador has been independent from Spain since 1822, and during the period under study has had democratically elected governments. These followed a brief period of being led by a military government, which ended with elections in 1978. Ecuador has had less political stability than most LAC nations. For instance, since President Abdalá Bucaram took office in August 1996, there have been ten presidents (or acting presidents), due to numerous political upheavals. Prior to that time, the democracy in Ecuador had been described as "fragile," marked by constitutional struggles, corruption scandals, and attempted coups.[11] President Correa is the longest serving president of Ecuador. Freedom House, an organization that evaluates political and civil liberties in nations around the world, has ranked Ecuador as "partly free" and "free" in the years from 1978 to 2015.[12]

Uniqueness—Geography and Environment

Ecuador is the fourth smallest nation in Latin America (283,520 square kilometers), about the same size as Colorado in the United States, and slightly smaller in land mass than Italy. It is made up of four distinct bioregions: the Galápagos Islands, the coast (*la costa*), the Andes (*la sierra*), and the Amazon (*el oriente*, the east, also called *la selva*, the jungle). Charles Darwin's visits to the Galápagos Islands, which were the basis of his 1876 book *The Origin of Species*, presaged the importance of the islands, and the country, in terms of biodiversity. The islands are now a major ecotourism destination. The coast contains the largest city and the main port, Guayaquil (see figure 2.1). The capital city of Quito, the second highest capital in Latin America (2,850

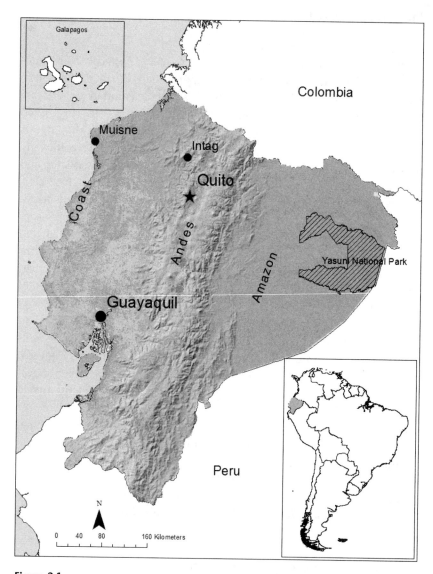

Figure 2.1

Map of South America with detail of Ecuador

Map created by Rebecca Boger using the following data sets: R. E. Bilsborrow, S. J. Walsh, and B. Frizzelle, 2012, LBA-ECO LC-01 National, Provincial, and Park Boundaries, Ecuador. Available online [http://daac.ornl.gov/] from Oak Ridge National Laboratory Distributed Active Archive Center, Oak Ridge, Tennessee. http://dx.doi.org/10.3334/ORNLDAAC/1057. P. D. Broxton, X. Zeng, D. Sulla-Menashe, and P. A. Troch, 2014a, A global land cover climatology using MODIS data, *J. Appl. Meteor. Climatol.* 53: 1593–1605, doi: http://dx.doi.org/10.1175/JAMC-D-13-0270.1. Digital Elevation Model (DEM) at 450 m pixel resolution. http://www.rsgis.ait.ac.th/~souris/ecuador.htm.

Figure 2.2
City of Quito, located in a valley and surrounded by volcanos

meters), sits among active volcanoes in the Andes (see figure 2.2). The Amazonian region, to the east of the Andes, is an area rich in petroleum and indigenous tribes.

Biodiversity

Because of its geographical diversity, and its location in the tropics, Ecuador's environment is incredibly rich. Scientists categorize Ecuador as one of the most "biodiverse" and "megadiverse" nations in the world on the basis of its high number of plant and animal species, and its high number of endemic species, meaning that they are native to that area. It contains over 20,000 plants, a fifth of which are endemic. It is well known for its orchids. The small nation also contains 10 percent of the world's plant species and 17 percent of the world's bird species, including rare birds such as the blue footed booby of the Galápagos (see figure 2.3).[13] All of this biodiversity exists in a very small area—only 0.2 percent of the earth's land area. This is part of what makes Ecuador a special, unique case. If we compare it to some US states, its lushness becomes even more apparent. California is the state with the highest plant diversity nationally. California has "6,272 plant taxa, including species and subspecies."[14] I

Figure 2.3
Blue-footed boobie in the Galápagos Islands

write from the state of New York, which has 3,899 plant species, a mere fraction of twenty thousand![15]

In the 1980s conservation biologists labeled Ecuador a "biodiversity hot spot"[16] and ranked it among the top "megadiverse" nations in the world.[17] This biodiversity designation had very real consequences for Ecuador.[18] Conservation biologists undertook these ranking exercises because they believed that a mass extinction of species would take place over the next few decades and they wanted to identify high priority areas in order to "determine conservation priorities in a more informed and method-ological manner."[19] Ecuador's richness drew transnational conservation organizations like USAID, the International Union for the Conservation of Nature, Conservation International, and The MacArthur Foundation. These groups and others invested in projects designed to protect Ecuador's biodiversity.

Some historical context for the biodiversity distinction underscores the paradox that Ecuador faces in determining its development trajectory. Norman Myers identified biodiversity hot spots in a 1988 article in *The*

Environmentalist as areas that contain two features: (a) "exceptional concentrations of species with exceptional levels of endemism and ... (b) [areas that] face exceptional degrees of threat."[20] This definition tends to zero in on tropical rainforests. Myers uses a comparative method for selecting hot spots. He contrasts regional numbers of plant and animal species. For example, in Ecuador, there are at least 20,000 plant species, 4,000 of which are endemic. If we compare this to that of temperate zone Minnesota, a US state twice Ecuador's size, one finds only 1,700 plant species, one endemic. Sources of "threats" include demographic and economic pressures. For example, Myers cites pressure from economic migration, which is migration to farm, log, and mine. Tom Rudel's study of the region, *Tropical Deforestation: Small Farmers and Land Clearing in the Ecuadorian Amazon,* showed that during the 1980s, migration was closely related to state policy.[21] People were moving, as "each of the governments in question perceives an incentive to speed up settlement of Amazonia as a means to assert sovereignty over the area with its abundant mineral resources."[22] With this recognition of threats, Myers's designations of biodiversity hot spots is closely linked to the economic choices of states. Thus biodiversity hot spots do not just exist in nature—they are created through a combination of ecological and political-economic phenomena.

While Myers examined biodiversity hot spots regionally, that same year, Russell Mittermeier, then with the World Wildlife Fund, created a typology of "megadiversity countries."[23] Mittermeier used the presence of closed tropical forests, primate diversity, and primate endemism to identify the "world's richest countries for living organisms in general."[24] He estimated that between 50 and 80 percent of the world's total biological diversity could be found in a small number (6 to 12) of tropical countries.[25] While Ecuador was not on the original list, which included Brazil, Colombia, Indonesia, Madagascar, Mexico, and Zaire, it was later added along with eleven other countries, including three others in Latin America: Mexico, Peru, and Venezuela.[26] Mittermeier also draws an economic link. Making a plea to conservationists in the Global North, he notes that most of the biologically rich countries are those facing economic problems, which do not have resources to establish protected areas/national parks on their own. The uneven distribution of biological diversity between the Global North and the Global South has been called one of the "great ironies of conservation."[27] There have been at least nine different ways that "global biodiversity conservation priorities" have been conceived.[28] The point here is that these early conceptions made a big difference for Ecuador.

Biodiversity hotspot designations have had very real funding outcomes. Conservation International (CI) (where Russell Mittermeier has been the President since 1989) puts forth the following analysis:

> ... [T]he impact of the hotspots concept in terms of investment in conservation has been dramatic. CI adopted hotspots as its central strategy in 1989, and in the same year, the John D. and Catherine T. MacArthur Foundation implemented the hotspots as its primary global investment strategy. In 2000, the World Bank and the Global Environment Facility joined CI in establishing the Critical Ecosystem Partnership Fund. The MacArthur Foundation became a partner in 2001 and the Japanese Government joined the partnership in 2002 .... In total, more than $750 million is estimated to have been devoted to saving hotspots over the last 15 years, perhaps the largest financial investment in any single conservation strategy.[29]

It is difficult to calculate a total dollar amount that the transnational community has spent to protect the Ecuadorian environment since the funding began in the late 1970s, but figures have been compiled for some areas of interest (notably, biodiversity) over a few periods of time. For example, in 1991, Ecuador ranked number five in the world in the amount of US-based funding received for biological diversity research and conservation projects from public and private donors, receiving $4.5 million that year (of $105 million spent in all nations).[30] That number only includes funds from the United States, not from other international bilateral or multilateral donors. The United States, however, has been a major biodiversity aid donor. One study lists it as the number 3 donor, following all units of the World Bank, and the Global Environment Facility, thus making it the number 1 donor in terms of nations in the period from 1980 to 2008. According to that same study other nations (not multilateral agencies) in the top ten included the Netherlands, Germany, and the United Kingdom.[31] A broader study that examined biodiversity funding from multilateral and bilateral agencies, NGOs, and foundations during the period from 1990 to 1997, found that Ecuador received over $96 million for 163 biodiversity projects. Following Brazil and Mexico, Ecuador ranked among the top Latin American and Caribbean countries receiving funds in terms of total receipts and dollars per hectare.[32] These numbers are incomplete, and only report funding for one issue area (biodiversity), but what they show is that in comparison to other nations, Ecuador ranks on the high end of receipts from foreign sources for environmental protection.[33] Ecuador is an example of a nation with high levels of foreign funding for the protection of its environment.[34]

There are two sides of the coin for biodiversity. On the one hand, Ecuador is able to use its richness to attract conservation dollars, bird lovers, and ecotourists who come to see its beautiful landscapes. On the other hand, its natural wealth can be used to fuel its economy in less sustainable ways. Its plentiful lands include oil deposits, which draw a completely different sort of international attention, and revenues that exceed the proceeds from transnational conservationists and ecotourists put together.[35] Based on these resources, Ecuador's economic trajectory has the potential for two very divergent paths.

Petroleum

Ecuador's state has been dependent on petroleum exports for revenues. Petroleum extraction, however, is a major cause of environmental destruction in so-called protected areas, and of social upheaval, especially for indigenous groups. Since Texaco found oil in the Ecuadorian Amazon in 1967, petroleum has played a key role in the state's decision-making. The national government's percentage of income from petroleum has varied, but always been high, often over fifty percent.[36] Petroleum is consistently Ecuador's leading export (58 percent in 2012; see table 2.1). Ecuador's petroleum exports have risen from 4,100 barrels a day in 1970 to over half of a million barrels daily (503,600) in 2012.[37] Following Brazil and Venezuela, Ecuador has the third largest oil reserves in South America.[38] The majority of Ecuador's crude oil is exported to the United States.[39]

As of 2015, Ecuador was the smallest oil producer of the twelve OPEC member nations. Nevertheless, in the period from 1970 (just after oil was discovered) to present, its percentage of daily crude oil production per day (measured in barrels) has increased at a faster rate than OPEC overall (12,183 percent increase versus 44 percent). Looking from 1980 to 2013, Ecuador still outpaces OPEC in its relative growth (147 to 28 percent, respectively).[40] Petroleum plays a leading role in the state's capacity to create economic growth. According to Ecuador's central bank, in 2012 crude petroleum was by far the largest export ($12,711,229 thousands of dollars in exports). For comparison, Ecuador's other main exports, in order of magnitude in dollars are (with the amount in thousands of dollars following each): bananas (2,077,351), shrimp (1,279,653), canned fish (1,116,059), natural flowers (713,934), cacao and its derivatives (454,815), and coffee and its derivatives (261,058).[41] Even though Ecuador exports the most bananas of any nation in the world (5,391.9 thousand tons in 2011),[42] its gain from that is only a fraction (16 percent) of that gained from crude petroleum exports (figure 2.4). Petroleum derivatives alone totaled almost half of the banana export dollars (1,080,729 thousand). Tourism is another

Figure 2.4
Bananas being loaded for export on the coast

important foreign export earning for the country, and it has been increasing annually. In 2012 Ecuador received over one million international tourists (1,272 thousand) and the international tourism receipts totaled $1,026 million, approximately 8 percent of that earned from crude, and just under half earned from bananas.[43] During the 2015 Superbowl in the United States, a football event famous for its commercials, Ecuador ran an advertisement "All You Need is Ecuador" (to the Beatles song All You Need Is Love) promoting tourism to the country. The state also declared 2015 the year of "touristic quality."[44]

In 1967, petroleum was found in the Ecuadorian Amazon by Texaco, a US-based corporation. From 1972 to 1990, Texaco and Petroecuador, the state-owned company, pumped more than two million barrels of oil from the region.[45] This caused dramatic political, economic, social and environmental changes. A key consequence of oil exploitation was that the state grew tremendously. In 1972, when oil exports began, the military took over the civilian government to "transform oil returns into reform and development."[46] Changes resulted from the military's reforms: income rose, infrastructure was developed, investments in education and health were made, illiteracy declined, and the percentage of the population with access to safe water and electricity increased.[47] During this early period new protected areas (national parks) were established. In the beginning, state investments helped the public. Thus early on the state eluded some of the negative consequences of the "resource curse." Some development gains were made. However, the state control over the petroleum industry resulted in unequal economic growth, making the rich bureaucrats richer. Some analysts argue that the state also outgrew itself. At the end of the 1980s, Ecuador had 60,000 industrial workers and 150,000 bureaucrats.[48]

Despite some social development, there was significant harm to the environment, which affected the culture and health of indigenous peoples. Petroleum's negative environmental effects on the Amazon have been well-documented.[49] Studies by the state's own environmental organizations (then called—DIGEMA) and by the World Bank acknowledged problems with the state's petroleum corporation in the protected areas.[50] Besides the direct effects of polluted land and air, fish kills, and negative health effects on indigenous people, roads that were built by petroleum corporations, in conjunction with government incentives, assisted migration to the Amazon. The rate of population growth in that region exceeded that in either the sierra or the coast.[51] A result of colonization is deforestation,[52] which increases extinction rates as habitat is destroyed in areas of high biodiversity.

The environmental effects of petroleum extraction were and are especially unsettling in that they occur in areas that are designated "protected" and in which a number of indigenous tribes dwell. The Forestry and Wildlife Law of 1981 prohibits petroleum exploration and other forms of extraction within the protected area system. However, the law has a provision that with the approval of the Minister of Agriculture and Grazing, extraction is permissible. In the past there have been mechanisms in place to work around such restrictions. For example, the boundaries to Yasuní National Park were adjusted a number of times to open certain areas to oil exploration.[53] At least three of the protected areas in the Amazon region have been the sites of oil extraction (Cuyabeno Fauna Reserve, Yasuní National Park, and Biological Reserve Limoncocha).

In the 1990s locals placed the blame for these problems on three sources: the government for not protecting its citizens, transnational oil companies for causing the contamination, and international banks for encouraging Ecuador's petroleum growth in order to pay the external debt with little regard for the local population (see figure 2.5)[54] The dumping of toxins, which created land contamination, illness, and loss of a way of life spurred a 1993 class action lawsuit against Texaco. The suit was filed by CORDAVI (Corporacíon de la Defensa de la Vida, Corporation for the Defense of Life), an environmental law organization, in New York on behalf of a coalition of

Figure 2.5
Anti-transnational corporate graffiti in Quito

five indigenous groups against the transnational Texaco for despoiling Ecuador's nature and indigenous communities. Chevron (which bought Texaco) has been found guilty in an Ecuadorian court, and ordered to pay $18 billion in damages, but has refused and has appealed the decision. In March 2015 the International Court of Justice in The Hague upheld the judgment. As I write, the issue remains unresolved, as Chevron will continue to fight. It is no coincidence that some of the main economic drivers in the country, namely oil and shrimp, have been sites of environmental contention and social movement activity. The state's proposed trajectory— to increase mining, especially copper—has also drawn social movement resistance.

The 1980s and 1990s were marked by neoliberalism and an open market approach to oil development.[55] This changed in 2006. Following Venezuela's lead, Ecuador revised its hydrocarbon law to require transnational companies to give 50 percent of their extraordinary income to the state. That same year, the state took over Occidental Petroleum's assets when their contract came to an end. When Correa came into office in 2007, he changed the hydrocarbon law again, upping the percentage due to the state to 99 percent.[56] Under President Correa's administration, more of the petroleum development is being carried out by the state than by foreign companies. Correa has used petroleum revenues, like Venezuela's Chávez, for social development. Under President Correa social spending for health and education has increased and poverty has decreased.

According to the US Energy Information Administration, in 2013 Petroecuador and two other national oil companies produced 73 percent of the oil in Ecuador.[57] Petroecuador has been responsible for a number of oil spills. Since 2009 the state has made loan-for-oil deals with the Chinese,[58] which some argue has led to China monopolizing an OPEC member's oil supplies.[59] Because Ecuador had defaulted on its other international loans, it had to look to new lenders/partners, and China's Development Bank provided Ecuador with a new strategy for borrowing.

The role of the state in oil extraction highlights its dilemma. The state plays a dual role: The government is both engaged in a process by which it needs to generate funds to sustain itself, provide resources for its citizens, re-pay its debts *and* it has committed to conservation of protected areas. In the 1980s and 1990s conservation provided the state with a politically acceptable reason, within a neoliberal framework, of protecting areas for future economic interests. When the government declares an area protected and under its jurisdiction, it gains control of areas with mineral resources, including petroleum (and copper, to be discussed in later chapters). Protected areas in the Amazon have served as petroleum piggy banks to fuel future economic development.[60] The 2008 Constitution prohibits extractive activities in protected areas,[61] as have earlier constitutions. However, when extraction is deemed to be in the "national interest," there are provisions to allow for it with congressional approval. The Yasuní-ITT Initiative is the latest attempt to find an alternative to extractive development that also enables social development. The ITT oilfields hold approximately 20 percent of Ecuador's known reserves.

To summarize, Ecuador is distinctive in that it has tremendous natural resources for such a small nation. The resources present the country with choices. Ecuador can focus on some combination of biodiversity protection and/or natural resource extraction as strategies for future development.

Other Environmental Concerns

In addition to the socioenvironmental problems related to oil extraction in the Amazon basin, some of Ecuador's more unique problems are related to its other economic development projects. Leading concerns include the destruction of mangroves due to shrimp farming on the coast, difficulties stemming from tourist development of the ecologically sensitive Galápagos Islands, and environmental health problems caused by pesticides used in the production of cut flowers. Another problem, which arises due to globalization and transnational influences, is the illnesses caused by fumigation along the Colombia border, which is part of the US "Plan Colombia" designed to eradicate coca.

Ecuador also has a number of environmental problems that are similar to those in other Latin American and Caribbean nations: deforestation, soil erosion, and industrial pollution. Ecuador has the highest deforestation rate in South America.[62] During the 1990 to 2005 period, Ecuador's rate was 1.4 percent compared to a 0.4 percent average for LAC. For the 2000 to 2010 period, the respective rates were 1.8 and 0.4 percent.[63] In the period from 1990 to 2000, Ecuador's forested area decreased from 43 to 38 percent.[64] Deforestation destroys habitats and contributes to species loss. Ecuador has 43 threatened mammal species and 93 threatened bird species.[65] Despite the high rate of deforestation, the percentage of Ecuador's land protected nationally is very high: 25 percent (compared to 20 percent in Latin America, and conservationists' goal of 10 percent worldwide).[66] While this is a high number, the quality of the protection must be taken into account. For instance, is there oil exploration in the "protected areas"? Ecuador's major cities (Guayaquil, Quito, and Cuenca) suffer from "brown" environmental problems associated with water quality, sewage management, air pollution, industrial pollution, and municipal solid waste.[67] Sixty-seven percent of Ecuador's 14.7 million people are urban dwellers, so these brown issues are more socially visible than the "green" issues of conservation.[68] Ecuador's environmental problems affect both pure "nature," and human health.

Four Eras in Ecuador's History

The strategy for examining the effect that transnational funding for sustainability has had on environmentalisms and the trajectory of Ecuador's development is to examine the key variables defined in chapter 1 over four periods of Ecuador's history. In each period the transnational funding has varied, as has the strength of the state, the types of environmentalisms, and the concrete environmental outcomes. Table 2.2 provides the overview of the strategy. This section explains how the four periods—origins, neoliberal boom, neoliberal bust, and citizens' revolution—were chosen and delineated.

Origins, 1978 to 1987

The year 1978 is a logical starting point for examining environmentalism in Ecuador for two reasons. The first is that Ecuador's first environmental organization, Fundación Natura (Natura), was founded in this year by a group of young, college educated Ecuadorians. Second, this year also marks the end of a military dictatorship, and the return to democracy, which has prevailed since then. The democratic state was relatively weak, in part due to its high level of international indebtedness to both public and private donors. Government revenues were dependent on petroleum extraction

Table 2.2
Key variables and four eras (cases) in Ecuador's history of environmentalism

	Origins 1978–1987	Boom 1987–2000	Bust 2000–2006	Revolution 2006–2015
Transnational funding				
Environmental sector				
State characteristics				
Environment and development policies				
Schnaiberg's syntheses				

and very few environmental policies were in place. Shortly after the founding of Fundación Natura, the United States Agency for International Development (USAID) provided Natura with its first large grant, which initiated transnational funding for the environment in Ecuador. During this phase a few other national groups were founded, including another key player in the environmental arena: Acción Ecológica (AE). Other groups also formed, but Natura and AE were significant in that they established two distinct lines of environmental action for future groups to emulate. By the end of the period, in 1987, environmental consciousness had increased to the level that three important events occurred: first, there was the creation of an umbrella environmental group—Comité Ecuatoriano para la Defensa de la Naturaleza y el Medio Ambiente (Ecuadorian Committee for the Defense of Nature and the Environment, CEDENMA)—whose function was to coordinate the work of all of the groups that had formed. Second, USAID cosponsored the first National Environmental Congress, which was attended by environmentalists, government employees, and business people. A third event that makes this a delineation point was the execution of the first of three debt-for-nature swaps. The origins era is characterized by the founding of a national level environmental organization and the beginning of transnational funding for the environment.

Neoliberal Boom, 1987 to 2000

The beginning of the neoliberal boom period is marked by the influx of transnational funds that was set off by the debt-for-nature swap. More funds flowed into Ecuador from two more swaps and from large environmental projects funded by USAID, other bilateral public donors, including the Netherlands, and from private conservation groups and foundations. Globally, this was an era of heightened environmental consciousness, highlighted by the 1992 UN Conference on Environment and Development (UNCED). Given the neoliberal principles prevalent in this period, such as the promotion of privatization, most of the transnational funding was directed toward private actors, such as nongovernmental organizations (NGOs), not public actors, like state agencies. As a result the number of environmental NGOs rose dramatically. Working for environmental NGOs in Quito became relatively lucrative for professional environmentalists. Other forms of environmentalism, such as "NIMBY" types (not in my back yard) and localized/place-based forms of environmentalism were also rising based on concrete grievances, such as health concerns based on oil contamination. Five indigenous groups filed a class action suit in New York against the transnational corporation Texaco for destroying their lands. Texaco claimed it did not violate any Ecuadorian environmental laws. The state was still very weak during this period. It had only limited laws and even less enforcement. The debt-for-nature swaps only marginally decreased the state's total debt load, which prevented it from taking any strong, independent actions. Nevertheless, transnational efforts to affect the environment via the non-profits yielded some policy responses. Ecuador participated in UNCED, expanded its national park system, and held a Second National Congress for the Environment in 1995. This second conference, like the first, was sponsored by USAID. USAID also sponsored a state environmental commission—Comisión Asesora Ambiental (Environmental Advisory Commission, CAAM). This era ended in 2000 when Ecuador suffered an economic crisis. The boom era is characterized by high levels of transnational funding and by subsequently large numbers of environmental groups.

Neoliberal Bust, 2000 to 2006

The economic crisis was not a single crisis, but a series of crises. The worldwide decline in oil prices, weather conditions that limited the banana crops, international debt default and bank failures culminated in a crisis that led to the dollarization of Ecuador's currency (the *sucre*). Dollarization—literally using the US dollar instead of the national currency—was another example of the weak and dependent state. Environmental NGOs were also debilitated because their major source of transnational environmental funding—the United States—was sidelined by the September 11, 2001, attacks. US public funding shifted to its wars, and overall funding to Ecuador dropped off. Concurrently large bilateral programs that had been scheduled to end, ended. Funding that had been plentiful was now scarce. Environmental groups had to adapt; many downsized, others closed down, and some sought ways to be financially independent. There was political instability amid continued resource extraction. A major loss to environmentalists was the building of the OCP pipeline from the Amazon across protected areas to the coast. In 2005 President Gutiérrez repealed the Supreme Court and the country was in a heightened political crisis. Social movement activists, including grassroots environmentalists, called for a national assembly. The Declaration that emerged from the assembly was a broad critique of the political, economic and environmental structures of Ecuador. The instability brought on by the economic and political crises provided openings for Ecuador to change. The end of this bust/crisis period is marked by the election of the populist, socialist, Rafael Correa to the presidency in 2006. The bust era contrasts with the boom era by the sharp decrease in transnational funding and the consequent decline of main-stream environmentalism.

Citizens' Revolution, 2006 to 2015

After President Correa was inaugurated, he called for the rewriting of the constitution. Many of the points that environmentalists had written into the Declaration made their way into the new constitution. It declared rights for nature, the first constitution in the world to do so, and the right to *buen vivir* (in Spanish)/*sumak kawsay* (in Quechua), generally translated as "living well." Transnational funding for the environment remained limited. Funds that did go into Ecuador were directed toward the new government, which was becoming increasingly strong and capable through Correa's leadership and his control of hydrocarbons and public investment. The state re-centralized and played a stronger role in society. The state also resisted international limitations posed by debt and transnational influences. It pushed international influence from the west away in favor of regional alliances, particularly those led by Venezuela's President Hugo Chávez. NGOs were still weak due to their fiscal difficulties and also because the state was holding them accountable to their rules, and extending its reach into their areas. NGOs protested what they perceived as the states' limiting of civil liberties through a number of presidential decrees. The lack of funds and the new state had consequences for environmentalism. Fundación Natura closed its doors in 2012. After over fifty years of working in Ecuador, in 2013 USAID declared that it was pulling out. The state sought ways to continue its program of trying to protect the environment while also decreasing poverty and improving social development. The state proposed the Yasuní-ITT Initiative at the same time it moved forward with plans to mine for copper and other minerals in previously undisturbed areas. In 2013 President Correa was elected to his second full term. The revolution era is most distinct from the previous periods in that transnational investment shifted toward the state, the state was strong, and in words, if not deeds, the state grappled with the contradictory attempts to both protect the environment and develop socially and economically.

History and Sociology: What Is Ecuador an Example of?

The roots of this analysis are sociological. By this I mean that the questions that drive the analysis assume that there are underlying structures that shape and pattern human behavior. Therefore I assume that if I can illuminate the relationships among transnational funding, environmental-isms, states' strength, and development trajectories in one nation-state, I can generate hypotheses about other like nation-states regarding how these variables relate to each other. Thus my goal is not simply an extended history of one country. The intention is to use the single nation to shed light on other nations. By breaking Ecuador's history into four periods, I am able to understand how changes in one variable affect the other variables in four cases, while controlling the context. Chapter 3 describes the main types of environmentalism that have existed in Ecuador over the periods of interest. These can also be applied to other nations receiving environmental aid. Though the sociological impulse drives this work, in the end, I am also presenting a history of environmentalism in Ecuador. It is by no means exhaustive, and it is limited by its focus on the sociological variables of interest.

I aim to use Ecuador as an example of and applicable to other nations like it socioeconomically and environmentally: indebted nations with low to medium income, and with natural resources that are at risk of depletion for development. In addition Ecuador represents a nation that is "high" on the intervention spectrum, meaning that it has received large amounts of transnational funding. The global processes that Ecuador has been a part over time also shed light on the relationship between the global political economy and environmentalism, with respect to three areas. First, the history of Ecuador's environmentalism demonstrates the effect of global trends, such as UN support of sustainable development, have had on developing nations. Second, it demonstrates how the international economic pressure to repay foreign debt affects the environment through degrading activities, such as resource extraction, and through opportunities, such as debt-for-nature swaps. Finally, it demonstrates how the expanding influence of "global" civil society affects national civil society, and vice versa. Understanding transnational environmental funding (aka global aid) is a means to understand transnational influences on a nation more broadly. Other forms of such aid include humanitarian aid, food aid, and military assistance. Understanding the effects of transnational environmental funding on a nation's movements and policies may also shed light on mechanisms at work in these other types of aid.

3 Ideal Types of Environmentalism

Taxonomy (the science of classification) is often undervalued as a glorified form of filing—with each species in its folder, like a stamp in its prescribed place in an album; but taxonomy is a fundamental and dynamic science, dedicated to exploring the causes of relationships and similarities among organisms. Classifications are theories about the basis of natural order, not dull catalogues compiled only to avoid chaos.

—Stephen Jay Gould, *Wonderful Life*, 1989: 98

The goal of this chapter is to present a typology of environmentalisms in Ecuador, with a focus on environmental *organizations*. In the spirit of Max Weber, I present four "ideal types." Ideal types are not simplifications or replications of concrete reality; rather, they exemplify typical features of a subject of study that logically fit together. They are composites based on the tendencies of the actors (organizations) being grouped. As such, there may be no single group that fits neatly into each one of the four categories. Recurrent patterns and relationships result in certain types. The utility of the ideal types approach is that it allows the analysis to transcend the historical particularities of each individual group to understand more general patterns, trends, and relationships. For instance, which environmentalisms are most influential at which times in history and why? How has this changed over time? How have relationships with transnational environmental funders altered environmentalism in Ecuador? This typology can also extend beyond Ecuador's boundaries to understand other nations' environmental movement organizations.

I delineate four ideal types: *ecoimperialists, ecodependents, ecoresisters,* and *ecoentrepreneur organizations*. Given the nature of the questions I am asking, namely what effect does transnational funding have on environmental organizations and the environmental movement in Ecuador, it makes sense to create a typology of groups based on their funding sources.

From there, the second level of sorting focuses on their level of organization (transnational, national, regional, or local), their main agenda, types
of projects, relationship to the state, public's view of them, and their position on the trajectory of development. The characterization of environmentalism in this chapter is both deductive—drawing on a 2007 survey of
organizations and interviews with activists, and inductive—drawing on
the work of sociologists and historians who have created classifications of
environmentalisms.[1]

Other Classifications of Environmentalism

Numerous classifications of environmentalisms exist. A common classification sorts groups by ideologies and/or agenda or discourses. Some of the
labels include shallow ecologists, deep ecologists, free-market environmentalists, reform environmentalists, radical environmentalists, ecopopulists,
greens, ecofeminists, social ecologists, environmental justice advocates,
conservationists, preservationists, post-material environmentalists, the list
could go on. Robert Brulle created one of the more exhaustive classification
schemes of North American environmentalism based on eleven environmental "discursive frames," including, in addition to some of those mentioned above, the environmental health frame and the ecospiritual frame.[2]
In Mark Dowie's book *Losing Ground,* he delineates the "Group of 10" US
environmental groups, characterized as being the most influential groups
because of their high level of corporate funding.[3] His intent is not necessarily to categorize environmental groups, but this delineation suggests that
size, power, and resources are dimensions that can be used for classification.[4] At the other end of the spectrum, Joan Martinez-Alier's book *The
Environmentalism of the Poor* defines two key types of environmentalism:
environmentalism of the poor (found in the Global South) and environmentalism of affluence. That characterization overlaps with work done by
Helen Collinson, Al Gedicks, and Bron Taylor focusing on the Global South
that highlighted "green guerillas," "resource rebels" and environmental
resistance movements rooted in "livelihood struggles."[5] These treatments
focus the connections between social class, resources and agendas. For
instance, the "green guerillas" resisting resource extraction are not organizations with big budgets, nor dues paying members, nor corporate funders.
Environmental movements from the Global North and the Global South
have been compared and contrasted in terms of their patterns of beliefs,
interests, and strategies.[6]

The environmental sector in Ecuador is diverse: it contains international, national, and local groups; some with many resources and most with very few. All of the nation's geographic areas are covered. The main issue areas are biodiversity conservation and sustainable development, though many themes are addressed, including environmental education, water pollution, and deforestation. It would be possible to find groups that fit into all of the categories mentioned above.

Four Unequal Types of Groups

In Ecuador there are (1) ecoimperialist organizations that fund the Ecuadorian environmental organizations from abroad; (2) ecodependent organizations, which are national-level organizations that rely on international funding; (3) ecoresisters, which are national, regional, or local-level actors that receive little to no resources from abroad; and (4) ecoentrepreneur organizations, also national, regional or local-level groups that receive little to no environmental resources from abroad and are distinctive for their innovative approaches to obtaining resources. An overview of the similarities and differences of the types is laid out in table 3.1.

Ecoimperialists and ecodependents are tied to each other by funding relationships. Ecoimperialist organizations provide funding to ecodependent organizations. Through this economic relationship, the agendas of the two groups become similar. These two types are co-dependent. In Ecuador, the initial connections were made during the Origins Era and the relationship played out extensively during the Neoliberal Boom Era. The relationship between these types is not static; it has altered the organizations over time. For instance, one of the consequences of transnational funding practices has been that ecodependent organizations have become more professionalized so that they can better report their project outcomes to their funders.

Ecoresistant organizations and ecoentrepreneur organizations eschew foreign funding, for the most part. This has increased the independence of these groups in terms of their agendas. Control over agenda is an important dividing line between these organizations and ecodependent organizations. In Ecuador, ecoresistant groups have existed since the Origins Era and have arguably been strongest in the Neoliberal Bust Era. Ecoentrepreneur groups emerged during the Bust, and depending on their success, they may gain more influence in the future.[7]

Table 3.1
Typology of environmental organizations

	Ecoimperialist	Ecodependent	Ecoresistant	Ecoentrepreneur
Source of funding	Home office in Global North	Ecoimperialist organizations and others	Little to no funding from ecoimperialist organizations	Funded locally through service fees
Level of organization	International	National and regional	National, regional and local	National, regional and local
Main actors	Professional conservationists	Professional environmentalists	Volunteers and a few paid staff	Technicians and financial professionals
Primary agenda	Biodiversity conservation and sustainable development	Biodiversity conservation and sustainable development	Depends on community and local extractive industries	Quality of life issues, including clean water and safe transportation
Type of projects	Land conservation and sustainable development	Land conservation and sustainable development	Defensive and alternative economic development	Urban, such as urban parks and water use
State's relationship to groups	Mostly cooperative	Mostly cooperative	Adversarial	Cooperative

	Negative	"Nonprofit mafia"	Mixed	Positive
Ecuadorian public's view of groups				
Approach to development trajectory	Does not address explicitly; thrived under the neoliberal model	Some against the neoliberal model in theory, but not primary focus of actions	Against neoliberal model; formulating alternatives; favors buen vivir/ sumak kawsay	Does not address explicitly; premise operates within market-based structure
Examples of Accomplishments	National parks established	Scientific inventories conducted; parks managed	Lawsuit against Chevron/ Texaco; delayed mining	Created public/private funds to ensure protection of watersheds
Examples	Nature Conservancy; World Conservation Society; USAID	Fundación Natura; EcoCiencia; Fundación Maquipucuna	Acción Ecológica, DECOIN, C-CONDEM, FUNDECOL	Vida para Quito, FONAG
Prevalence of type	Limited in total number	Most prevalent type, especially during the boom era	Fewer than ecodependents, more than ecoalternatives; less visible—not necessarily registered or explicitly "environmental"	Smallest type; may grow with increased state environmentalism and payment for ecosystem services (PES) approach

Each of these types will be sketched out a in the pages that follow and will be fleshed out thoroughly in chapters 4 through 7, where I explain the emergence of the various types throughout the history and demonstrate the rise and fall of the different types in conjunction with changes in the global/national political economy.

Type 1: Ecoimperialist Organizations

Transnational environmental groups in Ecuador, including international nongovernmental organizations (INGOs), bilateral and multilateral funding agents, and foundations are based in countries outside of Ecuador, and have offices in Ecuador, usually the capital, Quito. They bring resources (funding and otherwise) to focus primarily on biodiversity conservation, often with the secondary goal of supporting sustainable economic development. To this point, I have called them "transnational funders." I label them ecoimperialist because many Ecuadorians call them such because they establish themselves in Ecuador with their own funds to do what they want to do. Some outspoken national leaders view them as foreign intruders imposing their will on the people, policies, and land of Ecuador; in other words, gringos (a derogatory term for North Americans) meddling in domestic policies and development agendas. Of the groups in Ecuador's environmental sector, ecoimperialists have the largest budgets, often over $1 million. Examples of such groups are The Nature Conservancy (TNC), the Wildlife Conservation Society (WCS), and the United States Agency for International Development (USAID).

An example of a project led by ecoimperialist organizations is the Parks in Peril (PiP) program. PiP was a joint venture between the Nature Conservancy and USAID that ran from 1990 until 2007. The goal was to conserve biologically critical ecosystems. The program sought "to protect 50 million acres in Central and South America and the Caribbean by helping local nonprofit and governmental organizations provide effective park stewardship."[8] In Ecuador the program worked with national NGOs, including Fundación Natura, EcoCiencia, Fundación Antisana, and Fundación Rumicocha, to improve park management and expand the national park system. The program worked with NGOs rather than the government when the state was weak. Parks that were part of this program included Machalilla National Park on the coast and Podocarpus National Park in the southern region. The program was considered a success in that it conserved multiple areas and brought resources into the region: "In all, over its first 12 years, the program brought over $62 million to important protected areas throughout the region—$37.5 from USAID, and $24.8 from TNC and its local partner organizations,"[9] and more funds would follow in the next phases. By its own accounts, it protected 45 areas and conserved almost 45 million acres.[10] Even though the derogatory stamp of ecoimperialist is used for such groups, Ecuadorian environmentalists note that the transnational funding was critical in the consolidation and expansion of the protected area system, and without the funding, the process and the protection would not have occurred.

There have, however, been numerous criticisms of these groups, as their label implies. Though "ecoimperialist" is a strong term to use to describe these organizations, it reflects the opinion of some national and local organizations in the environmental community who see them as "forcing their will." There have been four main criticisms: First, these organizations impose their agenda. Environmentalists literally view these groups as inflicting a foreign agenda on Ecuador by funding and prioritizing land protection over Ecuadorians' goals. Second, they bypass Ecuadorian organizations. Prior to 2006, these organizations acted as intermediaries, channeling funds from their home offices to Ecuadorian NGOs, which would implement the project for the foreign-based INGOs, that is, in carrying out the priorities of the INGO. But some of these organizations have moved toward implementing their own projects due to concerns that their money was not producing results. For instance, the Wildlife Conservation Society does this. They implement projects with their own (Ecuadorian) staff. Ecuadorian NGOs that used to implement WCS's projects are bypassed, and they don't like it. A third criticism comes from indigenous groups and ecoresistent organizations. They believe that foreign organizations are trying to purchase land as a means of controlling water resources and to create private reserves, which is literally an imperialist objective. The Nature Conservancy is the main target of this claim since their focus in their home country, the United States, is to protect biodiversity through land purchase. However, this is not a strategy that they use in Ecuador. A final criticism has to do with the INGOs' practices within their home nations of cooperating with polluting multinational corporations. Environmentalists in Ecuador consider such relationships suspect and definitely unethical.

Type 2: Ecodependent Organizations

National-level organizations that are primarily funded by ecoimperialist organizations and whose agendas match up with those transnational funders are classified as ecodependent organizations. More than 50 percent of their budget comes from other countries. They have offices in Quito, but their focus is not necessarily on a narrow geographical area. Their budgets are higher than most environmental organizations in Ecuador and they are able to maintain full time staff. However, they are dependent on project-based funding provided from abroad, so their budgets vary quite a bit from year to year. An employee of such an organization described the work of these groups as "dancing to the rhythm of the donors." During the Neoliberal period these organizations proliferated and diversified in terms of their regional focus, issue area, and specializations. The most successful have become very capable and effective, including many of the well-known Ecuadorian environmental organizations, like Fundación Natura, EcoCiencia, and Jatun Sacha. Most of the organizations are politically similar and reformist in their goals. Their work fits into the dominant economic-political framework of the country. They cooperate with the state to try to get things done, using the system to achieve their goals. Due to their relationship with transnational donors and their relative success in carrying out the goals of ecoimperialists, some Ecuadorians view them with envy and skepticism, calling them part of the "nonprofit mafia."

An example of an ecodependent organization is Fundación Natura (Natura). Over time, this group has worked with numerous transnational organizations, including the World Wide Fund for Nature, the MacArthur Foundation, and UNESCO, on projects related to biodiversity protection, national park development, and environmental education. For instance, Natura worked with WWF on the first debt-for-nature swap. Natura handled the swap, which was partly used to manage eight protected areas; seven with the cooperation of the state and one (el Bosque Protector Pasochoa, the Pasochoa Protected Forest) managed directly by Natura. They also arranged the second swap in 1990, which was partially used for identifying, protecting, and managing new protected areas and creating a data repository for conservation information. This too was coordinated with state agencies, with Natura playing a lead role. In many cases the ecodependents' relationship with the ecoimperialists has been around shared goals, thus resulting in a "win-win" situation. The swaps were aligned with transnational conservationists' goals and with one of Natura's goals: enabling the execution of conservation projects.[11]

There are three main issues with the ecoimperialist-ecodependent relationships. First, is the inconsistency in funding, which results in the boom and bust of staffing within existing organizations, and the boom and bust of actual organizations, which have come into being and then closed, as ecoimperialist organizations initiated and then ended large conservation programs. The second problem is the organizations' lack of goal-setting autonomy, which is also related to the narrow focus of groups that are funded. Many ecodependent organizations started out with a focus on conservation but have shifted their agendas over time as ecoimperialist organizations moved toward "sustainable development." In this way the ecoimperialists are able to impose their agenda onto the leading national groups. Environmental organizations whose priorities are not conservation or sustainable development complain that they have not been able to obtain transnational funding for their priorities because they have not been able to master "donor speak." They add that the ecoimperialists "have plenty of money for their own project ideas, but not for ours." This is true of environmentalists concerned about urban problems, such as air quality. The third problem is that ecodependent organizations must compete for funds. For instance, transnational funders distribute requests for proposals that they would like to see completed. The ecodependent groups compete to secure these funds. This divides the organizations, which could be working together for a common agenda, thus limiting their interest in banding together to form an environmental "movement." These issues are discussed in greater depth in chapter 5 on the Neoliberal Boom.

Type 3: Ecoresisters

I have intentionally omitted the term "organizations" when referring to ecoresisters, to highlight the fact that environmental movement activists are sometimes part of formal organizations, and are sometimes not. Ecoresisters do not typically receive funding from ecoimperialist organizations. When they do receive foreign funding, it is funding that they specifically request in relation to a pre-defined, usually local project of their choosing. This is in contrast to ecodependents whose paid staff members respond to requests for proposals put out by the ecoimperialists. Ecoresisters most often work at the local or regional level in response to a specific grievance, such as the threat of mining and its consequent habitat destruction. They have a volunteer labor force. They create their agenda; funders do not. They address problems that do not have sponsors. Unlike NGOs, which tend to focus on projects, they focus on "processes." For example, through workshops, they teach communities how to monitor their environment, grab media attention, and pressure the government. In this way ecoresistant organizations facilitate the process of local popular organizations standing up to fight in defense of their territories and rights. These groups try to self-fund by creating economic alternatives, though these practices only provide a portion of what they require to resist. Ecoresisters oppose the dominant development model and seek independence from outside influences; they have created alternative visions for development and, in some cases, concrete steps toward making their visions reality, at least at a local or regional scale. Their primary goal is to resist the forces of "development," particularly resource extraction, due to its negative impact on the environment and communities. Ecoresisters are more populist, community-based and movement-like than ecodependents and ecoentrepreneurs.

An example of an ecoresisting organization is DECOIN (Defensa y Conservación Ecológica de Intag, Defense and Ecological Conservation of Intag). It was founded to prevent copper mining in the Intag Valley, which is situated in the cloud forests of the Andes. Along with the communities of that area, it successfully resisted a Japanese company's attempts to mine, and then a Canadian company's, and now it is up against the Ecuadorian state's mining initiative. It has received some support over the years from small international groups. However, its focus has been on creating self-sustaining economic activities: it has created community-managed reserves for ecotourism, a shade-grown coffee cooperative, and supported a women's group that produces handicrafts that are sold in DECOIN's store, Casa de Intag, in the popular tourist destination of Otavalo. DECOIN has also succeeded in having the county of Intag declared an Ecological County. It coordinates with other similar groups, including C-CONDEM, a confederation of organizations from the coast, which has one of its goals to limit mangrove destruction, especially for shrimp farming. Due to its resistance against state-led extraction, it has an adversarial relationship with the national government.

Ecoresisters deal with the "environment versus development" debate on the ground. In resisting extraction (development) for the protection of the environment, they must also deal with the realities that people need to make a living to feed and house their families. Thus ecoresisters sometimes see "brother against brother" when one is working for ecotourism and the other is hoping for employment in the mines. As ecoresisters attempt to block the state's efforts at economic growth through extraction, they stand in the way of the treadmill of production, and are pressured by both the state and citizen-workers. Their strategy of creating local alternative economies can satisfy some at the local level, though even this is difficult (is it better to have roads and schools and hospitals or nature?). There is also a problem of scale in defending local territories since local destruction will be felt locally, but the gains in revenue through local extraction has the potential to affect "development" nationally. Ecodependent groups call these actors "radicals" and criticize them for not achieving much: "all they do is talk, talk, talk." However, environmental leaders also call the ecoresisters "essential" because they voice a critique of development and extraction that would otherwise be absent. These groups are less visible than the ecodependent groups because they are not always registered with the state, and often they are community-based or social groups rather than "environmental" per se. These activists and their issues will be elaborated upon in chapter 6 on the Neoliberal Bust.

Type 4: Ecoentrepreneur Organizations

Ecoentrepreneur organizations are funded locally through service fees as a means of ensuring "sustainable" funding. For instance, they protect the watershed that the water company relies on in exchange for a fee. In some cases transnational funders have provided seed monies for these organizations. These groups are characterized by their pragmatic and innovative approaches to gaining resources. Their agendas tend to be more anthropocentric than biocentric. They focus on local issues relevant to communities' quality of life, such as access to clean water and green spaces, as well as human health. These human-focused issues are often called "brown" issues in contrast to "green" issues of conservation. They are both urban and rural. Because Ecuadorians either pay directly for these services or receive some payment for contributing to these services, there is a higher level of awareness regarding these activities and a generally more positive outlook.

A group that exemplifies this work is Fondo para la Protección del Agua (FONAG). FONAG is a public–private organization that was founded in cooperation between The Nature Conservancy and the City of Quito, with the goal of protecting watersheds in order to protect the city's drinking water. TNC provided seed funds and the city's water company (EMAAP-Q) collects funds via water bills from the city's residents. FONAG is essentially a financial manager. It collects funds from users and distributes funds to other organizations that protect the watershed.[12] This model has been adapted slightly over time and is considered very successful, so much so, that it has been replicated in other LAC countries, and continues to grow as a model. FONAG does not see itself as part of an "environmental movement" per se.

Ecoentrepreneur organizations are part of the most recent wave of strategies to protect the environment that can be classified under a broad category of payment for ecosystem services (PES). There are numerous forms. In the case of FONAG, users pay for the protection of their watershed. In a relatively well-known international program developed by the United Nations, Reducing Emissions from Deforestation and Forest Degradation (REDD), low income countries receive financial incentives to keep forested land forested in order to reduce carbon emissions. In short, it values the carbon in the forests by paying countries to keep it there.[13] The Ecuadorian government launched a successful program called Socio Bosque, which relies on this type of model: using a direct payment method to forest users to protect forests by not cutting the trees. These models can be carried out by private organizations or by states. The public, when they are aware of such groups, have a generally positive response to them. In line with their concerns about privatizing water and nature, in general, some ecoresisters have questioned the practice of valuing the cost of nature's services. These groups will be discussed in greater detail in chapter 6 on the Neoliberal Bust.

Utility of Typology

The typology of environmentalisms provides a tool for explaining what varieties of environmentalism are prevalent under different conditions at different times.[14] In this way it helps uncover causal relationships. The analysis in the following case studies will examine three main relationships. First, how the environmental sector is affected by outsiders (transnational funders/ecoimperialists); second, how the different types of environmental organizations interact with each other as a result of transnational funding, and third, how this translates into their stances toward environment and development policies of the state. The specific goal is to use these types to illuminate what is occurring in Ecuador. The broader aim is to generate hypotheses regarding transnational funding and social movement sectors, in general, to develop a theory that will apply to other nations and other movements.[15] This will be taken up again in the concluding chapter 8. The next four chapters lay out the history of Ecuadorian environmentalism in four periods, beginning with the founding of the first environmental organization in 1978, Fundación Natura.

4 Origins, 1978 to 1987: *Ambientalistas* and *Ecologistas* Emerge

We can so far take a prophetic glance into futurity as to foretell that it will be the common and widely spread species, belonging to the larger and dominant groups, which will ultimately prevail and procreate new and dominant species.
—Charles Darwin, *On the Origin of Species*, 1859: 347

The genesis of the Ecuadorian environmental movement can best be understood as it relates to local environmental problems, the interests of "the international environmental community," and the deficiencies of the Ecuadorian state. This chapter traces the movement chronologically from its origins in the late 1970s, through to its recognition as a relevant force in Ecuadorian politics in the late 1980s. After the founding of a few important organizations, namely Fundación Natura and Acción Ecológica, the movement grew and split into two dominant camps: the first became professionalized and worked hand-in-hand with international supporters, representing the ideal type "ecodependent"; the other took a radical stance against extractive development, mobilized communities and battled transnational polluters, typifying the category "ecoresister." I use interviews with environmental movement activists and primary movement materials to describe this early period from their point of view. Though the movement emerged from within the civil society of the nation, transnational actors played a critical role in the development of Ecuadorian environmentalism.

Not coincidentally, the advent of the environmental movement occurred alongside an increasingly powerful international neoliberal agenda. That agenda, discussed in the latter part of the chapter, provides a backdrop for understanding the state's weak role in environmental management. In particular, the state's debt was a liability through which transnational actors could both limit the state and build capacity for private environmental organizations that would serve transnational actors' interests; thus serving neoliberal interests from the Global North. The end of the chapter analyzes the emergence of the movement within the context of the international economic system.

From the Ecuadorian People—The First Environmental Organization

A small group of university-educated scientists and self-proclaimed "nature lovers" marked the start of the Ecuadorian environmental movement when they created the organization, Fundación Natura (FN or Natura), in Quito in 1978 and registered it with the state as a nonprofit organization (*sin fines de lucro*).[1] Their work focused on the conservation of species and ecosystems. The first period of the movement was marked by naïve optimism and a simple desire by educated Ecuadorians to raise consciousness in their country about their environment. Many of the eventual leaders of future organizations would be involved in Natura in some way during this period as volunteers or part-time staff. It became the dominant organization from which many others spun off.

One of Fundación Natura's first projects was a television nature show called "Education for Nature" sponsored by Ecuadorian businesses that aired on Sunday nights. One of the founders commented:

The companies that financed the program in television obviously had a sense that that was a good investment. Instead of funding *telenovelas* and the typical things that companies fund in television, they were funding a documentary, which was absolutely fantastic. If you can imagine the number of people who called on the phone every day saying thank you for giving us this program. And obviously we passed those messages to the funders of the programs and they loved it. They felt that they were not only making good business for their companies by promoting the image of their institution but they were also contributing to knowledge, to the education of the people by those documentaries.[2]

Fundación Natura was open to working with everyone. They saw hope in the private sector. They believed that the private sector damaged the environment due to ignorance, not because there was an inherently problematic relationship between industry and the environment. They sought to work with businesses for the good of Ecuador.

Natura employed reformist tactics. They sought cooperation, negotiation, and compromise. They attempted to change the system from within, and to create working relationships with the institutions of power, namely industry and government. They saw this as the best means to help Ecuador. A founder remarks:

We did not have a position against or for any sector of society .... We thought every sector had a responsibility towards the environment and towards what at that time was our definition of development, that later on became sustainable development a couple of decades later .... [We believed] that government should be supported; that we should negotiate. We could not or did not want to attack anybody without having the chance of discussing an issue, of reaching a compromise that would guarantee that we could reach our objectives without destroying each other. In that, our style was not to be confrontational ... until we saw that there was no other mechanism to reach an agreement.[3]

Another Natura leader noted that a strength of the organization was that it included people of all political persuasions.[4] Later, other groups would use confrontation and "radical" tactics, but in the very beginning, the movement focused on nature conservation and education, welcomed corporate sponsorship, and sought compromise.

Enter Transnational Funders

A few months after their founding, Fundación Natura entered a contract with the United States Agency for International Development (USAID) to create an "Environmental Profile of Ecuador." This almost immediately increased their staff from three volunteers to forty paid employees. Early activists consider the research done for the profile as critical for helping them understand the connections among different segments of the environment.

Our big stroke of luck was that we started Natura with a project, which was the Environmental Profile of Ecuador .... The fortune was that by producing the Environmental Profile of Ecuador, that we understood all the linkages. Not all, but the main linkages of urban development, agriculture, forests, fisheries, air, chemicals, law, policy. It was the most fantastic process of discovery for our team.[5]

During the period from 1980 until 1987, Natura received three additional grants from USAID for environmental education projects, through the project called EDUNAT, which made up the majority of Natura's funding. USAID regarded EDUNAT a "success story" and replicated the model elsewhere in the western hemisphere. In the Project Completion Report, USAID writes, "The ascension of Fundación Natura to the largest environmental organization in Ecuador can, in large measure, be attributed to the three phases of EDUNAT."[6]

Bifurcation of Environmental Organizations

Until the mid-1980s, Natura was the only active national environmental organization in the country. It was "the" environmental NGO. In 1985, the group Sociedad de Defensa de la Naturaleza (Society for the Defense of Nature, SODENA) was founded, also in Quito. SODENA supported a sub-group called Acción Ecológica (AE), which was and is considered the most "radical green" group in Ecuador. It's history states that its early work was *más sociales que ecologistas* (more social than ecological) even though it was also started by a group of biologists.[7] A member noted that their projects are focused on conflicts around mining, oil, mangroves, and forests and that little by little they became transformed into social ecologists in that they call into question "the very basis of the model of intensive resource extraction."[8] The members of AE are mostly women, and they are sometimes referred to as "eco chicas." A founder notes, "Women have been outstanding in the work; perhaps there is an affinity for the theme, because being ecologists, we question the dominant model and it is easier from a women's perspective."[9]

Formally registered with the state in 1989, AE fought (and still fights) against the government and industry's extractive development paradigm. For instance, Acción Ecológica has fought against oil extraction in the Amazon since 1989 when it started its Campaign Amazonía por la Vida (Amazon for Life), which focuses on the protection of the Amazonian environment, including the protection of its people, and helping the local communities organize for solutions.[10] Never has AE's work been funded by the United States Agency for International Development, an important difference from Natura.

The contrasts between Fundación Natura and Acción Ecológica embody conflicting themes within Ecuadorian environmentalism, which were present at the outset of the movement and have carried throughout its history. On the one hand, Natura tended to be more concerned with biological diversity and conservation, mostly the "natural" environment; environmental sustainability. Its concern stemmed from the founders' natural science approach to the environment, which was also associated with the concerns of the most powerful international environmental groups, which became Fundación Natura's partners and funders. Fundación Natura consisted of "*ambientalistas*," (environmentalists) who looked for solutions within the system, such as the implementation of environmental policies, who sought cooperation and compromise, and whose position was considered conservative. Acción Ecológica's concern focused on human-environmental interactions. AE included social and economic concerns in their ecological analysis, including the social and economic pillars of sustainability. These *"ecologistas,"* (ecologists) took an ethical position against the economic system, especially resource extraction, and particularly petroleum development, and argued for more fundamental/radical change. AE's approach was also more adversarial. They were effective at using the print media to draw attention to environmental problems. They were a "go to" source for journalists seeking an inflammatory quote about environmental issues. The definition of Ecuadorian "environmentalist/ecologist" was contested in the early period between Fundación Natura and Acción Ecológica. There was a stark contrast between the two conceptions.[11]

The ideological gulf between Natura and AE was wide. Even their work to educate Ecuadorians was directed to different ends. Natura educated to change consciousness in order to garner support for creating environmental policy. AE educated to mobilize actors and to help groups organize themselves to protect their environments, from the Amazonian rain forest to the mangroves in Esmeraldas. The early organizational bifurcation also played out in groups' relationships with the state in their support of environmental and development policies. Natura promoted better policies and enforcement (a managed scarcity synthesis) whereas AE sought an overhaul and thinking attuned to nature's and humanities' needs (an ecological synthesis).

In an interview, a founding member of Acción Ecológica reinforced the idea that the two types of groups were at odds, and described the difference in terms of ideology and constituency. She explained that there are groups, including Natura, that have a neoliberal view of the environment—"a World Bank view that sees environmental issues as obstacles to development" that can be fixed by market forces, such as privatization of lands for conservation. On the other hand, groups like Acción Ecológica work with "campesinos, indigenous people, fisherfolk and community women" and are part of a "popular ecological movement." These people have long been concerned with issues that were not labeled "environmental," and therefore these groups have been arguably much less visible than those that are established environmental NGOs. "There is a tradition of thinking that the environmental movement is just NGOs working on environmental issues and that is a bit poor, no? I think they [NGOs] play a role because they articulate, they generate information. But they are not necessarily an environmental movement."[12]

A leader of Natura explains differently:

Now when I think of the history of the environmental movement I also think of groups that later became organized and became NGOs [implying AE] but didn't like them [NGOs]. They thought that Natura was selling its principles by sitting at the table with the private sector, who was sitting at the table with the minister of mining or economy, whatever. And that started their [AE's] set up as an NGO by defining who are the bad, the good and the ugly. And we didn't have that [way of seeing the world]. All of us could be ugly and all of us could be good if we acted irresponsibly or responsibly. So that defined us as a different model that was not liked by many .... The radical NGOs started by attacking Natura. That was their main goal—to demonstrate that we were not legitimate in our approach.[13]

Esperanza Martínez, a founder of AE, has argued that there are three streams of environmentalism expressed nationally and internationally: (1) conservationists concerned with the conservation of nature, (2) environmentalists who focus on intervening in conflicts and proposing solutions in line with the system of production, and (3) ecologists that question that model of development.[14] Teodoro Bustamante, a one-time leader of Natura, describes two camps: (1) the reformers, who believe that the only way the system will work is to incorporate environmental considerations, and (2) the rebellious ones, who believe the ecological struggle is the most radical struggle against the system.[15]

These classifications align with the typology created in chapter 3. As will be elaborated below, the "conservationists" in Ecuador are largely the large international NGOs classified as ecoimperialists. The "environmentalists proposing solutions/the reformers" are the ecodependent groups. Finally the "ecologists questioning the model of development/the rebellious ones" fit the ecoresister type. Fundación Natura embodies an ecodependent organization. It relies on transnational funding to carry out projects largely focused on the protection of nature. It has a professional staff in its main office in the capital of Quito that works with the government and ensures its funding. Acción Ecológica represents an ecoresistant organization. It is grassroots and independent. Its primarily volunteer staff work in the office and the field. It trains communities how to resist nature-damaging development, and it has a specific campaign against petroleum extraction. If it takes any funds from the Global North, it has specifically requested the funds to aid in anti-extraction campaigns. Groups that formed in later periods would largely fit into one of these two molds.

In the late 1980s other prominent and long-lasting groups were also founded in Quito: CECIA (la Corporación Ornitológica del Ecuador [the Ornithological Corporation of Ecuador], now Aves y Conservación [Birds and Conservation]) in 1986, CORDAVI (la Corporación por la Defensa de la Vida [the Corporation for the Defense of Life]) in 1987, Fundación Maquipucuna in 1988, and EcoCiencia (EcoScience), Fundación Jatun Sacha, and Fundación Ecológica Arcoiris (Foundation Ecological Rainbow) in 1989. While Fundación Natura started with broad goals and a broad view of "Ecuador's environment," groups that followed began a process of specialization. For instance, CECIA and EcoCiencia were founded on principals of "science" and conducted research; CORDAVI litigated; Fundación Maquipucuna and Fundación Jatun Sacha were focused on action "on the ground," and both eventually purchased land for private preserves. Because of their focus on land preservation, Maquipucuna and Jatun Sacha's work moved away from the capital, though they kept offices in Quito. There was significant organizational growth during this period and into the beginning of the next.

In terms of the three pillars of sustainability—environmental, social, and economic—the early groups were heavily weighted toward the environmental. Exceptions existed. For instance, CORDAVI brought a lawsuit against multinational companies that had explored for oil in the Amazon's national parks and degraded the land and water of indigenous communities. CORDAVI started their battle in the Ecuadorian courts and then continued against the US corporations in US courts in 1991. CORDAVI and other groups fighting such development were against natural resource extraction for environmental and social reasons. The area in question was in Yasuní National Park (environmental reasons), and it was home to the indigenous Huaorani people (social reasons). CORDAVI's work integrated the themes. Nevertheless, at this time the majority of environmental organizations' missions were focused squarely on nature, animals, and conservation themes (figure 4.1).

While Quito was the hub of environmentalists' activities due to the fact that as the capital, it is the location of government and international agencies, notable groups emerged in other regions of the nation. On the coast, in Guayaquil (the largest city in Ecuador), a chapter of Fundación Natura was founded in 1984, as was Fundación Ecuatoriana para el Estudio de Mamíferos Marinos (FEMM, Ecuadorian Foundation for the Study of Marine Mammals), in 1986. In the *oriente*, a different sort of "environmental" organization was founded in 1980: Fondo Ecuatoriano Populorum Progressio (FEPP). Its objective was to "reconcile the conservation of natural resources and the survival of humans" by assisting grassroots organizations with technical capacity, monitoring programs, and legal aid in relationship to water and air pollution, deforestation, and soil erosion.[16] Again, groups were mostly nature and conservation focused, but CORDAVI and FEPP, both

Figure 4.1
Sign for Yasuní National Park taken from the Napo River. The sign reads, "The Forest Law prohibits hunting, fishing, colonizing, commercial plants and animals." The guard house near the sign reads, "Financed by The Nature Conservancy."

Amazonian based, showed that there were conservation concerns that included human faces, especially around petroleum development.

International *Origins*

Though I mark the start of the environmental movement with the founding of the national-level organization Fundación Natura in 1978, it is telling that an international NGO (INGO), the Charles Darwin Research Foundation, which focused its work in the Galápagos Islands, had existed since 1964 on the Galápagos island of Santa Cruz. However, it is not an Ecuadorian NGO; it is registered as an international nonprofit association in Belgium. The Galápagos National Park was the first national park in Ecuador, established in 1959. In part due to its importance in Darwin's *On the Origin of Species* (1859), and to its tremendous biodiversity, the area garnered international attention. The park became a UNESCO World Heritage Site in 1978.

Other international NGOs would eventually make their way to the Ecuadorian mainland, especially after there were more national NGOs with whom to "partner." For instance, The Nature Conservancy created a Quito office in 1989 and the South American office for the International Union for the Conservation of Nature (IUCN; UICN in Spanish) followed suit in 1991. Yolanda Kakabadse, a leading Ecuadorian environmentalist, later became the president of the IUCN. Intergovernmental organizations with environmental programs also had a presence in Quito, including the UN Environment and Development Program, starting in 1972. Bilateral donors, such as USAID and the German GTZ (German Organization for Technical Cooperation) also had major environmental programs with offices based in Quito. Literal signs of these actors could be seen throughout the country (see figure 4.2)

A Key Year—1987

Three important events occurred in 1987 that marked a shift from an emerging environmental movement to one that had achieved a

Figure 4.2
Sign outside of the protected Peguche Falls. Besides noting directions for native guides, information office, an ecotourism company, ecological trails, and environmental education, the sign shows which transnational funders (United Nations Development Programme) have contributed to these services.

recognizable level of development: (1) a national environmental congress was held, (2) an environmental umbrella group was formed to be an arbiter among the conflicting but complementary types of environmental groups, and (3) a large influx of international funds were generated for conservation through the country's first debt-for-nature swap.

In conjunction with national organizations, transnational organizations, including USAID and the World Wildlife Fund, sponsored a national meeting in Quito on the state of the environment (I Congreso del Medio Ambiente, First Congress on the Environment).[17] Approximately 350 participants from all sectors of society convened at the congress, including business, government, universities, and the few national environmental NGOs that existed. At the Congress an umbrella organization, Comité Ecuatoriano para la Defensa de la Naturaleza y el Medio Ambiente (CEDENMA, Ecuadorian Committee for the Defense of Nature and the Environment), was formed. It had multiple goals, including defending nature and the environment, taking legal action to do that when necessary, raising awareness that society needs a socially just and ecologically balanced environment, ensuring democratic representation regarding environmental decisions, demanding public discussion regarding development projects, whether public or private, to ensure the environmental impact is considered, and more.[18] Its aims encompassed environmental and social sustainability. The first president of CEDENMA, Vicente Polít, later remarked that at the time of the First Congress,

There were two trends on the subject [of environmentalism]: one, pragmatic, conciliatory and striving for technical solutions [ambientalistas, environmentalists], and the other of an idealistic character, contesting the system and seeking social solutions [ecologistas, ecologists] ... [This has] given a sense of 'technological optimism' on one side, and an 'ecological pessimism,' on the other.[19]

There was hope that CEDENMA could bridge the gap between these two sides. Esperanza Martínez, a founder of AE, remarked of CEDENMA:

It plays a fundamental role between the two streams: Acción Ecológica and Fundación Natura. There always tends to be two positions: the one (AE's) has been considered excessively radical, and the other (Natura's) has been labeled as conservative. In every moment the two positions come up against each other. For example when we speak of the activity in a petroleum block, the one [Natura's] tends to be conciliatory in the sense of talking, negotiating and reaching agreements with the company; the other [AE's] tends to totally reject. Between these positions there's the need to take intermediate positions. It is believed that CEDENMA is able to take the positions of the middle so that neither side protests too much.[20]

CEDENMA's creation provided an opportunity to bring together competing environmental ideas in a way that could move the environmental agenda forward.

Also in 1987 the first of three movement-changing debt-for-nature swaps took place in Ecuador. These need to be briefly contextualized and explained. Globally, in a relatively narrow time period (1987 to 1994), fifteen countries were the recipients of funds generated by debt-for-nature swaps. In a swap, an organization from the Global North purchases a portion of an indebted nation's (typically from the Global South) debt at a discount on the secondary debt market in exchange for a commitment by the indebted nation to establish a Conservation Trust Fund to carry out environmental projects. The indebted country's foreign debt is reduced, but they continue to make payments, though smaller than their original debt payments, into the Trust Fund. The beneficiary of the fund is typically an NGO within the country. In Ecuador's case, their debt was purchased by The Nature Conservancy, the World Wildlife Fund–US, the Missouri Botanical Garden, and the Frank Weeden Foundation.[21] The NGO recipient was Fundación Natura, which was intended to serve as a central agent to distribute funds to other NGOs and public programs. In the first exchange (1987), WWF bought one million dollars' worth of debt at a discounted rate on the secondary market for $354,000. They donated the debt note to Fundación Natura. In exchange for the debt note, the government provided bonds for the full price of the note, the interest on the bonds paid for Fundación Natura's ongoing programs, and the principal formed an endowment for them.[22] The second and third swaps generated over nine million dollars in conservation funds.[23] Debt-for-nature swaps were a successful mechanism for creating funds for conservation in Ecuador.

While much could and has been written about the pros and cons of debt-for-nature swaps,[24] there are three underlying conditions that explain why Ecuador became a target of these swaps, which in turn played a critical role in Ecuador's environmental history. First, Ecuador's government was heavily indebted to the international community. It felt economically pressured and the swaps were a release valve. Second, due to its high degree of biodiversity, Ecuador was on international conservationists' radar. They wanted Ecuador's species preserved for the good of humankind. Third, Ecuador's citizens had shown, through the development of organizations like Fundación Natura and CEDENMA, that there was national concern about the environment and national organizational capacity was developing to address their problems.

The *Congreso*, the formation of CEDENMA, and the first debt-for-nature swap, made 1987 a pivotal year for environmental organizations in Ecuador. The environment was on the political map. Government, businesses, civil society, and international civil society recognized the importance of "the environment" for Ecuador's future. The influx of real funds that the debt-for-nature swaps brought set up the boom years for the growth in the number of environmental organizations in Ecuador.

The State's Preoccupations

During this period the state was transitioning from a military dictatorship to a democracy; it was considered a "fragile democracy."[25] The government was weak in terms of its capacity to manage or administer, some say in part due to its history of clientelism and personality-based politics.[26] Revenues from petroleum were high, but volatile due to shifts in the world market. Just as Ecuador's biodiversity drew the attention, funds, and the influence of the transnational conservation community, its petroleum facilitated an influx of foreign funds that were likewise not in the control of the Ecuadorian state. Like other Latin American states that were also democratizing at this time, the political opportunities that opened up enabled a number of social movements to emerge, including the environmental movement and the indigenous rights movement.[27]

The Military Period
In the 1970s a military government ruled during an oil boom. Their policies concentrated wealth among the wealthiest, especially in urban areas. It wasn't a complete "resource curse," since there were some social advantages: increased schooling, decreased infant mortality, and increased life expectancy.[28] However, most Ecuadorians did not benefit from the oil revenues and in this early period, "development" was not achieved. In their detailed account of the politics of the era, *Ecuador: Fragile Democracy*, David Corkill and David Cubitt remark,

In the mid-1980s, Ecuador could look back on more than a decade of military or civilian government which claimed an explicit commitment to economic growth, development and modernization, which promised to work for social justice and respond to the long-postponed needs of the poor, and which were underpinned to a lesser or greater extent by the fabulous and unprecedented inflow of oil wealth. A quick overview of Ecuadorean society shows, however, that as far as the conditions of life for vast masses of Ecuadorians were concerned, the years of "development" and "social justice" had achieved very little ... [T]he bottom 40 percent of the

Ecuadorean population received around 5.2 percent of total income, while the top 20 percent took around 72 percent.[29]

During the military period, the public and private sectors also piled on debt, which would limit the development choices of future leaders.

Democratic Transition

In 1978, civilian elections were held and the people elected left-leaning President Jaime Roldós. He died in a plane crash in 1981, which some believe was an assassination, and Vice President Osvaldo Hurtado assumed the presidency. The period remained democratic. In 1985, right-leaning Febres Cordero was elected President, and in 1988, politics would swing back to the left with the election of Rodrigo Borja. While the citizens elected presidents from both ends of the political spectrum, the leaders were all limited in their actions by the country's debt burden. They were unable to deliver the goods to the people.

The Debt Load and Its Consequences

In 1970, Ecuador's total foreign debt was $242 million; by 1982, it had increased to $12.5 billion, more than a fiftyfold increase.[30] In 1982, the debt service (which is simply the interest payment without principal) to the International Monetary Fund (IMF) made up 79 percent of exports of goods, services, and income (table 2.1). This high debt forced Ecuador to renegotiate its loans with the IMF in 1982 and 1983. The IMF required structural adjustment. The conditions of the loan restructuring required "stabilization," which among other things meant devaluing the national currency (then the *sucre*) and cutting public expenditures.[31] Even after this, debt service took up a third of export earnings.[32] The transition of the Ecuadorian state during this period epitomized a shift from a developmentalist state to a neoliberal state.[33] IMF conditions promoted neoliberal policies, which included cutting social spending, privatizing public institutions, deregulating the economy, reducing labor protections, encouraging "open" and "free" markets internationally, including foreign direct investment, and focusing on export-oriented growth.[34]

The debt toll was negative for the society and the environment. Debt limited social payments for the good of the Ecuadorian citizens. Debt also stressed natural resources, since export earning was needed to service the debt and exports were often primary commodities, such as oil. Debt exacerbated the problems associated with oil that began before the debt crisis. The debt crisis, coupled with the state's dependence on oil revenues, led it to seek expanded oil development, and thus sped up the treadmill of production. Eventually, in 1992, Ecuador withdrew from OPEC because it didn't want to be bound to its production limits.

Neoliberal Strategies: Deregulation, Export-Oriented Growth, Foreign Direct Investment, and Resource Extraction

State policies focused on increasing exports and opening up petroleum extraction further to transnational corporations. Two actions, in particular, eased this relationship. First, in 1982, the state made changes to the hydrocarbons law that made it easier for actors from abroad to receive favorable contracts.[35] Second, in 1984, President Cordero forged an agreement with the US Overseas Private Investment Corporation (OPIC) that provided protections to US investors. Corkill and Cubitt report that "Foreign oil companies were among the first to benefit from the open door strategy. ... [M]ultinational companies [were] awarded up to 100 percent tax relief on equipment as part of a drive to double known oil reserves by 1988."[36] Ecuador had to meet its debt payments, and it sought to increase its funds by opening up to foreign investment in its most lucrative sector.

Jeanne Hey, an expert on small economies notes, "Ecuador during this period [1981 to 1988] was intensely dependent on the USA through the most prominent channels of dependence: trade, aid and direct foreign investment. ... Reliance on primary product export, low levels of industrialization and massive debt weakened the country's economy."[37] Some data from Hey's analysis support the argument: Regarding trade, Ecuador and the United States had a high volume relationship: in 1985 over 57 percent of Ecuador's exports went to the United States and over 35 percent of its imports were from the United States. Most of the exports were primary commodities, including petroleum, and petroleum revenues comprised almost 60 percent of the state's budget that same year. The United States also had high levels of direct foreign investment during the period from 1980 to 1988: averaging over $400 million per year, which amounted to 33 percent of direct foreign investment in Ecuador; by contrast, European investment was less than 21 percent. Regarding aid, the bilateral relationship was also strong. On average, in the period from 1984 to 1987, the United States sent over $55 million for economic and military aid. Finally, in terms of debt, Ecuador's had sustained a staggeringly high amount; in 1987, it was over $10 billion. Of that, almost 60 percent was owed to private banks in the United States.[38] Ecuador was under the influence of US economic forces. Cordero, President from 1984 until 1988, has been called "the darling of the international banking community" and Ronald Reagan held him up as a "model debtor."[39] Ecuador was subordinant.

Toward the end of the era, there were more problems, even after loan restructurings, and in part due to them. Economic crisis in 1986 was followed by protests and general strikes calling on the government not to follow the IMF's austerity conditions.[40] In 1986, the state suspended debt payments. Shortly afterward, in 1987, a major earthquake rocked Ecuador, causing the loss of human life, and destroying the primary oil pipeline. This hurt an already weakened economy and shut down oil production. Corkill and Cubitt assess:

> 1987 was [to that point] the most disastrous year in the short history of the Ecuador-ean oil industry. With oil output and revenues down by 60 percent through a com-bination of pipeline damage and the decline in the world oil price, Ecuador was in no position to keep up the interest payments on its foreign debt. ... Soon afterwards ... and following the Peruvian example, it announced that it would limit the level of repayments to a proportion of its export revenues.[41]

The period ends in 1987, not just for the environmental movement reasons above but because it coincides with these changes in the state's debt repay-ment policies.

In many ways Ecuador's political economy reads like that of other Latin American countries that followed the traditional development trajectory since the 1970s. Under the military government, Ecuador became severely indebted. The government borrowed large amounts of money in the 1970s, which led to a crisis in the early 1980s, as it was unable to meet debt payments. In the 1980s and 1990s it renegotiated loans with the IMF in exchange for agreeing to make structural adjustments. These included steps to liberalize the economy, increase exports, and reduce social spending. While these did not contribute to "development," in general, what this meant for sustainable development was that the social equity and environ-mental protection portions of "sustainability" were being squeezed out of the Ecuadorian state's economic equation. The options of Ecuador's govern-ment, to preserve and protect or exploit and ignore, in the face of immedi-ate problems to service the debt, led them down the path of exploitation of environmental resources. They resolved the nature-society dialectic with an economic synthesis. The state became more extraction-oriented just as the environmental movement emerged.

Environmental Policies

The focus during this period was not on new environmental laws. The environment was just making its way onto the agenda. Interestingly, though, under the military government and at the beginning of the democratic era, new protected areas were established. As stated earlier, the first protected area in Ecuador was the Galápagos National Park established in 1959. Two more were established by 1970 and the seventies witnessed a peak in new establishments: two in 1975 and a surge in 1979 (5 new areas). In the 1980s, four more parks were established. In addition to national parks, the system also includes other protected designations, such as ecological reserves (figure 4.3). A cynical view of all of the protection of lands is that it was simply a means for the state to control lands to exploit. The Ley Forestal y de Conservación de Áreas Naturales y Vida Silvestre (Forestry Law and Conservation of Natural Areas and Wildlife) of 1981 established a legal basis for a system of protected areas. This law placed the planning, management, development, administration, and control of these areas in the

Figure 4.3
Entrance to Cotacachi-Cayapas Ecological Reserve, founded in 1968. Home to 139 mammal species, 500 to 600 bird species, 125 amphibians and 111 reptile species.

Ministerio de Agricúltura y Ganadería (Ministry of Agriculture and Grazing, MAG). Though the state had an ambitious protected areas policy, it had mostly "paper parks." In other words, the parks existed in paper but were not protected on the ground. The state turned its head away when mangroves were felled in coastal parks and hydrocarbon extraction permits overlapped with protected areas in the Amazon. At this point Ecuador had signed international agreements for biodiversity protection, including the World Heritage Convention (1972) and the Convention on International Trade in Endangered Species (1973).

The International Political Economy and the Environmental Movement

This chapter links the international political economy to state dependency and the emergence of the national environmental movement. The international political economy contributed to the weakening of the Ecuadorian government. Even as the state expanded its financial resources through its international sales of petroleum, it was not able to finance public goods due to its international debt load. Ecuador's debt load put it under the thumb of the United States. This weak state was vulnerable to international pressures—pressure to alter policies, pressure to develop economically (from lenders and transnational petroleum corporations), and pressure to protect its biodiversity (from transnational conservationists and debt-for-nature swap brokers). The international political and economic forces encouraged the state to speed up the treadmill of production while the international conservation demands supported private NGOs to protect the environment. While international pressures were contradictory (produce versus protect), the pressure felt most by the state was the pressure to increase production. Private actors were urged to increase protection. From the perspective of dependency theory, which posits that relationships between powerful core states and weak peripheral states benefits strong states and elites in weak states at the cost of widespread "development" for the masses,[42] Ecuador was clearly dependent on and beholden to the United States.

Ecuador's engagement with the "international community" through its trade, aid, and debt affected its social movements. Despite export gains and significant aid from abroad, the majority of the state's revenues went to debt service, which meant that the state was unable to translate its gains into benefits to its people. Nationally this delegitimized the state and made it vulnerable. James O'Connor (1973) argues that a debt crisis creates trouble for the state since it cannot simultaneously repay debt and provide services to a nation. In this situation the state is vulnerable to "radical organizing." This line of thinking is in parallel with the treadmill of production theory. In the TOP theory, the state is understood as having dual and competing burdens: (1) creating the conditions that enable companies to produce and (2) protecting citizen-workers from the social and environmental damage that comes from production. The state must create conditions for the accumulation of profit so that it can tax, generating funds to sustain itself, as well as repay its debts. It must also maintain social harmony in order to keep its legitimacy with citizens. The state accomplishes this by providing social services to those who are not the recipients of accumulation. When the state is more attentive to corporations (or transnational interests) than to citizen-workers, a potential mechanism for change is social movements. In Ecuador's case, social movements were responding.

This analysis is supported by Suzana Sawyer's work. In her book *Crude Chronicles: Indigenous Politics, Multinational Oil, and Neoliberalism in Ecuador,* Sawyer summarizes the consequences that the implementation of the international neoliberal agenda had for the Ecuadorian state nationally:

> ... [S]tate neoliberal reforms backfired in Ecuador. Far from creating an environment of political and economic stability—the conditions necessary for democracy to flourish—neoliberal policies in Ecuador gnawed away at the country's social bodies and served to foment impressive resistance. Indeed, economic reforms undermined the very conditions that lent legitimacy and authority to the state's political system—its purported concern for its national subjects ... [T]he state jeopardized what little credibility it held.[43]

The combination of an international debt crisis, and the speed up of oil exploration and production for export, both had the effect of moving states away from meeting citizens' needs, and in making states vulnerable to citizen-led movements. In the parlance of social movement theorists, fiscal crisis opens the political opportunity structure (POS) and enables social movements to emerge.[44] While the state is more vulnerable nationally, its international situation also makes it more vulnerable internationally—to other states, its lenders, the IMF, transnational corporations, and transnational social movement actors, including transnational environmental NGOs. Transnational private actors literally take control of the lands from which they extract oil. Transnational conservationists literally take control of the lands they seek to protect for the good of humanity and the planet.

To put it another way, the international economic system contributed to the weakening of the Ecuadorian state in ways that made it vulnerable from both "above" and "below." From above, the weak state is beholden to the IMF, creditors, and to private transnational capital wishing to invest/extract in the nation. It is also vulnerable to conservationists' pressures, especially if they offer incentives, such as the reduction of debts. From below, the weak state is vulnerable to citizens-workers' demanding investment in public goods such as education, health care, social security and environmental protection. Labor movements and environmental movements can pressure states from below. They can also ally with transnational actors to apply pressure simultaneously from above and below to urge the state to take environmental regulatory action. In short, what this era demonstrates is the interplay among international economic structures, national political opportunity structures, and national and transnational social movement activity.

Most, though not all, of these pressures on the Ecuadorian state led it toward actions that accelerated the treadmill of production, already one of its internal goals: the IMF/creditors wanted their repayments, private capital sought investments in petroleum extraction, citizen-workers wanted jobs and growth in state revenues for the good of the people. CEDENMA argued that during this period, the government "exacerbate[d] environmental problems and severely affect[ed] the quality of life of Ecuadorians in the first attempt to implement a neo-liberal model of development in the country."[45] The Vice President of the country argued that concern for the environment should not put the brakes on development.[46] In Schnaiberg's terminology, Ecuador had reconciled the dynamic between production and environmental limits via an economic synthesis. Partially countering treadmill accelerations were the actions of transnational conservationists from above and more radical environmentalists—ecoresisters—from below. The weak state was porous: domestic and foreign actors could infiltrate it. In this period the Ecuadorian state was weak, but by the final era of this history it was strong. Spoiler alert. The strong state also speeds up the treadmill, but for different reasons: the good of the people. Later it seeks domestic legitimacy rather than kudos from transnational capital.

In the case of Ecuador, international economic conditions led to national social movement activity. This happened in other debt-ridden developing countries in the 1980s. Numerous countries renegotiated loans with the IMF in exchange for agreements to make structural adjustments, including steps to liberalize their economies, increase exports, and reduce social spending. These economic crises reduced debt-stressed states' legitimacy with their citizens and led to austerity protests around the developing world.[17] Because the debt payments benefit actors outside the nation, another layer of complexity is added to the case. In this situation, benefits of growth largely leave the country, whereas the negative consequences of it remain local. In an age of globalization, economic crisis generates vulnerability for the state not just at the national level, but also at the international level. State economic weakness opens the opportunity for transnational social movements.

* * *

The organizations that emerged during the origins period were native to Ecuador, though from the educated elite. They were urban professionals, not people living off the land. Fundación Natura would attempt to grow as a membership organization, but that was short-lived. Their growth would come from foreign funding that eventually created a dependency relationship, thus the categorization as ecodependent group. Fundación Natura would go on to be the most dominant organization over time. Acción Ecologíca's perspective was radical and confrontational. They would go on to ally with other radical movements, including the indigenous rights movement. They decried the extractive development trajectory and sought

Table 4.1

Summary of Origins Era

	Origins 1978–1987	Boom 1987–2000	Bust 2000–2006	Revolution 2006–2015
Transnational funding	Seed funds for new organizations and projects			
Environmental sector	Bifurcated into ecodependent and ecoresistent			
State characteristics	Weak, indebted, and resource dependent			
Environment and development policies	Environmental policies not implemented nor existing ones enforced; export-led development based on petroleum			
Schnaiberg's synthesis	Economic synthesis			

to disrupt it, thus making them ecoresisters. The diversity of Ecuador's environmental movement reflected the diversity of its plants and animals. There was no single dominant species from the start. At the end of this period the first president of CEDENMA quipped in 1987 that with the *Congreso,* environmental issues "rose from the cliques of insiders to the conference rooms and newpapers."[48] Early groups succeeded in putting the environment on the agenda. Table 4.1 summarizes this era in relation to the key analytic variables. Chapter 5 continues the chronology, outlining the boom years of the 1990s.

5 Neoliberal Boom, 1987 to 2000: The Rise of Ecodependence

Invasive alien species are animals, plants or other organisms introduced by man into places out of their natural range of distribution, where they become established and disperse, generating a negative impact on the local ecosystem and species. ... The impacts of alien invasive species are immense, insidious, and usually irreversible. They are causing significant damage to ecological, economic and health levels.
—International Union for the Conservation of Nature[1]

Invasive species are a harmful subset of so-called exotic, alien, non-native, or introduced species, and are one of the most serious global environmental challenges we face.
—National Environmental Coalition on Invasive Species[2]

This chapter examines international and national forces that shaped Ecuador's environmentalism during the height of neoliberalism. It looks at how the international environmental discourse of "sustainable development" interfaced with the international economic hegemony of neoliberalism. During the boom years, from 1987 to 2000, international, national, and local concerns coalesced to create substantial growth in the environmental movement sector in terms of both the number and the types of organizations in Ecuador. *Ecoimperialist* organizations used their transnational funding to grow *ecodependent* organizations, which altered their structures to become more professional, and conserved important habitats. The negative impact of the ecoimperialist funding was that the local ecodependent organizations' agendas were channeled by "so-called exotic, alien, nonnative" forces, and competition among Ecuadorian groups for funding weakened solidarity within the national movement, preventing a collective approach that would be critical of the extractive development trajectory. Nevertheless, ecoimperialists and ecodependents forged an alliance to fill the void left by the weak state, which was further weakened by its policy decisions to privatize and decentralize. The government's decisions were largely dictated by international economic actors. Similarly a state decision to create a new environmental ministry during this period was in response to the concerns of the international environmental community. Overall, the actions of environmentalists and the state were negligible in shifting the development trajectory away from Schaiberg's economic synthesis to a managed scarcity synthesis. Ecodependents, concerned about their own organizational maintenance, lost sight of the big picture. Even though the state espoused the rhetoric of "sustainable development," and there was need for it evidenced by rising inequality and environmental degradation due to petroleum extraction, the government continued to follow the prescriptions of neoliberalism by opening the country to investments from abroad, which would continue to increase natural resource extractive development. Amid these trends, under the radar, grassroots movements led by indigenous groups and emerging eco-resisters started poking holes in the state's development logic and generated some uncertainty about the nation's future trajectory.

International Context: The United Nations Conference on Environment and Development

International events set the stage for the growth of the Ecuadorian environmental movement. In 1992, at the United Nations Conference on Environment and Development (UNCED, nicknamed the Earth Summit), which took place nearby in Rio de Janeiro, Brazil, the world turned its thoughts toward trying to reconcile the competing demands of environmental protection and economic growth. The theme of the conference was sustainable development. The 1987 World Commission on Environment and Development had promoted the idea of "sustainable development" to address both the "environment problem" and the "development problem." The Commission's 1987 Report, *Our Common Future,* called for sustainable development, which it defined as "Development which meets the needs of the present without compromising the ability of future generations to meet their own needs."[3] At the time this was a major shift in the thinking about environment and development. The idea was not new, but its prominence was.

In Rio, representatives from 172 nations, including 108 heads of state, met to sign international agreements to promote sustainable development. This was the largest ever gathering of world leaders.[4] A parallel NGO event, the "Global Forum," was attended by over 17,000 people, myself included.

At the summit, over 150 nations signed two binding agreements: the Convention on Biological Diversity and the Climate Convention. The Convention on Biological Diversity is designed to prevent the "destruction of biological species, habitats and ecosystems."[5] Ecuador was the first Latin American country to sign it. Movement leaders from all types of environmental groups considered the Earth Summit a pivotal event in the history of the Ecuadorian movement. Even members of radical organizations saw this as a key moment and were optimistic because they believed that the agreements made in Rio de Janeiro meant that biodiversity and climate change were now on the agenda: "international priorities also mean resources and possibilities for action."[6] They were right. The question, though, was resources for which kinds of action.

State Environmental Responses

Governments around the world felt pressure to respond positively to UNCED. Ecuador wanted to be part of the international conversation. Numerous official state documents were produced to respond to information requests made prior to the conference and to agreements made at the conference with regard to making country-level data available. For example, the Ministerio de Relaciones Exteriores del Ecuador (Ecuador's Ministry of Foreign Affairs) in cooperation with the government of Canada produced La Gestión Ambiental en el Ecuador (Environmental Management in Ecuador) for UNCED. At that time Ecuador did not have a Ministry of the Environment. There were also follow-up reports, including an assessment of how well Ecuador was able to address "Agenda 21," the action plan for sustainable development that was adopted at the conference. The UN Food and Agriculture Organization (FAO) produced a report in 1995 suggesting that the Ecuadorian state had taken an important step in creating a state institution to coordinate efforts to address Agenda 21. The president created this institution, Comisión Asesora Ambiental de la Presidencia de la República (President's Environmental Advisory Commission, CAAM), by executive decree (and with the assistance of USAID, among others) just one year after the Earth Summit to advise him on how the country should proceed environmentally.[7] Even with the creation of CAAM, though, the state had very little capacity to carry out environmental projects. From its founding in 1993 until 1995, CAAM led the nation through a participatory process to formulate the Plan Ambiental Ecuatoriano (Ecuadorian Environmental Plan), which sought to move Ecuador toward "desarrollo sostenible" (sustainable development).[8] This included a plan for sustainable petroleum development. A year later a new ministry of the environment (El Ministerio del Medio Ambiente del Ecuador) was established by presidential decree.

During this time the Sistema Nacional de Áreas Protegidas (National System of Protected Areas) continued to grow. In 1996 two new national parks were added to the protected area system: El Cajas and Llanganates National Parks. These parks added to a system that already looked impressive, on paper at least, including areas recognized with UN designations: two World Heritage Sites (the Galápagos and Sangay National Parks), and two Biosphere Reserves (the Galápagos and Yasuní National Parks) plus a protected area—Cayambe Coca Reserve—which was considered one of the top ten biodiversity hot spots in the world.[9] However, the agency in charge of these areas was chronically underfunded.

Two years later, in 1998, the Ley Especial de Galápagos (Special Law of Galápagos) was passed, which was designed to improve the conservation of the Galápagos Islands. USAID officials were proud to report that Al Gore played a critical role in focusing worldwide pressure on Ecuador to pass this law. They called the passage "a US government success story." At the time, CNN reported, "'These islands mean so much to the world,' said WWF's [World Wildlife Fund's] President Kathryn Fuller. 'They are home to magnificent species found nowhere else on Earth. They remain an irreplaceable living laboratory of evolution for scientists, and a precious part of humanity's living legacy.'"[10]

The international gaze made a difference in Ecuador by affecting the state's actions. Then-president of CEDENMA remarked, "The international [community] obligates the government to act [on environmental issues] … or at least look like they're acting.[11] A German national working for the German Agency for Technical Cooperation (GTZ) argued that the GTZ's presence "at least keeps the [Ecuadorian] government aware that they must do something."[12] A founding member of the environmental organization CECIA commented, "If it weren't for eyes from the outside, nothing would happen."[13] At this moment foreign influence was seen as moving the state to action and viewed as potentially very positive for the environment. There were a number of important pieces in place, including environmental agencies and environmental laws. In this era and later, though, many interviewees commented that Ecuador's environmental management structure looks good on paper but not in practice. Laws needed to be enforced and agencies needed to do their jobs.

The Earth Summit pulled Ecuador in the direction of an emerging international environmental community. The international agenda spurred national-level state action and gave national-level environmentalists openings to create change. Though the Ecuadorian state showed interest in being considered a member of the international environmental community, it did not have the capacity to act effectively or independently, nor did it devote sufficient economic resources toward environmental ends. Its weaknesses enabled two other actors to take charge, thus further decreasing the state's role in the environment. First, international forces—ecoimperialists—would have a strong hand in shaping Ecuador's private, not for profit environmental sector (NGOs). Second, those national NGOs—ecodependents—which were well funded by the ecoimperialists through the debt swap, would fill the gap left by the state.

Growing Transnational Funding

Transnational funding for the protection of biodiversity and sustainable development drove the era. For instance, the Global Environment Facility provided over $7 million in support for its Biodiversity Protection Project, designed to strengthen the protected area system, in the period from 1994 until 2000.[14] USAID and the German GTZ both started large new programs in 1991: the German's was a forestry program focused in the *oriente*, and the Americans focused on finding ways to improve management around national parks and protected areas. International conservationists, including The Nature Conservancy and the International Union for the Conservation of Nature (IUCN) opened offices in Quito during the boom.

External international forces had played a role in Ecuador for many years. Foreign governments and international environmental organizations were drawn to Ecuador's megadiversity. USAID, in particular, had a long-standing interest in Ecuador and funded organizations and conducted numerous projects that were focused on Ecuador's environment. As was noted earlier, USAID funded Fundación Natura to prepare the country's first environmental profile and to work on environmental education. USAID was instrumental in organizing the national *congresos* and in the establishment of CAAM. Protecting biodiversity was a global priority for the bilateral donor. According to its own accounts, in 1994 USAID was the largest biodiversity conservation donor, funding projects in 40 nations, worth $74 million.[15] In 1987 that funding had been only $5 million. To that point its peak had been in the year of the Earth Summit with $90 million. It identified biodiversity as a "top priority for action."[16] The organization also funded several large projects that were coordinated with other groups, including the Parks in Peril project discussed in chapter 3. In the 1990s USAID sponsored one of its largest ever environmental projects in Ecuador, the Sustainable Uses of Biological Resources project (SUBIR). SUBIR began in 1991 and its first phase ran through 1997. Its design was a very conscious attempt to create sustainable development. It provided $9 million "to identify, test, and develop economically, ecologically, and socially sustainable resource management models in three Ecuadorian parks and their buffer zones."[17] The project was extensive and focused on six areas of effort: (1) policy analysis, (2) organizational development, (3) natural area management, (4) ecotourism, (5) improved land use, and (6) minority participation.[18] It was a tremendously ambitious project that sought to integrate the environmental, social-political, and economic aspects of sustainability. Ultimately, however, the project was considered by many to be a huge failure, including USAID representatives. Although the program was designed to promote sustainable development, covered a long period of time, and invested a lot of money, interviewees believed the communities were worse off and the infrastructure that was created made deforestation more likely. I heard many anecdotes about the economic and social irrationality of the program. For instance, women in the communities were given alpaca to raise, which they didn't necessarily want to do, and they ended up using family resources to feed the alpaca rather than their families. In another situation a local explained to me that families were given hogs to raise for food, but the proportion of males to females didn't make any sense from a breeding perspective.

USAID considers its role in Ecuador's environmental activities groundbreaking; employees take pride in having helped create the leading environmental organizations, strengthened institutions, worked with indigenous groups, and led policy processes.[19] According to USAID officials, staff members of national environmental organizations consider partnering with USAID a key element of successful environmental organizations' institutional resumés.[20] USAID's imprint is also visible on many of the state's environmental institutions. These accomplishments are reflected in USAID's annual reports. In its "60 Years of Cooperation" document, USAID touts its success in forming CAAM, helping to create the Ecuadorian Environmental Plan, the Fondo Ambiental Nacional (National Environmental Fund—FAN), the development of legislation, such as the Special Law for the Galápagos Islands, and the strengthening of nongovernmental conservation entities, including Ecociencia, Jatun Sacha, CEDENMA, Antisana Foundation, Rumicocha Ecological Foundation, Arcoiris Foundation, and the Charles Darwin Foundation, among other successes.[21] Due to the Ecuadorian state's weakness, foreign governments, through their bilateral aid organizations, could support NGOs, which would go on to play a strong role in Ecuador's environmental activities.

The Ecodependent Boom

International organizations bred new national environmental groups. While a number of NGOs rose from the grassroots, most emerged due to the sponsorship of international organizations that were interested in biodiverse nations. In the mid-1980s, there were only a handful of environmental organizations in Ecuador. By 1993, following the influx of funds, there were over one hundred environmental organizations. The *Directorio Verde: Organismos Ambientalistas en Ecuador* (Green Directory: Environmental Organizations in Ecuador; Varea et al.) profiled 124 such groups. Funding generated by the debt swaps and the global shift to sustainable development highlighted by the Earth Summit were key to this growth. New funding created opportunities. During this period, CEDENMA explained its existence as having two eras: one unfunded and one funded. The first was from 1987 until 1993 at which time they had no funds. The second era began in 1993 when they received funds from a contract with the SUBIR project to handle correspondence, faxes, copies, etc.[22] Other organizations experienced similar lifts from international contracts during this period. The director of a conservation organization noted, "In the 1980s, money went to Costa Rica. In the 1990s, money went to Ecuador, and groups were diversifying."[23]

Fundación Natura was the dominant Ecuadorian environmental NGO for the first ten years of its existence; then new organizations took off. Some, like EcoCiencia, were founded from Natura's ranks. Natura's founders look back and see this as a positive development for the movement, adding to its overall strength:

[At the time] there are no rivals in the sense that those other NGOs that do share more or less the same style grew up in the same nest and therefore we are always exchanging. We know ... the different strengths of the different NGOs. I think for example of EcoCiencia .... It was one of the most wonderful ideas ... because [Natura] could have a partner with whom to discuss the science part when [Natura] would continue on the policy side. There was a time when we were too big, trying to do everything, because there were no other NGOs which we could partner with .... I have always believed in the need for more organizations that would be based on objectives that went beyond personal interests, that were basically focusing on the interest of Ecuador, as a whole, as a team, as a conglomerate of people that needed support from different organizations. As I say today in 2007, I continue to think that we need as many. The dynamics of society tell you what is too much and what is not enough. Whenever anything succeeds it means that there was a niche in the organization and that expertise and that those assets were needed in society. When organizations fail it is because there was not as strong a structure to whatever was created or there was no space. There was no need for such a contribution.[24]

The new organizations that thrived found it in their interest to specialize and focus their agendas. While Fundación Natura was founded with a very broad agenda, new groups' agendas were narrower and focused by location, the types of problems they addressed, and their methods. Subsets of larger groups split off to form more focused groups. As Fundación Natura grew larger, a group of scientists from within it split off to form EcoCiencia, an organization focused on ecological research. That was one of a number of spin-offs. There were also new groups focused on law (Ecolex, 1998), private conservation (Fundación de Conservación Jocotoco, 1999), conflict resolution (Fundación Futuro Latinoamericano, 1993), and to publicize issues surrounding the environment (Corporación SIMBIOE, 2000), among others (see table 5.1). Regional specialization also took place. For instance, the Fundación para el Desarrollo Alternativo Responsable de Galápagos, an environmental organization focused on

Table 5.1
Sample of organizations founded during boom period

1988	*Fundación Maquipucuna*	Quito-based, working north of Quito in private cloud forest
1989	*EcoCiencia*	Quito, science and research
	Fundación Jatun Sacha	Quito-based, rural, private science reserves
	Fundación Ecológica Arcoiris	Loja (south), prevention of mining in protected areas
1992	*Fundación Ecológica Mazán*	Cuenca (south), ecosystem management
1993	*Fundación Futuro Latinoamericano*	Quito, conflict resolution
1996	*Fundación Ecológica Rescate Jameli*	Guayaquil (coast), animal rescue and endangered species
1998	*Ecolex*	Quito, environmental law
1999	*Fondo Ambiental Nacional*	Quito, trust for protected areas
	Fundación Para la Sobrevivencia del Pueblo Cofán	Quito-based with work in Amazon at interface of environment and indigenous issues
2000	*Corporación SIMBIOE*	Quito, environmental communication

finding ways to achieve sustainable development for people living in the Galapagos (2001), was established there. Fundación Ecologica Rescate Jameli in Guayaquil (the major city and port on the coast) in 1996 dedicated its work "To promote the flora and fauna of Ecuador with emphasis on species threatened by the destruction of habitat and illegal animal traffic." Fundación Ecologica Mazan was founded in Cuenca (the sierra) in 1992 with the mission: "Promote the protection and sustainable handling of the Andean ecosystem, by means of social processes that help create harmony between society and nature."[25] Part of the diversification was due to the shift in consciousness toward "sustainable development." The movement moved away from just looking at protecting species to "sustainable development" and protecting people. One of the big impacts of UNCED was to "add humans and stir" into the existing concern with "nature." This was described as "environmentalism with a face."[26] One of the organizations included in the *Green Directory*—Fundación para el Desarrollo Ecológico (FUNDECOL) exemplifies the intersection of environmental and human concerns. Founded in 1991, it is not registered as an NGO, rather as an *organización comunitaria* (community organization). Located in the coastal city of Muisne, its objectives are to defend the mangroves against the actions of shrimpers, and to prevent the indiscriminant cutting of mangroves. The organization focuses on human health and poverty, specifically as it relates to the destruction of the mangroves.

In explaining the rapid and vast rise in the number of environmental NGOs in Ecuador, a US Peace Corp volunteer (who was a volunteer with one of those NGOs) noted, "There are new generations of people [in Ecuador and around the world] who are eager to do things by themselves rather than channeling through the government, which has been the case." In the next breath, the volunteer noted another reason for the growth:

The unfortunate fact is that the government usually has a chronic shortage of funds which means they don't have enough staff, like park guards. They don't have enough money for gasoline and other things like that, which limits their work. Government entities are in a vacuum that is being filled, in part, by NGOs .... NGOs fill the vacuum [by] providing resources, park guards, courses, research, interpretation, environmental education and ... they've been pretty good at stimulating the passing of new regulations.[27]

An Ecuadorian USAID official, at that time, noted that USAID's focus on working with NGOs and the private sector on environmental issues, not just government agencies, was "a pioneering decision."[28] Another way of

Figure 5.1
Entrance to the Second National Congress on the Environment, 1995

looking at this is that the United States government promotes neoliberalism, which weakens the state and opens it to NGOs. The US funds the NGOs through USAID and thus takes control of the environmental agenda and operations of Ecuador.

I witnessed what was arguably the highlight of the boom period: the II Congreso Nacional Ecuatoriano del Medio Ambiente (Second National Congress on the Environment) held in 1995, a follow-up to the first Congreso held in 1987 (figure 5.1). Vicente Polít, the president of the environmental umbrella organization, CEDENMA, which was the main conference organizer, opened the second Congreso to a packed hall of over 700 representatives from NGOs, the state, and US development organizations. There were more than twice the number of participants than attended the first Congreso, and this one was much higher in stature. After Polít spoke, he presented Ecuador's President, Sixto Durán Ballén, who made remarks. The main purpose of the Congreso was for the new government agency, CAAM, to present the government's action plan (both USAID funded). Other goals included examining state policies and institutions, looking at the role of civil society in protecting the environment, and discussing the impact of "modernization" on conservation.

Professionalization

As groups proliferated, they became increasingly "specialized" and "professional." Groups became more professional to meet the demands of their donors. They needed to be accountable: file paperwork, prepare reports, and do financial audits. A successful NGO leader noted, "In the 1990s, money was easily available and there was the growth of groups. Early on, there was not a lot of monitoring .... It was easy to write proposals and we won lots. There was more monitoring after failures .... Donors were wising up and demanding accountability. Our donors showed up."[29] While number of groups grew, not all were up to the task of accountability. Those that did not do the work, and that could not account for the work that they did, struggled to survive or went under.

Organizations that sought transnational funding needed to become professionalized. Large donors like USAID had strict accounting guidelines that Ecuadorian organizations needed to meet. Due to these requirements there was an entire class of organizations that USAID could not consider funding because they did not meet USAID's minimum qualifications for accounting. International nongovernmental organizations (INGOs) required this sort of accountability, too. For instance, The Nature Conservancy's (TNC's) accounting system was very similar to USAID's because in Ecuador, almost half of TNC's funds are from USAID. A representative from an INGO noted, "We are strict in our choice of partners in terms of their financial/administrative and science/technology [capacity]. Partners are audited and need to pass to 'graduate'. We have the highest standard of responsibility, technical and administrative .... Groups that work with us must undergo audits .... It is very strict."[30] INGOs severed ties with national NGOs whose management, they believed, was not up to standards. Thus having professional skills, including auditing capacities, was key to national organizations' success in garnering funds. It is telling that Fundación Natura, the most prominent environmental NGO during this time, aimed for a high level of professionalism from the beginning, including professional salaries. A founder notes: "We always thought from the secretary, to the experts, we needed to be high quality and motivated by a good salary .... For that we were accused of treating our staff as though we were in the private sector and because the private sector is bad, we are also bad .... Our identity was that we had good people—well paid, and committed."[31] The accusers were from Acción Ecológica, which did not rely on big budgets and instead relied on volunteer labor.

Some groups saw the trend toward professionalization as positive. They believed that the strict accounting processes focused attention on outcomes and the business-like manner made them more efficient, and thus stronger, organizations. This sentiment wasn't unusual: "We are businesses. We need to be effective or fail."[32] These professional groups prided themselves on high quality work, good management, having the capacity to write reports and do audits. "We have a good reputation for managing money. We are squeaky clean, on time, and do well."[33] Another explained, "Even though NGOs are without *fines de lucro* [literally without ends for gain; commonly translated as "nonprofit"], at the end of the day, it is a business. They [other NGOs] act messianic hiding all of this. What is important is that conservation must be good business for technicians and for humans."[34] A former board member of a national NGO noted that many NGOs have major problems with money management, and spoke of one in particular: "They didn't listen to the board. They went broke. [They] blew all of their money on stupid things. Like all of the NGOs want a car .... You couldn't do this in a business."[35] The "business" analogy and traits that describe successful private sector organizations were used to describe successful NGOs: "[Our organization] had to learn to compete and be more effective, efficient, and less bureaucratic."[36] These were traits that contrasted sharply with the views of the government.[37]

Despite these arguments for the benefits of professionalization, many ecodependent organizations found the requirements of partnering with transnational funders to be overly bureaucratic and an exercise in paper pushing. One disgruntled director mentioned to me that he would like to write "blah, blah, blah" or "are you reading this?" on a few lines of a report he was writing to his organization's funders to see if anyone would actually notice. Many expressed frustration at boilerplate report writing and constantly being "accountable." "Maneuverability is limited, even more in [bilateral] government funded projects. For example, we will need to pay a fine if we are not there [in a protected area] for 15 days training guards. We have to take photos with dates, and get signatures, etc. ... There is so much time spent being sure you are documenting this, just for your survival."[38] On the other side of this, a bilateral donor complained, "Some groups are partners and some just see us as purses. [The ones that see us as purses] write back one line e-mails saying ... [your official] reporting only requires that we report back quarterly."[39] However, a director complained: "We get zero feedback or comments on the reports. Donors demand these reports but don't pay one iota about what's in the content."[40]

Even funders had some problems with their strict policies. For example, USAID had goals to work with indigenous groups to protect biodiversity and culture by conserving indigenous territories. Due to accounting rules, USAID used "BINGO middlemen"—shorthand for big NGOs, which tended to be the national NGOs/ecodependent groups—to implement projects at the community level and to distribute resources. In this case the BINGOs worked with the Huorani, the Cofán, and twenty-nine other indigenous groups and associations. USAID "can't do thirty one different contracts,"[41] so they provided funds to Fundación Jatun Sacha to manage the indigenous distributions. According to a USAID representative, they needed to use organizations that can "comply with regulations .... Not every Ecuadorian organization is able to comply. We need to trust how money will be used."[42] Another USAID worker told me, "There are high costs to this. There's only a small percentage of groups that can deal with implementing the projects. Not every group is able to pass audits .... USAID has the responsibility of being sure that the money is used properly."[43] Because the process is so difficult, they provide training to organizations, including indigenous groups, to provide technical support for what they consider "basic functioning": how to manage a board, do accounting, use office equipment, apply for funds. In essence, they teach indigenous groups, and others, how to fit into USAID's structure of an organization in order to be eligible for USAID's funding. This obviously has profound effects on indigenous ways of organizing. A leader of a local NGO asks, "How can community and indigenous groups who don't have the language, how can they do fundraising for their own projects without the influences of outsiders? It is hard .... You need to have a web page, references, lots of people working for you."[44] The funding process changed the type of organizations that could thrive in this period.

In addition to the technical capacities and organizational setups needed to carry out contracts and audits, there were other costs to receiving transnational funding. There were financial costs. One NGO noted that their notary fees for one project was $1,000. There were also costs related to having BINGOs serve as intermediaries. A director reflected that "Nonprofits began to fill a void, but now it is a business and very little money gets to where it is supposed to go."[45] There are in turn bad feelings among the NGOs. One NGO interviewee stated, "I hate USAID. They are degrading and horrific. I hate the Germans even more. I don't blame them because there must have been abuses. But we never embezzled. When you go into it, they assume you are wrong, a criminal. They are surprised if you do a good job."[46]

Thus, in the course of writing applications for funds, then writing reports on how funds were used, and undergoing internal and external audits, environmental organizations tied to global funding become professionalized. One of the unintended consequences of the ecoimperialist funding practices and the professionalization of ecodependent groups was that groups that were founded to protect the public good were constrained by their funding milieu and began working for the sake of organizational maintenance. Social movement scholars explain this as the Weber–Michels thesis, which argues that as movement organizations mature, they "become more conservative and ... goals will be displaced in favor of organizational maintenance."[47] At their origins many of these groups considered themselves environmental *movement* organizations, or at least nongovernmental organizations, two types of organizations that seek to protect the environment for the public good over the long term. However, they shifted their behaviors to resemble consulting agencies that exchange services for fees over short-term, fixed contracts. It was difficult for them to form alliances with other like-minded organizations under these circumstances. Bounded by the limitations of the system, they struggled to survive. Their survival mode prevented them from questioning the development trajectory as they focused inward.

A Green Agenda

In Ecuador's case transnational funders/ecoimperialists primarily funded "green" issues, such as biodiversity and land conservation in rural areas. Of the environmental organizations compiled in the *Green Directory*, "conservation" was the principal objective of 28 percent of the groups, the largest single category followed by environmental policy (23 percent). While locals were also in favor of addressing these issues, what was left out of this foreign funding equation were "brown" problems that affect Ecuadorians' immediate quality of life, such as air, land, and water pollution and urban issues.[48] This is despite the fact that a 2001 survey of Ecuadorians found that 90 percent agreed, "environmental pollution, especially in the air and water is a very serious problem." That same poll found that 72 percent of Ecuadorians were willing to contribute time "to protect and to clean the environment."[49] A study commissioned by USAID in 1995 detailed urban environmental problems due to industrial pollution, specifically poor air and water quality, in addition to problems with solid waste and potable water in the cities.[50] Also missing was funding to address extractive activity. CEDENMA's policy proposal at the second

Congreso in 1995 focused on eight themes, which are a good measure of the Ecuadorian environmental community's priorities at the time: (1) environmental law, (2) environmental education, (3) the urban environment, (4) the rural environment, (5) biodiversity and protected areas, 6) native forests and forest issues, (7) hydrocarbon activities in the Ecuadorian amazon region, and (8) mining. Though the transnational funding community was primarily focused on one of these (biodiversity), CEDENMA's interests spanned a range of topics, including urban issues and resource extraction.

Ramahandra Guha notes that this is a differentiation between environmentalists of the Global North and Global South: "While Northern greens have been deeply attentive to the rights of victimized or endangered animal and plant species, Southern greens have generally been more alert to the rights of the less fortunate members of their own species."[51] Due to the power of ecoimperialist funding, foreigners in effect set the agenda for Ecuadorian ecodependent groups. "Green projects" that promote "global interests" are funded, but "brown projects" that address "local interests" have not been funded, nor are interests that question extractive development. There are no NGOs that focus exclusively on brown problems in Ecuador. In addition to the lack of funding for brown projects, there was a lack of funding for ecoresisters and groups that questioned the extractivist economic development model of the state, which supplies the United States with important resources, namely petroleum.

Transnational actors started their work in Ecuador focusing on "pure" conservation; that is conservation without people, a model that was imported from US funder's early visions of conservation. This model shifted after the Earth Summit to include people in the picture; the model shifted to sustainable development, in line with the global trends and paradigm shifts. What this meant for the goals and actions of Ecuador's environmental organizations is that they shifted from an early strategy of creating protected areas, such as national parks, largely devoid of people, toward integrating people in and around protected areas into the economy of national parks, through practices such as ecotourism development and sustainable agriculture and forestry strategies. Many Ecuadorian organizations welcomed this as a legitimizing element to their work.

As part of this integration, ecoimperialists required ecodependent groups to demonstrate how conservation projects economically support local residents. This spurred money-making enterprises. In a private, transnationally funded reserve that I visited, I was taken to a workshop where women were making jewelry from locally collected natural materials, to a forested area where fast growing bamboo was being grown to construct buildings that were "sustainable," and (my favorite) to an area where organic sugar cane was being processed into alcohol that could be served to foreign ecotourists (figure 5.2). The leading national NGOs had successfully adopted humans into the environmental protection equation. A practitioner noted the change: "The environment in Ecuador is not just conservation. It includes a social and human aspect. The big NGOs now look at that area. It is not blaming people [anymore]. It is working with people .... You can't protect birds without humans, especially in lower income areas."[52] Another notes the economic pressure this adds: "Human well-being and human development is becoming more and more important and so economics is also becoming more and more important. How to make conservation more competitive? If conservation is not feasible, economically feasible, it cannot compete with other activities."[53] An insightful pro-sustainable development interviewee pointed out, "The problem with mixing conservation and development is that sustainable development implies growth."[54]

Figure 5.2
Organic sugar cane being prepared for processing into alcohol at an ecotourism site, providing jobs for locals

This shift in actions on the ground occurred because transnational funders incorporated a sustainable development agenda and funded it. Despite some ecoimperialists claims that they do not dictate the agenda - "We are not imposing any agenda on anybody"[55]—the evidence suggests that they are, at minimum, heavily influencing it by both what they do and what they do not fund.

Most of the transnational funders have explicit agendas and limited budgets that they must spend prudently, especially the international NGOs. For instance, The Nature Conservancy and Conservation International are clear about their agendas related to conservation.[56] For CI, one of the groups most squarely focused on a "green" agenda, their planning unit of analysis is the wildlife conservation corridor. This unit has a biological meaning, linked specifically to biodiversity. A representative explained their priorities:

We are looking for places with high biodiversity and high risk, high threat. We call them hot spots. We work in hot spots and we love to work with species. Some NGOs have dropped working on the species level. We still think that species level is one of the levels we want to work with. We want to identify exactly what species we are trying to protect. ... Protected areas are important and are the cornerstone of conservation. ... And that's our agenda and we are proud to say that we are trying to do science-based conservation, for science is important for us to learn and develop new tools. Partnership is important and human working is becoming more and more important. We are not a poverty organization or a rural development organization. It is not our main ability ....[57]

International funders also had funding limitations and could not meet all requests. "There isn't money for everyone. We receive piles of proposals. We must leverage funds. We can't change that. We can help Ecuador change what they want to change." Though wanting to help Ecuador help themselves, they can only help in their priority areas. In the next sentence this leader added, "Biodiversity conservation is the main focus. Protected areas and buffer zones and indigenous groups."[58] Thus the funders have a clear sense of what they will and will not fund.

There are various degrees to which international funders see their organizations as directing the national agenda, through inclusion and exclusion. For instance:

I would love to work in all of Ecuador, but I don't have resources for working in all of Ecuador. ... I need to focus my attention in some concrete areas. If that shakes the agenda, than probably I am shaking agendas. But it is not pushing them or imposing them. It is finding some priorities and so sorry that I don't work everywhere. I don't have funds to work everywhere.[59]

When asked about the process by which issues were added to the national agenda and which actors were involved, one director responded,

We have an agenda and it is ridiculous to say that we don't have an agenda...But if you don't have strong institutions, strong NGOs with their own agendas, the kind that say, "Ok, the national priorities for Ecuador are A, B, and C ...," sometimes you end up pushing your agendas instead of sharing agendas. My mission is to work [with Ecuadorian partners] to build a common agenda. See we have our own agenda. National NGOs have their own agenda. Let's work in this common agenda. ... And of course, sometimes it is clear that when you have resources you have power. That's true. That's something we cannot deny. ... The big challenge is to build this common agenda and my big hope is to have this common ground.[60]

This director related resources to power, and acknowledged the strong hand transnational funders had in agenda setting. Transnational funders self-consciously resisted being perceived as ecoimperialists. They lamented that they "have a bad image" and are "considered an arm of [US] imperialism," and were "misunderstood."

Transnational funders actively looked to find common ground with Ecuadorian NGOs. Others reiterated that theme: "How do we make [our priorities] fit with national priorities? We are careful in our development work to follow national priorities. If national priorities exist, we see where our agenda and the government agenda overlap."[61] The idea was to create partnerships, but the situation was complicated by financial power, as noted above, and political legitimacy. For instance:

Our main role is to support national NGOs and help [them] to be strong. By having strong NGOs, national NGOs, we hope that they can put together a common agenda. For us as international NGOs it is a very delicate situation because we are here to help, but we are not here to replace national NGOs. ... National policies come from the civil society, because I believe that public policies are not the question of the state, it is the question of the society. So that's a role for national NGOS, they should be the ones leading and participating in that process. We can help with information, we can help with something of support and also with some financial support to have stronger NGOS, but finally it is their responsibility.[62]

National interviewees, when asked generally about INGOs or bilateral agencies, would give plain responses such as, "They impose their agenda."[63] "They have a tremendous influence on the agenda."[64] A director of a large, influential NGO flatly stated, "[Some of] these groups suck up a lot of money and political space. They should go back to the US. They are not helping. They use us. They want us to be partners. There's nepotism, crony-ism, and corruption."[65] Another points out their double standards: "I would like to see international donors and INGOs involving national NGOS on their planning. You know, they plan whatever they want to do and come here with their own agenda and we have to fit the agenda." This inter-viewee continued by pointing out some of the hypocrisy in that the INGOs require the NGOs they fund to work with the local community to tackle problems, but the INGOs don't do the same with NGOs: "If we have to do it with them [the local community], then the international community has to do it with us."[66]

Many Ecuadorians questioned the political motives of environmental *gringos* (whites from the Global North) and began to extend their distrust to their partners—national ecodependent organizations. Following the Northern agenda is a concern to Ecuadorians because it means the move-ment "follows the wave of world environmentalists without an emergency plan to solve local problems."[67]

Another way the ecoimperialist funding affected the agenda was in what they did not fund. Transnational funding for the urban environment did not exist in Ecuador, despite the nation's mostly urban population, and the local concern regarding pollution. For instance, these photos show anti-car and anti-Texaco graffiti in Quito (see figures 5.3 and 5.4). There are numer-ous urban environmental issues, but not as many NGOs working on them as there are on rural, conservation issues. There are a number of explana-tions for this. One is that due to state decentralization, there is some work being done on urban environments at the municipal level.[68] In an opinion poll, though, only 14 percent of respondents believed that municipal gov-ernments helped "a lot," with most believing that they did "a little" (56 percent) and many believing that they did "nothing (30 percent).[69] A second and more compelling reason is that there is no consistent funding from international donors for urban environmental issues and thus no groups working on these unfunded issues. I have written about this elsewhere.[70] In sum, foreign donors are more interested in protecting the "global commons," in Ecuador's case, its biodiversity, than they are in local, city environments; thus relatively little money goes toward cities and therefore few NGOs work in that unfunded area. Interviewees support this view: "Organizations live according to external funds and there is very little fund-ing for urban work."[71] Another noted, "We didn't put emphasis on brown pollution issues because there wasn't money there." A few NGOs have small, side projects working on urban issues, but these are minor.[72] Urban environmental problems do not have transnational sponsors.

Figure 5.4
Anti-Texaco graffiti in Quito; "Don't buy Texaco" with indigenous woman, her child, and a school girl, 1994

Figure 5.3
Anti-car graffiti in Quito

Another area that some Ecuadorian environmentalists believe has been left out of the funding stream is the coast, specifically the mangroves. They blame this on ignorance: "International tendencies have been to give very little funding at the coast. Donors give money to sexy places, in this order: the Galápagos, the jungle, the highlands, and the coast. Some say there's not much to protect [at the coast], but they lack knowledge about the ocean ecosystems.[73]

Ecoresister Outliers

Groups that were not ecodependent nor focused on "green" issues emerged in response to crises, and to address local problems. They were not well funded, or funded at all, by groups from the Global North. During this period CORDAVI filed suit in New York on behalf of five indigenous groups against Texaco. The groups were organized locally as Frente de Defensa de la Amazonía (Amazon Defense Coalition, recognized by the state in 1994). The plaintiffs sought $1.5 billion in damages to clean up the contamination Texaco left behind after its oil exploration and drilling in the Amazon. Studies by the Ecuadorian government and the World Bank identified negative effects of drilling, including polluted land and air, fish kills, and adverse health effects. Another group working on local issues was Defensa y Conservación Ecológica de Intag (DECOIN), founded in 1995, north of Quito in the cloud forest, in direct response to a proposal by a transnational Japanese corporation to mine for copper in its community. Besides forcing relocation of four villages, the Environmental Impact Statement produced by the Japanese showed that drilling would literally dry up the cloud forest in the area, thus destroying the habitat of numerous species. Other groups like this—ecoresisters—that responded to very local conditions, popped up around Ecuador, but they are less visible in the historical record because (1) they did not always register as a non-profit with the government, (2) they were not connected to ecoimperialist funding and included in annual reports, and (3) they did not necessarily define their work as "environmental." Nevertheless, over time, the rising influence of environmentalism made the environmental label more lucrative than some other frames, such as human rights.

While there had always a relationship between the environmental movement and the indigenous rights movement, in the mid to late 1990s there was an explicit confluence highlighted by the case against Texaco. For instance, the Fundación Para la Sobrevivencia del Pueblo Cofán (translated into English by the organization as the Cofán Survival Fund) was founded with an office in Quito to focus on lands in the Amazon in 1999. The Cofán are a group of indigenous people in the Amazon. Part of the Cofán Survival Fund's mission is "To recover, to order, and to conserve for the future generation the ancestral territories of the Cofán." They do this "not for the single benefit of the Cofán, but also for Ecuador and the World."[74] The Cofán created an ecological reserve that they administer, which was the first indigenously administered ecological reserve in the world. During the 1990s indigenous groups experienced a shift in their outlook.[75] An indigenous leader told me, "The idea of being able to protect these lands against petroleum extraction, mining, and others just began to mature and to be possible during the 1990s, and it presented the possibility of demanding [the extractors] to leave."[76] Given the broad frame of the period—"sustainable development"—this confluence of indigenous rights and environmental protection made sense. It is also noteworthy because the indigenous were at the epicenter of the negative environmental and social impacts of petroleum extraction and thus had a critique of natural resource extraction as a development strategy.

Ecodependent Organizations Fill the Void Left by the State

National-level NGOs filled the vacuum left by the state's relative absence on environmental issues. There were real environmental problems on the ground that Ecuadorians wanted addressed. Locally citizens were seeing environmental damage with their own eyes, mostly the result of resource extraction. Of great concern was the contamination taking place in the Amazon by oil development. The state granted concessions to explore for petroleum in Yasuní National Park, the home of numerous indigenous peoples, including the Huaorani and Cofán.[77] In the north, widespread deforestation provided clear cut evidence of environmental damage. In 1995 a respected environmentalist cautioned "there won't be any forests in a few years."[78] Shrimp farming in the coastal regions was destroying mangroves. In the Andean capital electricity was rationed and residents with no ties to the land or connections to environmentalism interpreted the rolling blackouts as an environmental problem. In 1995 my Spanish language tutor explained Quito's electric rationing to me: "We don't have electricity in Quito because they don't have water in Cuenca to drive the hydroelectric plant. They don't have water in Cuenca because of haphazard, indiscriminant tree cutting. Since the trees are gone, the water doesn't get absorbed in the soil." For someone who claimed not to have an interest in ecology, this explanation seemed sophisticated, and was increasingly commonplace. Environmental issues, concerns, and analyses were entering everyday Ecuadorian consciousness. NGOs were engaged in research that documented the extent and rates of environmental destruction. They disseminated their results through their own reports and through the media. Citizens wanted protection, but the state was not seen as the agent to do this. Indeed the state was considered a big part of the problem: it encouraged damaging resource extraction as a means to economic development, such as the oil concessions in Yasuní National Park; it had perverse incentives, such as collecting stumpage fees for timber felled in protected areas. People looked to themselves and to NGOs as alternative sources of protection. The state was accelerating the treadmill of production, while numerous citizens and citizen groups sought to slow it down.

Ecuadorians were proud of their country and wanted to protect their biodiversity, but they didn't know how to do it. For that matter, no country had created "sustainable development" despite all of the rhetoric. Costa Rica stood out in the international community because its president, Óscar Arias (during his first term in the 1980s), had taken a stand to create sustainable development through ecotourism. In Ecuador there were many efforts to create ecotourism as an economic alternative to destructive economic practices. Tourism had been an important part of the Ecuadorian economy largely due to the attraction of the Galápagos Islands. In 1992 Ecuador received over 400,000 foreign visitors, almost 25 percent of whom visited a national park and the sector earned $192 million,[79] the fourth most important foreign exchange earner at the time. In the 1990s the "new town" area of Quito, where many foreigners visit and lodge, was flooded with travel agencies, many of which offered "eco-trekking," "eco-adventures," "ecotourism," and other brands of nature tourism (figure 5.5). Environmental NGOs also saw ecotourism as a means to promote livelihoods for people living in fragile environments, such as the Amazon, and as a counter to polluting industries, such as petroleum extraction. Ecotourism is not without its pitfalls,[80] yet it was a strategy worth trying. A number of environmental organizations were founded with the purpose of creating private reserves (e.g., Fundación Jatun Sacha and Fundación Maquipucuna) (figure 5.6). These groups and others developed ecotourism at their sites and sought to provide local jobs, and environmental protection; in other words, "sustainable development" on the ground. Ecotourism would continue to be a sustainable development theme, with USAID funding ecotourism development in the Galápagos and later as part of its CAIMAN project (Conservation in Areas

Figure 5.5
One of many Quito-based ecotourism companies in the tourist district of Quito in
the early 1990s

Managed by Indigenous Groups), which intended to help indigenous peoples develop capacity for national park management and ecotourism.[81]
People saw real environmental problems and sought real solutions to
them. The international environmental community (ecoimperialists) and
national-level NGOs (ecodependents) assisted them.

Global forces were interested and involved in Ecuador. Ecuadorians were
eager to act, but Ecuador's state was weak. Internationally, neoliberal economic and political forces sought to shift responsibilities from the public
sector to the private sector. In Ecuador and around the world, this meant
the not for profit sector grew. One interviewee during this period described
this as the "triumph of global civil society." It was a boom period for NGOs,
in general, as the numbers of NGOs around the world took off.[82] Sonia
Alvarez called this "NGOization."[83] Against this backdrop, the numbers of
NGOs of all types grew in Ecuador. One interviewee believed that there
were "over 5,000" NGOs in Ecuador in 1995; establishing an NGO was
seen as "lucrative." According to a government official, the United States,

Figure 5.6
Entrance to Private Reserve Maquipucuna, which is also an ecotourist site with a lodge, local guides, and trails; the pictured structure is made of locally grown sustainable bamboo

the Netherlands, Germany, United Kingdom, and Japan were sending "a lot of cash."[84] According to the same source, in the mid-1990s, there were over 500 NGOs in the environmental sector with five new ones approved by the state each month. International funding helped promote the growth of NGOs. The government also changed the law, making it easier to be officially recognized as a nonprofit group.[85] These two processes enabled NGOs to fill the gap that the state could not manage. One observer noted, there was "fast growth, but slow change."[86]

NGOs' work was not inconsequential. Environmental organizations both filled the void and affected the government's policies. For instance, environmental NGOs were behind the establishment of new national parks. In the early 1990s Fundación Antisana was created specifically to do the background work, including the scientific research and land acquisitions, to prepare the documentation for the government agency at that time, Instituto Ecuatoriano Forestal y de Áreas Naturales y Vida Silvestre (Ecuadorian Forestry Institute of Forests and Natural Areas and Wildlife),

INEFAN, which would declare the area around the volcano Antisana a protected area. The Nature Conservancy provided the majority of the funding for this task.[87] Once the area was established, the Foundation and the state entered into a public–private agreement to manage the park, including training and equipping park guards.

How Neoliberal Processes Promoted NGOization

The 1990s were a period of NGO growth in Ecuador and around the world. Neoliberalism played a key role in the promotion of NGOs. Hey and Klak characterize a neoliberal economy as one with "reduced state spending, privatization, international exposure, foreign investment, export orientation, labor code reductions, and market-determined prices."[88] McMichael's more general definition of neoliberalism is "a philosophy positing an individual instinct for economic self-interest, justifying elevation of market principles as the organizing principle of society, where private interest trumps the public good."[89]

Two political processes promoted the overarching neoliberal agenda in Ecuador during this period. These processes were also occurring around the developing world, and facilitated the growth of the private sector, including NGOs. First, the process of governing was intentionally becoming "decentralized."[90] What this entailed was "the transfer of decision-making power, administrative functions, and financial resources from central governments to provincial and municipal governments."[91] Decentralization was promoted as a means to improve governing in a number of ways, including better serving local communities, increasing accountability, creating opportunities for the participation of civil society, and matching local problems with local solutions rather than a one size fits all governing style.[92] While decentralization was being promoted for states, transnational corporations were merging, thus increasing the concentration of corporate power around the globe.[93]

The second and related process was the promotion of government–NGOs partnerships. International actors, notably the World Bank and USAID, promoted these arrangements to accomplish the governing tasks that had devolved to municipalities.[94] Deborah A. Bräutigam and Monique Segarra found,

The construction of government–nongovernmental "partnerships" in developing countries was a norm that arose at the World Bank in the 1980s .... Many bank staff came to privilege NGOs as partners in the political activity of strategy design and policymaking. Including NGOs in these processes was viewed as an implicit means to promote a more open and accountable model of governance.[95]

These two processes—decentralization and the promotion of public–private partnerships by transnational agents—worked hand in hand to lead to the exponential growth in the number of NGOs in Ecuador, and in much of the Global South.

In Ecuador the impetus for decentralization came from the international, national, and the local levels. Internationally conditions attached to loans from the World Bank and IMF promoted decentralization.[96] Ecuador's weak position vis-à-vis its debt made it vulnerable to those forces. Bilateral aid programs also sponsored decentralization programs, including the Germans, Swiss, Dutch, and Spanish; and multilateral agents, including the UN Development Program, the EU and the Inter-American Development Bank, also participated.[97] The United States sponsored a project in Ecuador titled "Decentralization and Democratic Local Governance Project." Among other things, its goals included teaching citizens how to hold local officials accountable.[98]

It would, however, be inaccurate to suggest that decentralization was forced on the Ecuadorian people. Nationally these plans were met with some favor because the central government was perceived as ineffective. Keese and Argudo (2006) argue that the problems of a centralized national government were underscored in Ecuador in 1997 when President Abdalá Bucaram resigned under a cloud of corruption and inefficiency. While efforts to decentralize had already been underway, in 1997 the Congress passed the Ley Especial de Decentralizacion del Estado y Participación Social (Special Law of Decentralization of the State and Social Participation), which transferred most government functions to the county (canton) governments.[99] Indigenous groups, through their confederation—CONAIE (The Confederation of Indigenous Federations of Ecuador)—and related movements, had been calling for more local control, and a bottom-up participatory politics.[100] Thus, at the national and local levels, there was support for some forms of decentralization.

The leaders of this era also promoted the economic neoliberal program that dovetailed with decentralization and privatization. Presidents Rodrigo Borja (1988–1992) and Durán Ballén (1992–1996) continued and expanded the economic neoliberal policies begun in the earlier period, including reducing trade barriers, opening the country to foreign capital (especially US capital) and reducing domestic subsidies.[101] Observers note that the period between 1989 and 1994 was Ecuador's major period of trade liberalization, making it one of the most "open" economies of Latin America.[102] The Durán Ballén administration created the Consejo Nacional de Modernización del Estado (National Council of Modernization of the State), funded by the World Bank, to carry out modernization and decentralization policies.

While Ecuadorian political actors made these choices, they were greatly influenced by the world stage. Ecuador did not want to be left behind. There was the growing hegemony of a "Washington Consensus"[103]—a view that promoted neoliberalism and saw the "powerful state" as "injurious" and less effective than the private sector.[104] To reiterate the point from chapter 4, it wasn't just ideology that allowed this to happen, it was also debt and the vulnerabilities it entailed. In 1994, Ecuador renegotiated its loans again with the IMF, considered the strong arm for US interests, which pushed for its neoliberal policies.[105]

A specific example of Ecuador's deference to the United States was its 1992 withdrawal from OPEC. While the reported reason that Ecuador left OPEC was the high membership fee and the limits on production,[106] critics noted that Ecuador withdrew from OPEC as a means for the Durán Ballén administration to please the United States, "the unambiguous ideological leader of the hemispheric movement. While Ecuador's withdrawal from OPEC had few measurable consequences for the Ecuadorian economy, its perceived effect was to distance Ecuador from third world solidarity in primary exports and to signal its growing free market orientation."[107]

The multilayered push toward decentralization, and the international encouragement for private actors to intervene, combined to promote the establishment and growth of NGOs. New NGOs were launched because they could access resources that had in the past been directed to states. It was a big opportunity for the sector. NGOs took on a larger institutional role in social life. For instance, in an analysis of Ecuadorian NGOs, James Keese and Marco Freire Argudo note:

[T]hey have played an ever-increasing role in grassroots organising, service delivery, and policy making. NGOs have captured considerable institutional space as governments restructure, scale down services, or simply fail to meet the needs of marginalised groups within society .... NGOs also act as intermediaries, providing links between governments, donors, other NGOs, and local communities.[108]

Though they note some benefits to having these roles filled, there are significant disadvantages to NGOs filling them, including "permit[ing] the central government to abdicate its responsibilities."[109]

There have been numerous critiques of this NGOization. Latin American scholars argue that the institutionalization of issues and organizations is "depoliticizing," "deradicalizing," and leads to "de-movementization" of social issues.[110] This critique is right in line with social movement scholars' analyses of the consequences of external support for social movement organizations. Doug McAdam and others argue that elites offer assistance to organizations as a means to moderate grassroots efforts, and that external support narrows organizations' choices.[111] Social movement theorists call this "channeling."[112] Extending this line of thinking beyond borders, neo-Marxist James Petras has argued that foreign funded NGOs in Latin America are an arm of imperialism. While the World Bank and other international organizations can enforce neoliberalism "from above," these agents also fund NGOs to produce neoliberalism "from below." In this way, "The NGOs became the 'community face' of neoliberalism."[113] Thus transnational funders channel social movement organizations in the Global South in similar ways that dominant/core/Global North countries channel subordinant/peripheral/Global South nations. In terms of environmental issues, this suggests that claims of green imperialism are not unfounded.

A related critique of "neoliberal NGOs" asks who they represent.[114] For intergovernmental and state agencies, they are often used as a proxy for true citizen involvement and are intended to represent "civil society." However, this is problematic. For instance, in Ecuador, analysts note:

The rise of NGOs has been mirrored by the decline of groups such as labor unions and peak business associations, which previously had privileged access to policy-makers. Service delivery NGOs are less likely to be membership organizations and less likely to represent constituents. The promotion of partnerships that privilege NGOs while ignoring representative democracy may ultimately be an unintended political side-effect ....[115]

In sum, NGOs are being used to address some public concerns, but members of the private groups are not publicly elected nor necessarily representative of some given population. The role of NGOs in civil society and "democratic" governance thus should raise questions, as I have argued elsewhere in regard to land conservation.[116]

In Ecuador the continuation of the neoliberal program that promoted state decentralization went hand in hand with the growth of a particular type of organization and a particular issue area: ecodependent NGOs that focused on the "green" agenda. It looked like green imperialism. This is a similar process to what Sonia Alvarez describes as happening to feminist NGOs during the same period. In 1999, she wrote:

Neoliberal social and economic adjustment policies, state downsizing, and changing international regimes have dramatically altered the conditions under which feminist and other struggles for social justice are unfolding in Latin America today. The restructured terrain … has triggered a significant reconfiguration … favoring particular actors and types of activities while actually or potentially marginalizing others.[117]

Consequences of Transnational Funding for Environmentalism and How the Movement Addressed Development

A consequence of ecoimperialist funding during this period was that ecodependent organizations dominated the environmental scene in the 1990s. The most important and most influential Ecuadorian organizations were those that partnered with transnational actors like USAID. The agendas of ecodependents were channeled by foreign forces into the green agenda. For the most part only professionalized groups received funding. What this meant for environmentalism was that organizations became self-centered, competed for funds, and any "solidarity" or "movement" was weakened. Thus the ability of environmentalists to effectively alter the proposed development trajectory was likewise debilitated.

There were notable successes during this era, but problems were brewing. There was inter-organizational discord among the ecodependent organizations. Funds for Ecuador's debt-for-nature swaps were channeled through a single organization—Fundación Natura. However, with the proliferation of newly professionalized groups, numerous other organizations believed they should be getting a piece of the pie. This created friction among competing NGOs.

Environmentalists believed that Fundación Natura was too big, too bureaucratic, monopolistic, and unable to manage large sums of money. Even INEFAN, the government agency in charge of protected areas, expressed resentment that Natura, and not the government, received the debt for nature funds. Further fueling the flames, there was the perception that funds were being "squandered" by Fundación Natura.[118] Even by their own assessment, Natura grew too big.[119] Natura dominated the sector because of their control of these funds, but they were not the only ones to feel the heat about their transnational relations. Other recipients of funds were also under scrutiny. Another NGO founder noted,

We were very successful in a few years and grew very fast, which was not necessarily very good for us and for the relationships with other organizations. Because of, you know, jealousy, and because there was some competition …. When you start to have some success then you have problems because then, of course, you start competing with other NGOs. …We gained some funding from USAID and that's when the problems start because when you start to gain some resources, you gain some enemies, too.[120]

NGOs acted like private sector entities competing for market share. "Specialization decreased competition," but it still existed. The bifurcation of groups that was evident in the Origins era prevailed during the boom. The president of CEDENMA reflected at the second Congreso in 1995 on the value of the two positions:

These visions, however, have been paramount to the development of the environmental movement. To the state and society, they contribute data, research, solutions to existing problems, and propose an image of a better future for the nation. ... At this point in the environmental history of the country, it is not possible to express a judgment about the ... legitimacy of one or the other side, as both have been ... necessary for practical or political reasons.[121]

Early competition among organizations over resources and ideological differences previewed a future of discord among groups. Resentment grew between groups that received the international funds and those that did not. The division partly mirrored the mainstream/ecodependents versus radical/ecoresisters dichotomy. The radical groups had already labeled mainstream Ecuadorian NGOs as "ugly" and their compromises with *gringos* as supporting a neoliberal agenda, but that was only part of it. Most troubling was that the groups that were most alike ideologically and could potentially work together—the ecodependents—were being divided by the funding structure. This got even worse in the next period.

The competition over funds weakened solidarity among like-minded organizations. This limited their ability to coordinate to act in a concerted manner. A director commented, "Competition in some ways is healthy for improving an organization, for making new challenges, new tools, to try to do more creative things. But what really matters, what worries me, is that we do not have a common agenda. The environmental movement is quite fragmented."[122] Numerous NGO leaders questioned whether an environmental movement even existed. For instance, a senior environmentalist in a prominent NGO remarked, "I hesitate to say there is an environmental movement as there ought to be ... one that faces problems and brings us to agreements, so that we lobby Congress, and the Ecuadorian government, and that pushes for projects that will benefit Ecuador. I do not see that in the environmental movement."[123]

Organizations were perceived as working independently for the good of each organization's survival. More than once I heard from interviewees from all types of organizations, that though NGOs in Ecuador are legally described as nongovernmental/nonprofit organizations, *sin fines de lucro* (without gains/profit as their ends), that in reality they are nongovernmental/nonprofit organizations with *lucro sin fines* (gains/profits without ends); the word play implying that NGOs exist for their own ends.

The public perceived environmental NGOs negatively. So did journalists and others in influential positions, who called these groups part of the "nonprofit mafia."[124] Ecuadorians began viewing environmentalists as people who "just want to make money," thus leading to distrust.[125] They were also seen as helping nature and animals, and not humans. Ecuadorians imagined NGO employees were earning "scandalous salaries." A 2001 public opinion survey asked, "In your opinion, have NGOs helped a lot, a little, or nothing to protect the environment?" "A lot" received 11 percent of responses; "a little" 58 percent, and "nothing" 31 percent.[126] The environmental movement had an image problem. It was exacerbated by the fact that environmental organizations were not membership organizations. Natura started out trying to be, but it didn't work out. An Ecuadorian woman who saw my US passport when I was in line at the airport asked me disdainfully if I was an *"ambientalista"* [environmentalist]. Another time, after I had given a public lecture in Quito on the role of NGOs in Ecuador, I was hounded by a reporter from one of Quito's daily newspapers (*El Comercio*) to give him negative quotes about NGO ineffectiveness, implications of embezzlement, and the like. (I didn't, but told him to report anything I said in my talk.) An ecotour guide of seventeen years in the Galápagos commented of environmental groups "They're all here [the Galápagos] to make money. They give something, but there is always something they want back." Though Ecuadorians cared about their environment, they did not respect the ecodependent organizations that had formed privately to protect it. The environmental organizations' relationships with transnational funders were actually counterproductive to building environmental consciousness or support. With funding from foreigners going to NGOs rather than the state, and all of the distrust that entails, it made it harder to create a mass base for environmentalism. In this way the funding structure undermined the domestic political legitimacy for ecodependent NGOs. Nevertheless, NGO directors argued, "Without NGOs, the environment is in trouble."

There was also a critique of the radical/ecoresisters, but of a different sort. Acción Ecológica was frequently quoted in the mass media to represent the environmental movement. This led to some public opinion problems for the environmental movement in general:

The environmental movement did not work with people early enough. This is why people are not very aware or conscious. People take one side or the other. You see this with companies. NGOs say companies should go away, they are the devil, at least this is Acción Ecológica's interpretation in the press .... Acción Ecológica and others in the movement are destroying the movement. The public, with the black and white information they are given, take the side of destroying the environment in the Galápagos and the jungle because environmentalists are blaming me [the people]. There is a lack of self-consciousness. The NGOs hurt themselves in the long run.[127]

The limits of an "environmental movement" to create a unified front prevented it from shifting the development trajectory. There was no consensus among organizations with regard to the "big picture."[128] The ecodependent organizations could not even unify on key issues such as whether they should unite to work with or against the government on big projects such as the development of a new oil pipeline from the Amazon, across the Andes, to the Pacific. That lack of coordination, for example, led them to lose that battle and the OCP pipeline was built in 2001.

The infighting and organizations' efforts focused on attaining resources for their own projects and organizational maintenance sidetracked them from having a larger analytic focus on the development model, even though individual environmentalists were concerned about the dominant development model (extractivism) and saw how their participation with transnational actors limited their capacity to shift it. For instance, one informant noted:

International agencies focus on birds, mammals, plants, ecosystems. They don't have a focus regarding communities and the environment. They talk a lot and have a good discourse .... But this type of focus on a specific species of bird or animal or ecosystem allows the model of development [extractivism] to continue.[129]

Representatives from USAID said themselves, that they had no intention of questioning an extractive economy: "We believe there is good in projects and in behavioral change in people. We don't oppose timber and oil. We need to do it right. We need to comply with laws and use the state of the art technology or we deplete the resources."[130] In other words, resource extraction is fine if it is done right. "Greening" oil extraction prevented disruptions to oil production. Some national actors saw the difficulty in this position. Was it better to work within the system to better it or to try to alter the structure? Working within the system to "green" industries, Fundación Natura attempted to partner with the timber industry to alter their practices. They were perceived as well intentioned, but the force of the extractive economy was far greater on the businesses than any pressure the NGO could apply. They could not succeed.

The national actors saw this irony. An informant explained what he believed were misplaced goals:

If you went to the town of Borbon [a town in which there were numerous sustainable development projects] in the 1980s and 1990s, all of the NGOs and international aid groups were there: USAID, Care, Fundación Natura, Conservation International, The Nature Conservancy, World Wildlife Fund, the Ministry of the Environment, universities, CEDENMA. All of them were there with money. And every day, wood left this area. Every day there was logging—legal, illegal, and unsustainable. This isn't about poor people cutting down the forest. It is about those with resources taking the natural resources for a profit. The model of development is the problem and I don't know if it will change. If we maintain the model, the environment will be destroyed.[131]

This informant was not a member of a radical/ecoresister group. Instead, this quote is from an Ecuadorian who had worked on the ground in conservation in the Amazon region for many organizations over the years, including a few of the national organizations, an international NGO, and a multilateral development agency. He complained that most state spending was oriented to pay the debt rather than to pay for health, education, and the environment. The actual state investment in the environment and resource management is minimal. He continued:

The model is wrong. We need to look for ways for the state to see a different form of development. It isn't just money. International politics and commerce also play a role .... The countries of the South provide energy, minerals, petroleum, water, wood, industrial plants, to the North. The exchange is open, free, without control; economics driven. We need another international form .... We need an alternative model. We need a new model that improves the environment, decreases poverty, increases equality, increases participation, in which the focus on sustainable development is distinct.[132]

Despite this broad analysis, the movement was limited by its day-to-day concerns. Instead of uniting against the system, Ecuadorians critiqued NGOs and environmentalism. Some Ecuadorians critiqued foreigners who were funding the system and promoting "sustainable development." Skepticism of foreign environmentalists grew.

An event that marked the growing resentment against *extranjeros* (foreigners), *gringos*, and especially foreign environmentalists occurred in the Galápagos in 1995. Local fishermen, armed with machetes, rounded up North American researchers at the Charles Darwin Research Station.

The fishermen were angry that the government, on the recommendation of scientists working at the Research Station, was preventing the fishermen from harvesting sea cucumbers from the Galápagos marine reserve. Sea cucumbers are a delicacy in Japan and have a high market value. The allowable catch set by the government was half a million a year. At the time of the takeover in 1995, at least seven million sea cucumbers had been harvested. *Gringo* scientists convinced the government to cut the fishing season short. The fishermen targeted the scientists, as they represented ideas of protection, which the fishermen viewed as limiting their ability to economically survive. Who were they to say?[133] Who should decide the balance between protecting the environment and protecting the economy? Who was to say how Ecuador should deal with its environmental problems? Hadn't North Americans already cut down their forests, drilled for their oil, and overfished their waters? What did they know? Foreigners had not successfully achieved any balance or "sustainable development."

While most Ecuadorian environmentalists were not able to harness their critique of the extractive development model into any concerted actions, Ecuadorians, such as these fisherman who were reliant on the environment for their livelihoods, acted on what they saw as foreign imposition of sustainable development into Ecuador.

The proliferation of private NGOs and the justification of development by calling it "sustainable" went hand in hand with the neoliberal development model. A shallow interpretation of sustainable development didn't force systemic change. It could be adapted into the existing political-economic institutions. Laura Rival's (1997: 2) early analysis of this is apt: "The concept of 'sustainable development' is being used to justify forms of development which are in no way sustainable, such as Ecuador's oil policy of unbridled extractivism. The naturalization of this drive—'there is nothing we can do to stop oil development in the Amazon' —can then be used to advantage some companies in the bidding competition."

Vicente Pólit, then CEDENMA's president, pressed for a deeper interpretation of sustainable development, focused on the economic and social justice pillars, and questioned its compatibility with the current model:

To defend the quality of life, nature, and the environment means fighting the causes of poverty. This requires a change in the neoliberal model that produces and carries poverty to extremes in the country. The neoliberal model is incompatible with sustainable development that looks for harmony among the paths of economic development, nature and natural resources. ... Internationally, it means justice in

North–South relations, the elimination or cancellation of the external debt, the real participation of the poor countries in the advanced centers of international decisions, concrete actions for development, beyond words and speeches.[134]

Representing CEDENMA, Polít publicly delivered one of the strongest statements against the development model at the opening of the II Congreso. He denounced the state's neoliberal model, and argued that the four most important changes that had happened since the first Congreso were all related to extraction in the name of payment of foreign debt: (1) increased petroleum exploration and extraction that threatened indigenous territories and protected areas, (2) investment in shrimping for export that put the mangrove ecosystem at risk of extinction in four coastal provinces, (3) the high rate (second highest in South America) of deforestation, especially from primary tropical forest, and (4) changes in mining legislation that favors foreign investment.[135] He also noted that sustainable development is not the same as developing sustainably. Paraphrasing his exact remarks, he argued that sustainable development (*desarrollo sostenible*) is a quantitative concept measured by economic growth and part of the neoliberal discourse. By contrast, developing sustainably (*desarrollo sustentable*) is a qualitative concept, part of environmental science, and is defined by social democratic organization based in the regeneration of natural resources. Developing sustainably improves the quality of life within the carrying capacity of ecosystems and integrates the destiny of human beings with the system that guarantees our permanence.[136] Acción Ecológica would also question the concept of sustainable development, arguing that the concept is used to justify almost any proposals that favor economic growth and the exploitation of natural resources.[137] Many believed that sustainable development was simply a new label to justify old practices rather than an alternative to neoliberal development.

The groups that take foreign funding to protect the environment fail to act together against the worst environmental offenses. The unintended consequence of transnational funding was the weakening of the environmental sector's critical edge. Ecodependent groups succeeded in protecting small segments of the environment. They planted trees and completed scientific inventories of bird species. But the movement did not focus on the economic development model. It did not target the damaging extractive industries that caused environmental destruction. The non-state actors opposed to its negative socioenvironmental consequences were divided and unable to create a collective movement opposing that path. Transnational funding conquered any movement potentially capable of addressing such big issues as Ecuador's development model. The science of naming biodiversity hotspots takes into account economic threats; yet the funding for protection did not focus on the environmental destruction caused by economic development projects, especially those focused on extraction. The extractive, state-permitted development modeled continued on.

End of the Boom: Crisis, Indigenous Uprisings, and Alternative Visions

In 1995, Ecuador and Peru engaged in a military dispute (again) over Amazonian territory, which caused a spike in government spending. The government suspended its international debt payments. This was the beginning of a prolonged crisis, which peaked in 1997 when President Bucaram's incompetent and corrupt government resigned amid demonstrations and allegations. The President was declared "mentally unfit to govern" following structural adjustment uprisings. In 1997 and 1998, a Constituent Assembly was formed by Ecuadorians, which operated alongside a contested, politically elected assembly, to review the country's constitution amid the political turmoil. The Confederation of Indigenous Nationalities of Ecuador (CONAIE, formed in 1986), were important actors in the Constituent Assembly, after having led major indigenous uprisings during this era. In 1990, there was a major protest by the indigenous of the highlands, and in 1992, a major lowland indigenous march, both in part responses to neoliberal adjustment policies.[138] The 1998 Constitution that emerged from those assemblies contained a number of CONAIE's demands, and enhanced indigenous rights. Environmentalists were also able to advance some environmental themes in this constitution. An outcome of CONAIE's grassroots movement was the creation of a political party (Pachakutik) that successfully entered electoral politics.[139] In 1998, President Jamil Mahuad was democratically elected, but the crisis continued.

That same year oil prices dropped, El Niño repeatedly flooded the agriculturally important coast, there was a run on banks, and the banking system failed. It was considered the "worst crisis in over a century."[140] Rochlin compiled data that illustrate:

Between 1998 and 2000 .... The country's GNP shrank 7.3 percent, foreign investment fell 34.7 percent, and imports declined by 38.4 percent. In 1998, there were 42 banks in the country, by the year 2000 there were only 26. Between August 1998 and December 1999, the Mahuad government spent 23 percent of the country's GNP to rescue the banking sector. Social spending fell 50 percent as a result, and the minimum wage fell 25 percent.[141]

To stop the economic slide the Muhuad administration decided to dollarize—exchanging the national currency, the *sucre*, for US dollars. Two weeks later a coup attempt led by CONAIE and the military forced the president to resign. Thus, during the late stages of the boom, the political-economic situation was unstable. The instability created openings for organized others to fill some political space. The indigenous movement led; not the environmental movement.

Transnational Influence, Neoliberalism, and Ecuador's Environment

During the boom years funding from ecomiperialists poured into Ecuador and generated the founding, growth, specialization, and professionalization of ecodependent organizations. The involvement of ecoimperialists channeled the agenda of the national movement. Ecodependent organizations were focused on the North's agenda of biodiversity preservation and later sustainable development. Together, ecoimperialists and ecodependents succeeded in protecting land and slowing degradation, but the national ecodependent groups had not created a self-made agenda nor a coherent movement, and had not addressed underlying causes of degradation, namely resource extraction. Financial incentive structures prevented them from mobilizing against the dominant development model. The irony of the ecoimperialist-ecodependent relationship is that international involvement intended to strengthen these groups and their work weakened the mainstream movement. It would not be too much of a stretch to liken transnational funders to invasive alien species: "introduced by man into places out of their natural range of distribution, where they become established and disperse, generating a negative impact ...."[142]

However, the global link also has had some positive influences. International funding and international political influences, such as the UN Conferences, have helped national environmental organizations put environmental issues on the national agenda. The Convention on Biodiversity was especially important for bringing attention and resources to Ecuador, given its status as a biodiversity hotspot. Al Gore, who was repeatedly referenced as a great environmental leader, and the UN Intergovernmental Panel on Climate Change and other international bodies were noted as putting important elements on the agenda. These influences are based not on funding streams but on ideas. While these provided a context for action, what happened on the ground, materially, was more directly tied to the ideas that became incorporated into funding streams, as in the case with biodiversity protection. Without international funding, most Ecuadorian environmentalists believe the environment would have been degraded at even higher rates and many believe that environmental groups would be considerably weaker.[143] Table 5.2 summarizes the era in relation to the key analytic variables.

At an even broader level, international political-economic processes, namely neoliberalism, weakened states and strengthened NGOs. In many ways this meant that "foreigners" had a lot of power and influence on Ecuador's policies and practices, not just in the environmental realm. Environmentally, international groups were charged with being ecoimperialists. In the Galápagos Islands and elsewhere, locals spoke out against the Global North's attempt to control Ecuador's environment. Anthropologist Arturo Escobar critiques what he calls the "dominant biodiversity

Table 5.2
Summary of Boom Era

	Origins 1978–1987	Boom 1987–2000	Bust 2000–2006	Revolution 2006–2015
Transnational funding		Multiple funders and large amounts of funding primarily for NGOs		
Environmental sector		Many new NGOs (ecodependent) founded that are focused on conservation agenda; ecoresistant organizations forming under the radar that are building grassroots support for social-ecological issues		
State characteristics		Weak, indebted, following neoliberal model		
Environment and development policies		New environmental ministry and Law of the Galápagos, expansion of national parks, continued resource dependence		
Schnaiberg's synthesis		Slight shift toward managed scarcity		

discourse" that is articulated by the "West" (what I'm calling the Global North). The discourse propagates international conservation projects based on the Western conception of biodiversity, which he calls the "resource management dominant view." Ecuador was a perfect example of this in which the Global North was directing the understanding of human's relationship to the environment. In the boom era, environmental issues became "global," and funding moved from North to South to "protect" and "manage" environments. When the national government became unstable, this conception was challenged and alternative conceptions of the nature–culture relationship started to be powerfully articulated. Not coincidentally, neoliberal policies and practices were also being questioned.

In reference to the treadmill of production, and the three syntheses Schnaiberg elaborated, this era marked a slight shift from the economic synthesis toward a managed scarcity synthesis, in word. The rhetoric of sustainable development forced the state to at least look as if it were taking action to protect aspects of the environment, through actions such as the creation of environmental institutions, new protected areas, and limits on fishing. It was, though, just a green wash. These actions were relatively easy for the state to take because their revenues were not affected by the changes, nor did the costs negatively affect the fortunes of industrialists. Petroleum and logging—two of the main extractive industries—were not touched by the state. Additionally land that was "officially" protected by the state was encroached upon by petroleum companies, miners, loggers, fishermen, and colonists. In instances when state agencies charged with protecting the environment competed with agencies charged with economic development, the economy almost always won. Even though environmental policies were enacted, the growth coalition, fueled by international debt requirements and led by the state, took precedence over attempts at sustainability.

Chapter 6 explains the turn from neoliberal boom to bust and the rise of environmental groups that were less attached to an international system of funding than the ecodependents described in this chapter. The next chapter shows why ecoresisters emerged and how they differ from ecodependents in terms of their issue areas, agenda and projects/processes.

6 Organizational Bust, 2000 to 2006: Opportunities for Ecoresisters and Ecoalternatives

Another world is not only possible, she is on her way. On a quiet day, I can hear her breathing.
—Arundhati Roy

This chapter analyzes the decline in transnational funding that began around 2000 and the consequent shrinking of the mainstream segments of the environmental sector *(ecodependents)*. Grassroots and radical activists *(ecoresisters)*, who had long been an overshadowed aspect of the movement, came to the fore. While these activists and their groups existed almost since the beginning of environmental mobilizations in Ecuador, the decline of both international support (from *ecoimperialists)* and *ecodependents'* strength coupled with a crisis of the state, created an opening for such groups to thrive. *Ecoresisters* are largely independent of international funding, and thus, relatively autonomous in their agenda setting. They have the capacity to set their own terms and resist the dominant environmental and developmental agendas. These groups have a radical critique of the extractive development model. They present alternative views and visions for the future that are more aligned with an ecological synthesis. They have natural alliances with organizations in the indigenous movement, and have pressed for development focused on "living well" (*buen vivir/sumak kawsay*).

Theoretically the independence of these groups is analogous to the independence of the state in terms of their capacity to act on their own terms. Dependent states form policies on the basis of their terms of dependency, and based on their subordinate position in the international setting. The same is true of nongovernmental organizations. Some theories of globalization, such as world polity theory, suggest that hegemonizing forces have led major institutions to have similar structures, policies, and practices.[1] This is true for dependent states and dependent environmental groups. The *ecoresisters* highlighted in this chapter suggest that organizational independence facilitates alternative visions and practices. The resistance to dominant forces and ideologies, by organizations such as DECOIN and C-CONDEM in Ecuador, suggest that another world is possible.

A fourth and the final kind of group in the environmentalist typology is also explained and illustrated in this chapter: *ecoentrepreneur* organizations. Like *ecoresisters*, these groups are relatively independent from international funding structures. In fact, by design, these types aim to be regularly replenished at the local level through taxes, user fees, and payment for ecosystem services. These groups represent yet another alternative for organizing for sustainability.

Transnational Funding Declines

Around 2000 and 2001, funding for Ecuador's environment from abroad took a sharp decline, which had a devastating effect on national *ecodependent* organizations that had relied on foreign funds. There were three main reasons for the funding decline. First, with the 2000 financial crisis and dollarization, there was a loss of confidence in Ecuador's political-economic system. Funders were reluctant to give and it was harder for organizations to do their work. An Ecuadorian NGO director reflected, "Dollarization hit hard. Everything was more expensive. Many groups disappeared in early 2000. In the late 1990s, there were hundreds, perhaps 300 groups."[2] Second, after the terrorist attacks in the United States in 2001, US funding shrunk as US interests were diverted to the Middle East. Not all *ecodependent* groups were able to adapt to these financial shocks. When funding from the United States dropped off with "Bush's war" and "$600 billion spent on Iraq, ... groups disappeared or downsized .... In general it was a down period."[3] Some groups folded altogether; others kept going, but without paid staff or regular funding. A few groups were protected to some degree by their long-term relationships with international NGOs. One group that grew during this period—Fundación Jatun Sacha—noted it was able to do so because of support from the popular local base in the areas where it held nature reserves.

However, it wasn't just "Bush's war" that created the downturn. The third cause of the contraction of funds was that by the end of the 1990s, two large-scale bilateral projects were coming to an end. USAID's SUBIR project, which had flooded the country with environmental funds, and a Dutch project in Loja called Programa Podocarpus, which also boosted numerous environmental groups, both ended in the late 1990s. Many groups closed their doors for good when these projects concluded. Despite project aims to create some social sustainability by way of organizational continuity, when the projects ended, so did many of the organizations that the projects helped get off the ground. An informant called these organizations "USAID babies." "With project-based funding, the project finishes and the work is gone. ... The SUBIR project had lots of money, but when USAID left, everything disappeared. ... You work to develop trust in the field and [you want to] stay there, not just for a project. [Our NGO] tries not to do what USAID has done. Conservation is a long process."[4] Another interviewee, commenting on the Dutch program, noted that the growth and decline of groups in tandem with project-based funding is a common process.[5] Thus the *ecodependent* groups revealed their vulnerability to geopolitical shifts and private and public funding agents beyond their control.

The OCP Pipeline: A Real and Symbolic Loss to the Movement

The financial downturn for ecodependents coincided with the beginning of construction for the OCP pipeline (crude oil pipeline, Oleoducto de Crudos Pesados) in 2001, which would carry heavy crude oil from the rainforest town of Lago Agrio across the Andes, to Esmeraldas, a port city on the Pacific coast. It cuts through an internationally recognized "important bird area," protected forests, and the town of Mindo, an ecotourism destination. The pipeline was backed by the International Monetary Fund, multinational oil companies, the German government and the Ecuadorian government. Numerous local protests arose over the pipeline, including protests around the Mindo Cloudforest where locals were beginning to reap the benefits of their ecotourism enterprises.[6] These were NIMBY (not in my backyard) protests. National-level NGOs —*ecodependents*—however, were criticized by locals (and themselves) for not mounting a stronger campaign against the pipeline. Rather than rally together to prohibit its construction, organizations competed for the contracts for the environmental concessions. In the end the national groups ended up winning the contracts to reforest the areas alongside the pipeline. Though the clash raised environmental consciousness across the nation, the loss devastated environmentalists. This, numerous interviewees, cited as a major failure of the "environmental movement."

A foreigner working for an international environmental group was surprised by the development of the pipeline:

It was very interesting to me when I first came here, that none of the major international NGOs or even national NGOs were willing to get up and say "This is completely unacceptable. We're dead against this." They would not. They sat on the sideline and watched and they waited to see which way the wind would blow. It wasn't until the government had actually taken the decision to go for the pipeline and put it through some sensitive areas that the NGOs jumped on site and said now we need to work … to find out what's the best mechanism that we can secure resources to make sure the pipeline has the minimal impact on this area.[7]

This, however, was not the perspective from *ecodependents*. A leading Ecuadorian environmentalist explains:

There was a huge concern among the people …. Environmentalists were saying this was not a good project for Ecuador in general. … One way to stop it was to review the Environmental Impact Assessment [EIA] and explain what was wrong with it, but we didn't receive enough time for reviewing it. … NGOs tried to prove there was no public consultation regarding the project before it was approved, with no luck after all.[8]

She further explained that in NGO meetings with the Ministry of the Environment about the EIA that the Ministry declared those meetings were "consultation":

All of the environmental organizations involved felt cheated by the Ministry. … We learned a lot from the process. … It shows we have to be very careful when there are these economic interests. The Ministry of the Environment in general is a weak institution, and it was used by the Ministry of Energy any way they wanted.[9]

What eventually came out of the OCP process was an "Ecofund." Officially, it is a $16.9 million fund to be used for biodiversity conservation in Ecuador through until 2022. Fondo Ambiental Nacional (FAN, the National Environmental Fund), a nonprofit organization, manages the fund. Organizations submit proposals to FAN for projects, and FAN evaluates projects and distributes funds. According to its documentation, projects are primarily for conservation "for the long-term benefit of the Ecuadorian people." An interviewee notes, "FAN is paying directly for park rangers. This money is from petroleum. It is a way for petroleum companies to know that the Ministry of Environment won't be hard on them. They pay them off nicely."[10] In essence the Ecofund served as a means to greenwash the process and the responsible corporation and to appease the detractors. Patricia Widener details the process that led to this fund in her book *Oil Injustice: Resisting and Conceding a Pipeline in Ecuador*. She makes some important points about this process that are worth repeating. The first is that in this process Northern NGOs introduced Southern NGOs to the process of adopting corporate-environmental agreements. This is not a process that had been practiced in Ecuador, and many nonparticipating NGOs actually regarded this work with the pipeline constructors as cooptation and unethical. Second, the process by which national NGOs negotiated the Ecofund led to feelings of betrayal and mistrust among national NGOs, which hurt their willingness to collaborate as allies. Finally, by using the Ecofund strategy the NGO community "had adopted ... a capitalist and development worldview that then restricted their choices before them."[11] Widener argues that other options were available. "Had the environmental NGOs in Ecuador identified points of solidarity with the laboring poor of Lago Agrio [who were fighting against OCP for rights to participate in oil decisions], rather than the conservation NGOs of the North, their impact and import may have been strengthened rather than diminished."[12] Big development projects couldn't unite environmentalists. In fact their response to them created animosity among environmentalists, fragmented the movement, limited other potential alliances, and furthered the extractive development program. Other choices, such as cooperating with the poor of Lago Agrio, could have led to a unified front against the development of the pipeline.

OCP wasn't the only failure. The environmental movement also lacked a unified response in a similar event that again pitted the Ministry of the Environment against the Ministry of Energy. In this case the Brazilian oil company Petrobras was granted the rights to develop a road into Yasuní National Park through the indigenous Waorani Ethnic Reserve. They started the road in 2005. An Ecuadorian working for an international NGO offered disbelief that the Petrobras/Yasuní/Waorani debacle could not be a unifying event for environmental groups. "What was amazing ... [is that] all the institutions involved in the discussion, all the environmental groups would tell you that the road was a bad idea for sure. And somehow we couldn't get together and present with a common front to the government."[13] Eventually, in the next era (2008), after changes in national leadership and a number of indigenous marches on the capital, Petrobras withdrew after having started the road and invested $200 million in the area.[14] This area in Block 31 was transferred to Ecuador's Petroamazonas.[15]

The resource blocks in the protected areas are sites of heightened tension because the state has the right to open the areas to petroleum exploitation and mineral concessions. In this context often "the state does not view the park as a park, rather they view it as a petroleum block."[16] Given its distance from the capital, the state can ignore environmental devastation in lieu of revenue. Locals then are left to defend these spaces.

However, they too can be subject to economic trade-off and the tactics used by multinational companies. "In the jungle, oil companies go to indigenous protest areas before exploration. The communities learned to ask for a 'toll,' for instance, motorboats and schools. NGOs and the government haven't done anything for them in terms of social aspects."[17] Another added, "In the petroleum areas, they get services. They have potable water. They get better money [with petroleum] than with sustainable development projects."[18]

Ecodependent Strategies to Cope with Funding Bust

When transnational funding declined, environmental organizations had to close up shop, downsize, or try new strategies.

Strategy 1: Shut Down

Ecodependents were vulnerable to external changes over which they had no control. For instance, the Dutch's large-scale, multiyear project Programa Podocarpus in the provinces of Loja and Zamora-Chinchipe was designed to build the capacity of environmental organizations. Before the project began, there were approximately ten environmental organizations in the region. The Dutch injected a lot of money and during the project period, new groups were founded. The number of environmental organizations in the area grew to somewhere between forty-three and sixty-five (the range of numbers given by various interviewees). After the project ended and the external funding ceased, the original ten organizations were the only environmental groups that remained, including Fundación Arco-Iris and Fundación Podocarpus. The others failed. One interviewee who had worked on the project explained, "When the funding ended, the other [NGOs] closed their doors. ... After five years, you don't see those NGOs."[19] The newly created NGOs folded after the project ended despite the fact that one of the project's goals was to strengthen these groups. They didn't have a plan for long-term financial sustainability. There was not even a chance to extend this project and thus the organizations' lives and work because at higher levels the Dutch government decided to eliminate their Ecuador program. They chose to have a bigger impact in fewer countries, and Ecuador wasn't one of them. In 2003 they drafted an exit strategy. Ecuadorian organizations could not control any aspect of the Dutch's departure. Forces beyond national control altered their focus. Even Dutch nationals working in Ecuador at their embassy were surprised by this change in course.[20]

The bilateral donors were shifting their priorities. A similar process was at work with USAID. For instance, in 2007, USAID would receive only one-third of the funding for Ecuador that they had received in 2006, and that had been on the decline. In the environmental sector, USAID was viewed as having diminishing strength because it was "putting more emphasis on themes of democracy and in themes of drug trafficking."[21] Similar processes also occurred in the private sector. A US-based international NGO director noted, "Funding is a major issue. Even with private donors, you never know. It is driven by the US economy. Now there is investment in Iraq. USAID money is diminishing very dangerously."[22] "Funding organizations change priorities."[23]

Up to this point many Ecuadorian organizations had developed a dependency on foreign funding. In 2007, I surveyed the organizations in the Ecuadorian environmental sector that had survived this period (the 2007 Ecuadorian Environmental Organization Survey). At that time the degree of foreign funding dependency remained high. Of the population of 176 organizations, 45 percent responded to the survey ($n = 80$). Fifty percent of responding groups received at least half of their funding from foreign sources, including foreign foundations, international NGOs, and foreign governments.[24] Ninety percent of the organizations believed that international funding was "somewhat" or "very important" in resolving the problems they were working on.

Because of the deep dependency on transnational funding for the environmental sector, the number of organizations has paralleled the amount of funding available. In other words, the number of organizations grows during times of high funding (boom) and declines when funds stop flowing (bust). The incursion of funds creates the impetus for new organizations, many of which eventually fold when funding ceases. This boom-and-bust cycle is internationally, not nationally, driven. Given its global nature, it is likely that this cycle occurred in other nonprofit sectors and in other countries.[25]

Strategy 2: Shift Agenda

A second and related consequence of organizational dependency on foreign funding is that environmental organizations shifted their emphasis to ensure funding from international organizations. This strategy of agenda shifting is one of organizational survival. It has meant, simply, that environmental organizations in Ecuador have altered their missions to meet donor desires. In the previous chapter I discussed how ecoimperialists bring their agendas with them and how they attempt to find partners who share their agenda. In the bust era, national organizations consciously shifted their agendas to follow the money and to fit within the international organizations' purview. Ecodependents morphed into what ecoimperialists wanted. Since funding organizations control resources they have the potential to influence the grantees' actions and agendas. Organizational theorists call this resource dependency.[26] From the point of view of the grantees, shifting their goals to meet donors' interests is a strategy to stay alive. Instead of folding when their funding ends, they shift and adapt. They figure out how to sustain themselves. In sustaining their organizations through this strategy, ecodependents allow foreign interests to trump Ecuadorian organizations' original goals.

What this has meant for the Ecuadorian environmental agenda is that when there is funding for strict conservation (i.e., conservation of flora and fauna except humans), groups work on strict conservation. When the international funding trend was for "jobs and conservation" (aka sustainable development), groups work on sustainable development. When women were added to the international mix, Ecuadorian organizations added women, and so on. If there's no funding for air pollution or sanitation, groups do not work on air pollution or sanitation. "The funding [of national issues] depends a lot on international tendencies. If someone says at the international level that we need to pay attention to 'X,' there will be money for 'X,' like the international hotspots."[27] Another director observed, "There is a trend. International organizations found that 'communities' were the fashion of the time, and all of the financing went to the communities. After that, the women were the fashion, then to the feminist movements went all of the money. Then it arrived for the environmental movement. The time [now in 2007] is for democracy, or something ...."[28] According to another informant, when transnational funders wanted projects with alliances, such as environmental NGOs allying with social NGOs and universities, NGOs started doing that. When funders wanted income generating enterprises, such as artisanal works and ecotourism, groups started doing that. Groups have a lot of resentment about this.[29] In chapter 5 this process explained why there were no urban-focused environmental groups: urban pollution is a problem without a sponsor. A lot of time was spent on concerns from abroad rather than on the concerns of the Ecuadorian people.

From a different point of view, a national director said, "The national organizations don't have their own strategy for conservation, they look outside to international organizations."[30] This suggests that the ecodependency of national organizations is disempowering and that national groups are the ground soldiers for northern concerns.

At the very least, dependency on foreign organizations prevents Ecuadorian organizations from making independent choices. An informant noted that groups that want to survive are "dancing to the rhythm of the donors."[31] Another said that environmental organizations "live according to foreign funding." A savvy but disgruntled leader of a small organization commented:

We learned how donors work. ...You need to know the discourses of what the donor is willing to give. You can have the best idea for a project, but they're focused [on their issues] and not going to fund it [your project]. ...You need to have skill and knowledge and know the trendy words. ... They [INGOs] have plenty of money for their own project [ideas] but not for ours. ... You need to know what the NGO is looking for.

In a case where this director requested funds and was turned down, she commented, "They wanted oranges and I wanted carrots."[32] Organizations whose priorities do not match international NGOs' priorities complain that they have not been able to master "donor speak."

National groups can sometimes move the donors closer to nationals' priorities:

There is learning on the NGO side on what donors want to hear. There is a language on how we can persuade donors. ... The baseline of projects comes from donors. Sometimes it is general, such as capacity building. They may have an idea, and if you want to change it, you must give them a believable alternative.[33]

Others have noted outright that they won't do what donors what them to do just because the donors want it. For instance, a scientist working for a national organization said, "Many times, their [international organizations'] strategies are not necessarily the needs that we as a country have. Therefore in some cases they are interested in conserving an ecosystem that from our point of view is not necessarily a priority. There are other questions more important." He followed, "In my experience, international organizations have never made an imposition on what we did. Never. Because every time they have told me this should be done, and we have said, 'but those are not our needs, we are looking for this.'"[34]

This stance, however, was not often represented in interviews. In the 2007 Ecuadorian Environmental Organization Survey, over half of the groups had shifted their issue areas. Of those groups, over 70 percent did so based on the available funding. Other top reasons included needing to secure available resources, and donors' priorities. The shifting was prevalent among ecodependents. An informant noted of this period:

Institutions became so desperate for funds that they would change their initial motivations. ... EcoCienca is an example of that because EcoCiencia [stands for] the Fundación de Estudios Ecologicos. At the beginning it really was an ecological studies organization and then they were forced to pursue funds wherever they could and as a result, right now they barely do anything that you could call ecological studies. They do a lot of social stuff. They do a lot of planning, a lot of GIS. They do a lot of training also, which is really important, but I doubt that they actually do ecology studies anymore. And that has happened to a lot of organizations. They go to wherever the funds are and they change their initial motivations because they need the funds.[33]

The shifts also were the results of global trends in ideas, as mentioned above. The trend in conservation moved to incorporating people, to sustainable development. Scientists—biologists in particular—who were interested in studying flora and fauna founded many Ecuadorian organizations. When sustainable development forced the question of how conservation worked with people, organizations shifted toward social scientific work. Thus funding structures played a role, but especially in how they promoted the ideas of the day. Of the shift toward including humans, one natural science director noted:

So things started to change. ... We had national pride. The idea that we can't just focus on parks conservation but we actually have to do something with the people and for the people, that was the first change, the first evolution in the movement. ... It became this wider approach, about an environment, in general. And when you talk about environment, you are talking about many, many more things, like how to deal with development; development that is necessary. But you have to do it within a way that the natural resources are effected, but not in a very bad way.[34]

The funding was the mechanism by which the ideological shifts were translated to the ground.

Some national NGOs are criticized for acting as if they were the national chapter of international organizations. They get this reputation when they have continued funding from a transnational donor. Some INGOs are fluid with their partners, changing from time to time, and some are more set. In 2007 The Nature Conservancy had eight partners in Ecuador: seven NGOs (Fundación Natura, Fundación Antisana, Fundación Charles Darwin, Fundación Jatun Sacha, EcoCiencia, the Conservation Data Center, and Fundación Rumincocha), and the Ministerio del Ambiente, the government's environmental agency. Other INGOs, like Conservation International, change over time. The Nature Conservancy receives some funding from USAID, which limits who they can choose as partners due to their stringent reporting requirements. For the most part, donors have not been risk-takers in their giving. They have relied on their traditional partners, reinforcing relationships, and bolstering reputations. The ecodependents gather strength, expertise, and capacity through their funding, which in turn builds their reputation and begets more funds. However, informants complain of nepotism, cronyism, and corruption. It is hard for smaller groups with different agendas to break into this structure.

Birdlife International is an INGO that fosters regional agenda development. They work with only one partner in each country where they work. In Ecuador that organization is Aves y Conservación (A&C). The national partners sit on regional boards that make the decisions about how Birdlife International undertakes and implements its agenda in the region. This is by far the most democratic international environmental organization working in Ecuador. According to a representative from Birdlife Ecuador, "It takes a long time to get decisions made, but when they are made, they tend to stick. We find that a large number of the partners really feel that they fall into the agenda. It is not imposed on them because they've actually helped develop it."[37]

Even with this partnering strategy, though, Aves y Conservación, as the sole partners of Birdlife International, according to BI's Director, "Agree to advance certain agenda items. They are in essence, the Birdlife in Ecuador. They are the franchise. They represent Birdlife so they are Aves y Conservación–Birdlife International." Because BI chooses partners with whom the agendas align, this does not necessarily require a huge agenda shift. A&C is the national chapter of BI. A bigger issue for Aves y Conservación is that BI requires them to be a membership organization. As such they are the only national membership organization that I have identified in Ecuador. Their membership is very small and they do not provide services to members. They struggle to keep the minimum number required by Birdlife, and in 2007 had almost 100. In the past, Fundación Natura tried to be a membership organization, but it didn't last. Although A&C has a sugar daddy of sorts, the partnering requirement of membership obliges A&C to create itself in the image of Birdlife International, which has a very different context. BI is a European organization. In England, Birdlife's partner is the Royal Society for the Protection of Birds. It has four million members and a $20 million budget. This doesn't make sense for the Ecuadorian context.

Like most of Latin America, Ecuador does not have a tradition of group membership in environmental organizations, nor does it have a tradition of philanthropy. Unlike big US-based environmental organizations, such as the Sierra Club, Ecuadorian NGOs do not have members who donate funds and receive a T-shirt, a tote bag, and a bumper sticker. They also lack corporate sponsors to fund specific campaigns. Their funding streams are insecure:

It is not like in the U.S. where you have your foundations with a trust fund. Then at least you have permanent funding for at least your operational costs. So at least you can think. You can devote more time to thinking and analyzing and proposing new things. ... At [national NGOs] they try to survive and have to beg for resources.[38]

Given that there are so few national-level funding sources, national organizations compete with each other to attain international funds. "There is no support locally therefore NGOs are always caught in the money part. ... All of the NGOs are competing for the same funds. It diminishes the power of the NGOs."[39]

Environmental organizations' funding survival strategy reinforces the North's agenda. The Ecuadorian leaders of these groups do not deliberate and agree on a national agenda. Instead, the national agenda mirrors the international agenda. National organizations did not choose their issues; they lacked social sustainability: choice. External resources drove changes. Shifts in agenda were not due to internal changes in leadership or mission or changes in objective environmental conditions. Control came from the top down. The agenda-shifting strategy provides evidence of green imperialism. Neither science nor on the ground needs drove the agenda; economics drove the agenda. This, however, was not true for groups that are detached from the international funding structures discussed later in the chapter.

Strategy 3: Proyectismo

A third survival strategy directly linked to agenda shifting was what interviewees described as *proyectismo*. Lacking corporate or membership funds, environmental organizations respond to "request for proposals" (RFPs) from transnational funders. The requests are for projects that ecoimperialists want completed. The plus side of this process is that concrete goals are accomplished, such as the training of park guards and the reforesting of denuded lands. However, there are many negatives. The first is that the ecodependent groups configure their projects into what donors want to receive funding. Their work is then driven by the project guidelines and timelines. Funded organizations prepare contract "deliverables," meeting the project objectives, rather than their own goals. This is an extreme but common version of agenda shifting. Through this process, organizations support themselves by working from project to project, constantly responding to RFPs from donors to sustain some variant of their work. Ecodependent leaders disdainfully refer to this as *"proyectismo"*—going "from project, to project, to project." An interested foreign observer noted, "The behavior of NGOs is mercenary. The economy doesn't allow anything else."[40] Another cynically commented, "There are no projects that work. It is a way to get money."[41] A bilateral donor stated, "When an NGO maintains its original philosophy, it survives. The problem is when NGOs look for projects, just [looking for] payrolls."[42] National directors really dislike the process. They complain that too much of their time is spent in their offices in Quito searching for funds and writing reports, rather than in the field doing work or forming alliances with like-minded organizations focused on their environmental agenda. "Groups are in Quito to get money. ... We need to grow more in the field than in the office."[43] Another said, "You wear yourself out getting funds. ... I write proposals like crazy."[44] This creates a short time frame and lack of vision. "If you are in day-by-day survival, and you need to find new projects ... you start to not have time to think and to work with [other organizations]."[45] A long-time NGO leader, who has served in multiple roles laments, "One of my main concerns is that very often we are not looking at the long-term needs, strategies and goals of the country.[46] These groups are aware of these downsides, but project-based work is an adaptive strategy that allows them to survive in the Ecuadorian context.

Proyectismo has led groups to complain that other organizations are "self-serving" and "each out for their own selves."[47] In the process of looking for funds for their own projects, organizations sell their services and expertise. They become more like contract consultants than movement organizations. They are professional and pragmatic about it. "A contract is a contract. We don't care. We do it for money. We'll do it right, but [we] want funds for our own projects. We don't like services [i.e. services for hire]. There are risks and we must bow down and we can't say what we want. It pays well if handled right, but it can be horrible."[48]

Directors raised questions regarding the degree to which these environmental organizations should be classified as non-profits versus simple businesses or consultants.

I think it is very bad if NGOs become consultants .... There are rules for consulting firms. Of course, they have the right to work and you need some consulting firms as part of the society. But they are not *sin fines de lucro* [nonprofit]. They are for profits. They basically produce something and leave. But supposedly, NGOs should not do that. They are nonprofit and they normally should be there for a least a longer period of time. Over and over we have seen that conservation projects require

long-term approaches. ... At least be long enough and have a long-term commitment to those communities. Once you start to work as a consultant, you start to
behave as a consultant. The long-term commitment is very weak and it becomes
very opportunistic, because consultants' nature is very opportunistic. And in this
case—NGOs and conservation processes—you need longer processes. That's the
difference between conservation *process* and conservation *projects,* which I think is
a big difference.[49]

This distinction between process and project was elaborated numerous
times, with everyone preferring processes to projects. It is also a distinction
made by ecoresisters to show how they differ from ecodependents. For
instance, Acción Ecológica prides itself of teaching communities and grassroots organizations about resistance processes that can be continued and
replicated locally without foreign funds.

The director cited above was very concerned about the lines being
blurred between NGOs and consultant groups, especially as NGOs moved
into microenterprises.

I think it is very important to call thing what they are. If you really want to be
consultancies, create a consultancy firm, behave as a consultancy firm, and lead
us as a consultancy firm. If you want to be an NGO, you need to liberate people.
And if you want a business and test markets, then grow a business. And if you
have the social conscious, environmental consciousness, let's donate some of the
profits to conservation and conservation NGOs. But the problem is when you
start mixing everything. It creates problems. It's not good for the environmental
movement. It's not good for the enterprises. And it's not good for the state or the
consultancy.[50]

He wasn't the only one who was concerned about this. Others raised
ethical questions. "One of the issues is ... when do you [an NGO] become
something else because you are looking to wherever the funds take you ...
[These organizations] are doing consultancy. They are doing environmental
impact statements for oil companies or any other destructive industry
because they need to get the money."[51]

Ethical issues were raised a number of times, especially in regard to the
"soft" conditions that are attached to projects. Bilateral donors fund their
nations' priorities. An NGO director explained how his NGO's issue areas
were limited by conditions of bilateral funding. He used the example of
flower production, which is controversial in terms of its pesticide use and
its labor practices. He said, "If we have a priority to work against the production and the export of flowers, and for the Dutch [bilateral donors] it is
not permitted because they have an interest in the theme of flowers, by this
manner there is a brake on this work that we are not able to overcome,

because they are deciding our priorities."[52] Bilateral donors affect issue areas and nationals' practices. The donors are in a position of power and can strong-arm recipients. I asked a group of USAID representatives what they considered "good partners." One responded,

Good partners are those that work with us. We have an open relationship. We don't tell them what to do, but there is some tough love involved. For instance, as part of Parks in Peril, we supported community park guards. We told our local partners ... that they needed to find independent funding for them. They said, "We're too busy. We'll do that the month before the funding runs out. We don't have time to do that." So in the end, we wrote down that we'd all think about this and then we made them write a plan .... Originally, the groups resisted finding funding for this part of Parks in Peril. There was a rebellion. But then they did it.[53]

This response reveals power relationships: USAID controls the purse strings and can make demands. NGOs can push back at donor requests, but in the end, the donors prevailed. According to the USAID official, the park guards were an NGO priority.

The proyectismo funding process also has inter-organizational consequences. It increased the competition that had existed within the movement. Due to competition for funding, organizations are less likely to work together, less likely to see similarly minded organizations as allies, and as a consequence the environmental movement sector has been fragmented. Ecodependent organizations' behaviors are privately motivated (i.e., maintaining the organization) rather than publicly motivated (i.e., protecting the environment for the public). Rather than working for a common agenda, groups are competing for paychecks. Economics trumps ecology. The scientific research and scientific reports that environmental organizations prepare for donors are often proprietary, which impedes information sharing. The competition to secure limited project funding also creates incentives for withholding scientific information. A researcher at a national ecodependent organization told me, "We don't want others to know our secrets or our donors. We are competition."[54] A director of an international group explained: "Competition for funds is so fierce that I think they tend to become afraid that if you share information then that could result in you losing opportunities for future projects. It's a survival strategy. ... For me it's very sad."[55] In the end the transnational funding practices create disincentives for cooperation. They have limited groups' interest and ability to work together to pursue mutual ends. Like-minded groups that could potentially be working together for a common agenda are split. The codependence between ecoimperialists and ecodependents breeds competition rather than cooperation among national groups.

There is competition for project money, and there is competition to be aligned with a transnational funder. The larger NGOs have become "favorites" or "chosen partners" for certain funders and "as a result of that alliance, it acts as a conduit for, in some cases, quite significant funding."[56] There is a funding bias toward organizations in the capitol of Quito. However, "There are hundreds of NGOs. Most are not partners [with international organizations] and therefore are resentful. In Cuenca and Guayaquil, they feel left out, excluded and angry."[57] Even within Quito, though, a director notes: "Quito is a small town. [People] criticize projects because their organization competed for funds and didn't get them."[58]

Transnational funding does not need to breed competition and resentment. A few project directors mentioned the collaborative work that was being fostered by the MacArthur Foundation. For instance, "Fundación Natura and Arcoiris have money from the Macarthur Foundation. It was not a condition of the grant to work together. It was actually a request from MacArthur to try to share the information for conservation. And we did."[59] This same director notes, "It has been a policy of mine to share all of the information that we have. I think you have to share it with NGOs freely whenever they ask, sometimes even when they do not ask. If we see that they are needing something, we hand over information. It is our policy." It is notable that this NGO has a solid international partner, and thus a degree of financial stability. Another noted that private organizations like MacArthur and universities contribute to dialogue and social learning among the groups more so than organizations like USAID that are rigid in their reporting requirements. The World Conservation Society's staff were also working on this: "[Cooperation] is something we are trying to make a big part of our role here. We think that sometimes lacking is the sharing of information and transparency and the sense of the need of getting together with the other institutions to share information and make something bigger out of the collaborations. That's something that we are trying to work on very, very hard."[60]

The lack of cooperation and coordination is linked to limited time due to constant scrambling for funds, and a lack of trust, due to the same. Another INGO director cites cooperation as his biggest challenge in Ecuador. "Purely cooperation [is the challenge]! Cooperation of coordination. There are too many NGOs. Too many fractured agendas. There are plenty of amazingly capable people in this country and at some point there needs to be the meeting of the minds to determine really, what is the agenda for the movement?"[61] A national leader agrees: "We need to coordinate a national strategy ... no one is coordinating. ... But with all that we do, we can't. Who implements? Who will do it? We cannot do it ... that's too much."[62]

The national umbrella environmental organization, CEDENMA, works to bring organizations together. Its official role is literally "To politically group and represent the collective opinion of Ecuadorian Non Governmental Environmentalist Organizations, whose goal is the conservation of the nature, the protection of the environment and the promotion and attainment of sustainable development." In this era, sixty-three organizations made up CEDENMA. It brought organizations together in National Congresses and other assemblies to discuss the environment. But CEDENMA competes against the structure of *proyectismo*. Despite CEDENMA's efforts, interviewees consider it "a fragile umbrella" and dismiss its work as "just talk."

Increasingly, international groups were also competing for these funds as they began to implement their own projects rather than serving as intermediary organizations, passing funds to national NGOs. For instance, the Wildlife Conservation Society (WCS) implements projects directly, with their own staff, without engaging Ecuadorian NGOs. This practice has led to complaints among Ecuadorian NGOs, despite the fact that the employees of WCS are Ecuadorian. In discussing the German Aid Agency (GTZ), which has also started implementing its own projects, one director described them as more competition—"like one more NGO." This is seen as unfair. "These international organizations are now competing for the same funds that the rest of the organizations have to, so there are less resources."[63] This frustrates Ecuadorians who are well-educated and capable of doing the work. The international groups defend themselves. One defense is that they are able to tap funds that the national groups cannot: "So, for example, if we have this millionaire in New York who gives money to [an INGO from the United States] and some of his money comes to Ecuador, that's not money that these [Ecuadorian] organizations could get anyway. So the idea that we're competing for funds is not real. I don't think so."[64]

Proyectismo was one way that organizations adapted to scarce resources. However, it counterproductively compromised their missions, ethical stances, and ability to be part of a cooperative movement for the environment.

Strategy 4: Generate Regular Income
A final strategy organizations used to respond to declining international funding was to identify new sources of income by providing regular services

for a fee. A prominent example of this is what Fundación Natura started during this period. Fundación Natura incorporated a branch of the organization to become Fundación Natura, Inc., which contracted with the city of Quito to manage municipal waste. This provided them with a steady source of income, but it would later lead to their demise.

Organizations were reflexive about their funding and attempted to develop long-term, sustainable strategies. Fundación Maquipucuna (FM) is an example of an ecodependent group that had to drastically downsize during the bust phase. They creatively attempted to adapt. Fundación Maquipucuna is interesting because they have headquarters in Quito, but work rurally and have a strong field presence. Other organizations like this include Fundación Jatun Sacha, Fundación Jocotoco, and Fundación Paramo. The field-based groups often have private land and experiment with alternative economic development practices. They are aware of the volatility associated with dependence on international funding. They strive to be independent and self-reliant, though they haven't achieved this status. Many successfully supplement their international funding. For example, Jatun Sacha charges a fee for volunteers to work at their reserves on small-scale sustainable development by raising pigs, shrimp and cacao. In 2006, they had 870 volunteers, which generated $350,000 for their reserves. Fundación Maquipucuna uses its biodiverse private cloud forest reserve in the Chocó-Andean Corridor, a biodiversity hotspot (over 200 plant species, 50 mammal species, 340 bird species), for ecotourism and sells its own organically grown, bird- and butterfly-friendly coffee. Most national groups have creative strategies such as these, and wish to develop them so that they can do more of the work that's on their agendas. Environmentalists have a lot of hope for these independent enterprises. A conservation leader who promotes this says, "Tour operators in Quito are promoting ecotourism. This is very postitive. I love ecotourism. It is the best mechanism for conservation. ... Many communities are involved and have taken over on their own. ...The local groups really do a good job and are successful with ecotourism."[65]

These projects also have the potential to help the local communities. For instance, in 2006 when I visited Reserva Maquipicuna, which is approximately two hours northwest of Quito, they were employing ten people full time at the ecotourism site plus some others part time. They were all Ecuadorian except for one Columbian. The Foundation was also working with eight local communities, including the buffer communities of Yungilla, Santa Lucia, and Santa Marianita, on developing organic gardens; promoting a women's cooperative—Colabri (Hummingbirds)—

that makes handicrafts out of tagua, coconut, and local seeds; a greenhouse for orchids; and other means of self-sustenance. The reserve was bringing 1,000 school children a year to the reserve for environmental education.[66] In 2003 they welcomed 2,400 ecotourists and 3,000 hikers.[67] Their promotional literature reads, "Saving the Cloud Forest. Supporting Viable Communities."

Maquipucuna's director noted: "I risk saying we are becoming self-sustaining. We are getting there. We have some permanent expertise and jobs."[68] Their ecotourism pays for itself, as does their reforestation project. However, not all of their projects do. Environmental education does not, and conserving land through purchase is not self-sustaining. On the pros and cons of international funding, the director commented that if there were no external funding, they would:

... overcome it, but it wouldn't work out as well. We wouldn't have as much of an impact. We need to get more funding before it is too late [because the clouds for the cloud forest recharge over their reserve]. We can't do this without external funding. Without foreign investment that land would be gone. The government doesn't have the money to do it.[69]

From its founding in 1988 up into this era, FM had received funding from a wide variety of sources including multilateral aid from World Bank's Global Environmental Facility, the UN Development Program, and the Food and Agriculture Organization; bilateral agents including the British Embassy, the German bilateral aid agency, and USAID; transnational conservation groups, The Nature Conservancy and the World Wildlife Fund, and foundations, including MacArthur and Butler, among others.[70]

Despite all of their external funding, and very much because they saw the limitations of it, their funding strategy was intentionally designed to promote self-sustainable development. From their literature:

Our approach to sustainable development embraces a new business model that harnesses environmental performance—the efficient and restorative use of the four types of capital—to make our part of the world more secure, equitable, prosperous, and sustainable. We actively engage business, civil society, and government to design integrative solutions. Maquipucuna's primary role in this process is to be a facilitator and enabler of economic development in this poor and marginalized region by bringing it actively into the global development process by:

1. building human capital (i.e., training, environmental education, establishing day care facilities, and increasing gender equity);

2. establishing social capital (i.e., networks, community-based conservation and development, support and creation of local microenterprises and producers associations, fair trade contacts, and an international environmental education program);

3. recognizing and utilizing natural capital (i.e., ecotourism, "bird-friendly" shade-grown organic coffee and cacao, native bamboo, tissue culture of endangered orchids and bromeliads, trading carbon offsets derived from forest protection and restoration); and

4. providing financial capital (investments, infrastructure, microfinancing). [71]

Fundación Maquipucuna was a leader and an innovator and has been recognized with global ecotourism awards. Like other ecodependent groups, a recurrent theme for them was how to achieve economic sustainability for their group. Many organizations would prefer to receive less funding than they would receive on a short-term project on a regular basis over a longer period of time. They would like to create endowments and fund themselves from the proceeds rather than working in boom-and-bust fashion.

In sum, there were numerous responses to the bust in funding: ending operations, shifting priorities, *proyectismo,* and adapting by generating funds through other mechanisms. The transnational funding dominance created dependence, mission shift, lack of autonomy, competition, de-movementization, and lack of impact on slowing extractive development. However, organizations that were less influenced by the transnational funding structure have generated a different set of consequences: organizational independence, autonomy, group learning, unity, and resistance to economic development dependent on extraction. Later in the chapter I will discuss ecoresisters and new ecoentrepreneurial groups that emerged and grew during this period. For the most part these groups eschewed eco-imperialist funding to focus on local/national sustainable operations and funding structures.

An Environmental Movement?

Continuing a theme from the boom era, the bust period and its consequent struggles deepened the question regarding the existence of an environmental movement. For some, there absolutely was:

I think there are many [environmental movements]. Ecuador is so diverse. There are many needs and ecosystems and approaches to conserve. There are radical organizations like Acción Ecológica that say this is the project. And then you have Fundación Natura saying this is the project. It is not a consensus movement. Definitely an environmental movement.[72]

Others were less certain. An INGO director mused:

I still have my doubts about whether we can talk about a real movement. You know you have all of the real movements. You have the women's movement. You have many social movements going on. I'm not sure if we can talk about our environmental movement in Ecuador. Does it really exist? That's something that at least should be a question mark there. Supposedly a movement includes the construction of some common ground, that is missing right now at least.[73]

Another INGO interviewee quipped: "If you define the movement as a very coherent group of institutions that have some common goal and that really share information, then I don't think we have that."[74] In book one of a three-volume edition examining the environmental movement in Ecuador, *Ecologismo Ecuatorial*, Ecuadorian Anamaría Varea and her collaborators argue there is not a strong environmental movement in Ecuador due to NGO fragmentation and lack of a common agenda.[75]

Pondering the movement's ups and downs, one national director reflected:

[Some] people would say there was never a movement in reality, which I don't share that vision. I think there were moments when the environmental movement maybe was stronger and some moments it was very weak. It has been an up and down. It has not been stable. For example, the First National Environmental Congress was I think a very important moment for Ecuador. CEDENMA organized that and the second one. In the second one, it was very interesting to see people trying to create a common agenda. ... That for me was one of the tops of the movement. I think at that moment it was a movement. ... CEDENMA was invited to be part of several boards of different decision making processes. ... At that time everybody was for CEDENMA. Then Acción Ecológica left CEDENMA because they were, I think, they are basically against everything. ... During the 1990s, the big five [national organizations] were against ... mining, against the oil industry ... against the shrimp farmers. Right now the fighting is among ourselves.[76]

Mainstream environmentalists regularly blame Acción Ecológica for the downfall of the movement. The same director continued:

Acción Ecológica has gone to a different kind of battle. They are coming from the discourse of imperialism. That agenda has become more important than the environmental one. ... The main problem is they turned on the mission of the environmental movement. ... They basically divided the environmental movement into one group of NGOs—basically Acción Ecológica with several locally based NGOs, grassroots organizations—and the other NGOs and the international NGOs, which use, according to them, the national ones to build their imperialistic strategy, or something like that. ... It is much more complex than that, but my main impression is that right now, we don't have really a common agenda.[77]

In this era the biodiversity law was being debated. It was a dividing factor and one that Acción Ecológica took a stand against. They argued that it was a way "to steal all the traditional knowledge and sell our resources to the multinationals of the *gringos*."[78] On the other side, there were groups in favor of the biodiversity law. Mainstream groups believed:

We have lost the ability to sit at the table and say, "Ok, let's discuss what you really mean by that. What is it that you are opposing, or are you just opposing because you want to oppose? Or because you want to be next to the indigenous people's movement of the world who say that all the gringos steal biodiversity knowledge?"[79]

Radical views and obstructionism were considered to contribute to the movement's weakness.

The wide ideological spectrum among Ecuadorian environmental organizations was seen as having pros and cons. Routinely, "mainstream" environmentalists had two reactions to Acción Ecológica. Many cringed when asked their thoughts: "All they do is complain, protest, and criticize and they do not produce any alternatives." But many others respected them. Ecodependents working within the system argued "[Acción Ecológica's] role is entirely necessary. ... They make us aware of other positions." Acción Ecológica could also be used to espouse strong "radical" opinions, freeing other groups to appear "mainstream" and move forward with some work. This is known as the "radical flank" effect.[80]

Plenty of environmentalists argued that Acción Ecológica and the grassroots communities that they work with are the "real" movement. An interviewee sums up this position:

I don't think that Ecuador has an environmental movement. There are environmentally focused NGOs that work on the theme in the environmental sector. It is the small groups that are movements. There is not a national movement. ... Instead, there are initiatives. ... But there are exceptions: DECOIN and Acción Ecológica. They are more like movements in their activism and protest. Other NGOs are compromised by their funding.[81]

In sum, the practices of ecodependent organizations did not qualify to most as movement-like. Instead, their reality was simply, "projects, projects, projects." For ecoresisters, the process mattered and they worked at the local, grassroots level to develop "real movements."

Consequences of Decentralization: Local Environmentalism

A foreign environmentalist working for an international NGO told me:

If you want to see what an environmental movement looks like go to Mindo. That's where they are … walking the talk. … The community over the last decade has really taken to heart this issue that the environment has a place in community, and they are not just talking about it, they are actually doing it. Those are the people that actually chained themselves to the pipeline. They stopped OCP people coming down to their community. They really advanced this tourism idea. They're interested in innovative ways of working with civilians.[82]

Mindo is a top ecotourism site for international visitors to Quito seeking one and multiple day trips (see figures 6.1 and 6.2). The Mindo community, like others I will discuss later in the chapter, are seeking to integrate environmentalism into their lifestyle and their livelihoods. They are seeking ways of "developing"—improving and getting better, not necessarily growing—their communities. Mindo is one example of how a local community is incorporating environmentalism.

According to interviewees, what was happening environmentally at the local level was more successful than what was happening at the

Figure 6.1
Ecotourism business in Mindo

Figure 6.2
Ecotourist in Mindo

national level. City-level regulations were being put in place in Quito, then Tena, then Machalla, and so forth. Ironically, this was in part due to the decentralization of the state, brought about by the neoliberal agenda. Small groups of environmentalists within municipalities worked with local governments to move environmental agendas forward. These groups were not necessarily registered as environmental nonprofits, but worked within local councils. Larger, national groups also started working with local governments. This was a major trend noted in the 2007 Ecuadorian Environmental Organization Survey. Survey commentators noted that this trend had pros and cons. On the one hand, it was welcomed. Environmental organizations believed the local level had good human resources; they also believed that they could be more successful at the local level. At the national level, the national ministry had serious problems. On the other hand, working at the local level meant that policies would be more piecemeal.

Environmentalists regularly criticized the National Environmental Ministry from numerous angles. First, they argue that the Ministry is severely underfunded. This is not the Ministry's fault. Nevertheless, that weakness matters when it has to negotiate with other ministries, such as the Ministry of Energy and Mines. In intragovernmental debates over whether to preserve or exploit the environment, the environment is at a structural disadvantage. When the state has an inherently contradictory role of protecting and exploiting resources, this is especially problematic. An interviewee provides an example: "Petroleum is an environmental disaster. The Ministry of the Environment is so weak that it cannot stand up to the petroleum interests. There are highways and drilling in the protected areas."[83]

Another major complaint was that the Ministry is very difficult to work with. It works at a much slower pace than donors and NGOs, thus limiting the progress that many groups could make on their own. This is a problem when the Ministry controls key pieces of information and legitimization. For instance, an NGO may need a signature from the Ministry or a key piece of data to move a project forward or to secure funding from a donor. They request it from the Ministry, but the requests "don't seem to faze the government agency" and they get to them "when they feel like it"; sometimes after the signature or data are no longer meaningful.[84] Related, the third common complaint is that the Ministry is corrupt. I heard more than one story about having to bring chocolates in order to secure a meeting with officials. These criticisms of the National Ministry came at the same time that more and more cooperation between the Ministry and NGOs was occurring.[85]

Environmentalists were enthusiastic about working at the local level because of the excellent human resources. Individuals who were trained in environmental NGOs were now working in local governments, in tourism agencies, and in local consultancies where they could make a difference. The knowledge and commitment of these locals was considered a strength of the movement. Environmentalists are now on the inside of local governments. Building human capacity and getting activists on the inside was something that Fundación Natura had hoped to do since their founding: "From the private sector to NGOs and from science and academia to government, it's very good to deal with everybody because sooner or later those decision makers are moving around into different posts where they can influence policy."[86] Another long-time activist noted of this trend:

There is a real movement, it has social bases, it has local groups, it has relationships with local governments, with parishes. There is youth sufficiently strong in the spectrum of the organizations. There are those who speak, opine, demand, and ask questions about environmental themes. Now what is still to be seen is if the movement can more or less influence the theme of politics.[87]

The long-term changes that the movement has sought appeared to be paying off in terms of human resources and incorporation into the local level.

While most survey and interview respondents spoke positively about the trend toward actions at the municipal level, there were concerns noted about decentralization. For instance, one respondent commented that it "weakens the responsibility of the central state to conserve the natural patrimony."[88] It also cedes more power to the private sector—both the nonprofits and the for profits. This was noticed elsewhere, as well. In 2002, when world leaders gathered in Johannesburg for the Earth Summit +10, Ecuadorian observers saw a shift in the direction toward private business participation in environmental management:

I believe what happened was very important. Businesses participated at the same level as the state. ... This was very important because it opened the option for businesses to work through big NGOs to manage conservation and the environment. That signified who was making the decisions. This parallels national themes. You see, the Ministry of the Environment in Ecuador was always weak. It was born without functions. Over time it has become weaker and weaker. Now it has no reason to exist. ... In the last meetings of the Convention on Biodiversity, the companies appeared, like large conservations NGOs, like the executors of the Convention on Biodiversity. ... That is terrible.[89]

Thus, while decentralization provided local opportunities, if one stepped back and looked at the big picture, it begged the questions: who should decide how to best manage the countries' resources and who should do it?

Ecoresisters Emerging: DECOIN Rejects Mining, C-CONDEM Rejects Shrimp Farms

During this period grassroots organizations resisted economic development actions that were focused on resource extraction and converting environments for economic gain. I illustrate two groups that exemplify these struggles to demonstrate how these organizations are fundamentally different from ecodependent ones in terms of their (1) concerns and primary agenda, (2) resources (human and financial), (3) practices, and (4) goals as they relate to the development trajectory. Kuecker (2007: 95) calls the example of DECOIN, "A case study of grassroots resistance to neoliberalism."

The development of mining has been growing internationally, and especially in Latin America.[90] Ecuador is no exception to this trend. As the state sought new sources of foreign exchange income to repay international debts, mining looked promising. In 1992 the state granted rights to the Japanese company Bishi Metals, a subsidiary of Mitsubishi, to explore for metals in the Intag valley. Intag is located in the Andes to the northwest of Quito. It is a biodiverse region, rich in cloud forests, which create an environment for hundreds of orchid species, rich animal life, and beautiful waterfalls (see figures 6.3 and 6.4). It is also home to the olinguito, what observers describe as a cross between a bear and a cat (it is actually in the raccoon family), which was discovered in the Intag valley in 2013 and is the first new carnivore species discovered in the Western Hemisphere in thirty-five years.[91] The deal that was being made between the state and the transnational corporation was not transparent: communities in the valley were not informed of Bishi Metals' plans. When some locals discovered what was going on, a priest and a landowner organized

Figure 6.3
Cloud forest in Intag

Figure 6.4
Biodiversity in Intag

community resistance. As the citizens learned about the mining activities, they became concerned about the possible negative impacts on their communities. Soon after, Bishi Metals discovered a large copper deposit. Though it was not made available to citizens, a Japanese environmental impact statement (EIS) predicted that exploiting the site would require the relocation of four communities, create massive deforestation that would dry up the cloud forest, stress the habitat of dozens of threatened mammals and birds, and contaminate rivers and streams with heavy metals. When citizens discovered the EIS, there was a grassroots education campaign that increased resistance to mining. There were a series of confrontations, and in 1997 the locals burned down Bishi Metals' camp. The company left Ecuador. However, this would not be the end of conflict over copper in Intag.

In the period from 1997 until 2002 local opposition to mining increased, though there was no immediate threat. A group had formed in 1995 with the primary goal of keeping mining out of the community: Defensa y Conservación Ecológica de Intag (DECOIN). A key strategy they used to fight mining was to create alternative sources of employment. This was critical because the prospect of mining jobs was "pitting brother against brother." DECOIN helped organize a women's craft group and a

Figure 6.5
Handicrafts in Casa de Intag, Otovalo

coffee cooperative: AACRI (La Asociación Agroartesanal de Caficultores Río Intag) (see figure 6.5).

The idea to build positive alternatives to mining practice was central to their fight.

Intag stands out because we said no to mining. But we also said no to mining, and we want *this*. And we were able to generate *this* with the coffee and the tourism and now the women's group making soaps and so forth and so on. So we played a part in this alternative development. We created a coffee co-op and tourism in Junín. Now just think about it. Junín would have been wiped off the map.[92]

Junín was one of the four communities that would have been relocated if Bishi Metals had continued.

A second key and intentional strategy of DECOIN's was to raise environmental consciousness so that the reason for protecting lands made sense to everyone in the community. "Forest conservation is really important. But if you don't have people understanding why it's being conserved, sooner or later it'll be invaded."[93] One of the ways they did this was through a watershed project. DECOIN purchased lands over the copper fields and turned the properties over to the local communities for watershed protection. This directly benefited the communities because their water was cleaner and fewer people had water-related illnesses. That made sense to people. The watershed project generated buy-in and understanding about the value of a protected ecosystem. "Where their water's being protected, the community will do anything to protect that land. ... They're completely committed. They're really, really committed."[94] Communities also developed ecotourism projects in the protected lands.

The goal of these activities is development that meets the needs of the local people (not transnational corporations) and protects the local environment. Given its dual strategies of creating economic alternatives to mining and conserving the land, I asked leaders whether they were an environmental organization or a community group. The response was: "Why can't we be both? We're all part of a community, this community, it's environmental—this biological community."[95] DECOIN lobbied successfully to have the county declared an "ecological county."

The activists in Intag were local residents. The incentive for them to participate was literally to block the mining companies from the lands that they relied on for their livelihoods. They were deeply committed to the process and volunteered their time because they were protecting their ecosystem and livelihoods. Unlike ecodependent groups whose staffs were dependent on foreign funding, the activists in DECOIN and other ecoresister groups continued their work despite the transnational funding bust, since they were not reliant on funding.

In the meantime the World Bank was working with the government of Ecuador to rewrite the mining laws, incorporate pro-industry reforms, and conduct a geological survey of the country, which would ease the way for mining companies in the future. Given its pressure to repay debt, the state allowed the World Bank to lead those actions. The Minister of Energy and Mines noted: "This is a very deregulated system, very hands-off on the part of the state. The Ecuadorian government has turned into a facilitator rather than a policeman, as we used to be."[96] The Bishi Metals' concession in Intag was sold to Ascendant Copper, a Canadian-based company, which took over the site and conflict ensued. Ascendant used strong-arm tactics, including death threats, to get some locals to approve of the project. The state was not an innocent bystander to these activities. Police arrested activists on what most observers to the situation consider to be trumped up charges.

DECOIN organized regional protests against Ascendant and a march in Quito. In 2005 the community burned Ascendant Copper's camp to the ground. Paramilitaries attacked the community resisters, but the community literally blocked Ascendant's access to its site. Eventually this episode would end with Ascendant Copper leaving Ecuador.[97]

In addition to its local resources (volunteers) DECOIN had an intentional international strategy and sought collaboration with other groups. They did not respond to requests for actions by the international community. They asked the international community to assist in their plight. The request was from the local to the international, from the bottom up. They received some funding and groups assisted them by applying political pressure (e.g., writing to the Ecuadorian government) and economic pressure on the corporation. Leaders noted that they do not do anyone else's project. "We won't get funding if it's not compatible."[98] But they were not naïve about their situation. "You have got to have the focus, the international attention on your fight, or you lose. You just go away."[99] DECOIN maintains several websites, including one written in English.

DECOIN's initial funding was from individuals, then the coffee cooperative funded the organization, but that was eventually separated. A German NGO and a British Group (Rainforest Concern) provided funding to purchase lands. The land acquisitions were done "on a shoestring." The Threshold Foundation in California provided funding that "was flexible." Foreign students who have visited Intag's ecotourism sites returned home, raised money, and sent it back to DECOIN and the community.

Acción Ecológica was instrumental in helping DECOIN create international ties. For instance, Acción Ecológica took Intag leaders on a tour of a mine in Peru to view the environmental destruction and to meet with the local communities to learn about mining's social consequences. DECOIN was also in close communication with similarly minded groups, such as the NGO Mining Watch in Canada. Regarding Mining Watch, a leader noted: "We're always in close communication. I've been to Canada, I've met them. They've been here. We're tight with them."[100] These close connections are for sharing information and coordinating strategies, not for funding purposes. In the next era Mining Watch Canada would help in DECOIN's battle by working to have Ascendant Copper delisted from the Toronto Stock Exchange.

A participant explained the contrast between DECOIN's actors and work and that of national environmental NGOS:

We're friends, we're neighbors. We live here, so we care about the people. ... Fundación Natura, EcoCiencia, they don't care about the people. They just care about their objectives. ... NGOs in the cities, their main mission is to survive, you know. That's why they'll get money and do whatever needs to be done. But from the beginning, I even told our colleagues, I said, look, it doesn't matter if we survive [as an organization] or not. What really matters is that people develop this environmental ethic, conservation ethic. Really, if we're successful, what's the use? What's the purpose of DECOIN if we're already succeeding?[101]

DECOIN has been an informal member of CEDENMA but cannot be an official member because it is not registered with the state. Since it is considered radical, a lot of groups do not publicly support it, but it is supported behind closed doors. A leader of the organization noted, "Fundación Natura would never have anything to do with us."[102] DECOIN has good relationship with other like-minded groups working on similar issues, including groups in different regions like C-CONDEM, which works along the coast.

C-CONDEM (Coordinadora Nacional para la Defensa del Ecosistema Manglar, Coordinating Committee for the Defense of the Mangrove Ecosystems) is similar to DECOIN in that they are fighting to keep shrimp farming out of the coastal region so that the communities along the coast that have long relied on the mangroves can continue to do so. C-CONDEM is a confederation of smaller groups, such as FUNDECOL (Fundación de Defensa Ecológica, Foundation for Ecological Defense), that represent gatherers and artisanal fisherpeople in the provinces along the coast: Esmeraldas, Manabí, Guayas, and El Oro (figure 6.6). According to C-CONDEM's website, its

Figure 6.6
Fisherperson in Muisne

goals are to defend and restore the mangroves as well as to use local, traditional knowledge to create community policies for managing the ecosystems. C-CONDEM's defense of the mangroves is environmental and cultural. Besides the work they do locally to protect the mangrove ecosystems, they provide cultural education, through activities such as sponsoring a musical group that performs to educate about the heritage of the mangroves.

Like DECOIN, C-CONDEM was founded in response to development that was being driven by the state's interest in earning export dollars, which came at the cost of local environments and livelihoods. According to Christine Beitl, despite the fact that the Ecuadorian Forestry Law prohibits mangrove destruction:

These policies were weakly upheld in light of export-led growth and global demand for cheap shrimp cocktail that drove the conversion of public mangrove areas into private shrimp farms throughout Ecuador and many other parts of the developing world, resulting in widespread environmental degradation, welfare impacts, and social conflict.[103]

Mangrove areas had been accessible as public goods. Also according to data reported by Beitl, since 1985, 25 percent of Ecuador's mangroves have been converted to shrimp farms and in areas such as Muisne, three-quarters have been deforested.[104] According to a remote sensing report, the increase in shrimp farms from 1984 to 1995 (89k to 178k hectares) corresponded to a decrease in mangrove forests (182k to 147k hectares).[105] Shrimp exports rose during this period and became a main export earner, along with oil and bananas. The industry crashed in 1999 due to the white spot syndrome virus, a disease that occurs in cultured shrimp.

The state was an outspoken supporter and defender of shrimp farming despite the fact that it broke its own laws and wrought environmental destruction and social conflict. The state went so far as accusing a member of Acción Ecológica, Gina Chavez, of betraying her country because she testified at the United Nations that shrimp farming in Ecuador and around the world limited the food sovereignty of coastal communities. The Ecuadorian government's UN delegation recommended that she be brought up on charges of treason.[106]

Also like DECOIN, C-CONDEM considers their role primarily "for the people, but the people are inseparable from the ocean and the mangroves."[107] Their website opens with a quote that (paraphrased and translated) says that mangroves are not trees, but they are thousands of men, women, children, old people who inherited the land from God; they are a way of life, of singing, of smiling.[108] In other words, the lives of the people living among the mangroves are synonymous with the ecosystem. Like most of Ecuador's indigenous groups, C-CONDEM and its members have a worldview that sees people as interconnected with and not separate from nature; it is integral to their lives.

C-CONDEM's leaders believe its most important sources of support are the communities and people in the confederation. Again, this characteristic mirrors DECOIN. C-CONDEM was founded in 1998 as a result of a meeting called by the local group FUNDECOL. Greenpeace International assisted that effort. Swiss Aid and the US-based NGO Heifer International provided some financial support, but C-CONDEM members told me they are not like the "elite NGOs."[109] Rather than receiving funding from international organizations, they coordinated strategies with their international partners. C-CONDEM was instrumental in creating REDMANGLAR, an international network of organizations dedicated to protecting mangroves. In this way they used their local knowledge to scale up, and to reach their arms out to similar coastal areas in other countries experiencing mangrove destruction.[110] "We were very small, but to this moment, we have a very strong voice."[111]

One of the international strategies used to draw attention to the destruction of the mangroves was a shrimp boycott. Participants from North America had different motivations than C-CONDEM. Esperanza Martínez, a leader of Acción Ecológia, another one of C-CONDEM's allies, noted that in the North, there was a boycott of ocean caught shrimp because it kills marine turtles. In the South, there was a boycott of farmed shrimp because its production threatened the largely female human population of conch collectors, limited an important source of protein of coastal populations, and destroyed the mangroves. In other words, in addition to being ecologically "absurd," shrimp farming violated local populations' livelihoods.[112]

C-CONDEM has succeeded in establishing national laws to protect the mangroves and to have communities collectively manage mangroves. They are currently seeking to create what they call an *economía propia* (own economy). Their goal is economic *independence*. Like DECOIN, they support community-based economic activities. One of their main activities is directly selling fish to restaurants in Quito, which are willing to pay top prices for fresh, high-quality products. They also teach marimba dance lessons and support *turismo comunitario* (community tourism). This is different from ecotourism. In four of the communities where they work, travelers can stay with families, and get an experiential education into their way of life and the rights of people and nature. C-CONDEM's influence in national politics was another victory for the group, which will be discussed later in the chapter.

At issue in the struggles of DECOIN and C-CONDEM has been the question of *who* decides. The communities of Intag have chosen *not* to have mining; however, transnational corporations and the state have chosen mining. The communities along the coast have chosen *not* to convert mangroves to shrimp farms, but private shrimp farmers and the state have chosen shrimp farms. Esperanza Martínez, a founder and spokesperson for Acción Ecológica, has written that sovereignty should be a criterion of sustainability, in terms of *who* decides.[113] According to this stance, the community should decide how their lands should be utilized, not some outside group, not even the Ecuadorian state.

In their discussion of the conflicts that have arisen over new mining projects, Anthony Bebbington and his co-authors argue:

These struggles are frequently over the meaning of development. ... These can become struggles *against* development oriented towards economic growth, and *for* development as a process that fosters more inclusive (albeit smaller) economies, respects citizenship rights, demonstrates environmental integrity, and allows for the co-existence of cultures and localized forms of territorial governance.[114]

This is true in Intag and along the mangrove coast of Ecuador. In another piece, Bebbington and colleagues argue that social movements that respond to extractive development are pushing back at both the ideological and material forces of development: "When movements have emerged to contest the development of extractive industries, they might be understood in these terms: as vehicles for contesting *both* the colonization of lifeworlds *and* the material threats to livelihood."[115] These cases of ecoresisters demonstrate that the dominant development discourse, which relies on resource extraction, was actively opposed and other visions were consciously being constructed.[116] These visions would become institutionalized in the next era.

Political Crisis Creates Opportunities for Ecoresisters

This period of neoliberalism was bad for the poor, and especially bad for the poor indigenous groups; these groups lacked social welfare support, and the inhabitants of the Amazon were fighting off the intrusions and disruptions of multinational oil extractors.[117] The nation lacked a strong and effective state. In April 2005, environmentalists seized a key opportunity. President

Lucio Gutíerrez, who was widely considered to be both ineffective and authoritarian, created a national crisis when he repealed the newly appointed Supreme Court. This led the government to declare a state of emergency, which was followed by national protests. Gutiérrez stepped down (and was later arrested, then released) and his Vice President Luis Alfredo Palacio became president.

The political crisis created a political opening. In social movement lingo, the political opportunity structure (POS) shifted; the weakness and chaos of the state cracked open a space where social movement actors could voice their grievances. In May 2005, to address the rapid changes taking place, CEDENMA assembled a group of environmental and social organizations in the first National Environmental Assembly (Asamblea Nacional Ambiental, ANA). The other organizations that helped coordinate this meeting were not the internationally funded national environmental groups (though these groups were members of CEDENMA). The lead organizers were from regional groups whose focus was divided among environmental issues, social issues, and issues of democracy. These groups included C-CONDEM, Coordinadora Zonal de INTAG (of which DECOIN was a part), Amazon Defense Front (Frente de Defensa de la Amazonía, FDA), Forum of Water Resources (Foro de los Recursos Hídricos), Ecuadorian Coordinator of Agroecology (Coordinadora Ecuatoriana de Agroecología, CEA), and the Plurinational Federation of Community Tourism of Ecuador (Federación Plurinacional de Turismo Comunitario del Ecuador, FEPTCE).[118] There was diversity among the organizers. For instance, FDA was focused on oil issues in the Amazon and led the suit against Texaco while FEPTCE promoted community-based tourism in farming and indigenous communities. There were radical ecoresisters and mainstream ecodependent groups. The participation of the wide swath of groups in the ANA broadened the "environmental movement," beyond simply the environment, to include productive groups, indigenous groups, human rights groups, and community organizations. While the main convener, CEDENMA, was explicitly an environmental organization, the themes went far beyond the environment. The assembly articulated a more *social* environmental movement for Ecuador. It also shone a light on groups that were actively resisting resource extraction. These groups had been gaining influence. In response to an open-ended survey question about changes that had taken place in the environmental movement, a respondent noted the rise in "the expression of local communities defending their rights against oil, mining, hydroelectric, etc."[119] These groups were represented at the ANA.

Over 1,000 people came together for the assembly in a theater in Quito. A long-time leader of the movement notes of ANA:

It is a really important point, because [we saw] for the first time, the existence of an environmental movement that was more than nongovernmental organizations (NGOs); NGOs saw the emergence and the presence of social organizations, grassroots organizations, of farmers, of communities, large local groups. ... This is the first time you see the environmental movement with a more social basis; less tied to the technicians and professionals who often form the NGOs.[120]

Observers remarked that the ANA was a big leap forward for the environmental movement in terms of its national importance. The same leader quoted above remarked that the group had taken a radical position, which was not a problem; however, he was concerned that part of the group had adopted a "belligerent " discourse without scientific evidence, and that was a problem. Despite this, he believed the environmental movement was stronger at this time.

The national environmental assembly was held with the idea of having a public space where different points of view related to the environment could be aired. A participant explains:

You know in Ecuador, in the environmental issues, we have different approaches ... how to do the management of environmental issues, the management of resources. For example, some people think Ecuador has to have policy related to no oil in protected areas. Others think that oil is possible, with stricter norms or environmental assessment plans.

With the assembly, they created the space to think about strategy. She continued:

What is the strategy for joining the different political points around the environmental issues, from organizations like Acción Ecológica to Fundación Natura, [organizations] with different political colors?... It was interesting and the first time we analyzed the political role for the environmental movement ... and what is happening with the environmental agenda for the country.[121]

The ANA was a turning point. It was the beginning of a political movement. It was the voice of another world that was possible.

A formal declaration emerged from the ANA, which was a broad critique of the political, economic, and environmental structures of Ecuador. It was not a narrowly focused environmental agenda. It began with criticisms of the state's political economic model that "supports the accumulation of capital which excludes the majority of the Ecuadorian population and benefits a few sectors, mainly transnational corporations and international organizations."[122] It continued by arguing that the state has relinquished sovereignty and given power to foreign interests, and has perpetuated neoliberal and neo-colonial policies through its extractivist economic and political development. The authors assert that the environment and people of Ecuador have been systematically violated and excluded from participation, and that natural resources are threatened with extinction. The ANA Declaration demands referendums on numerous issues, including free trade agreements, requests direct representation, and specifically demands the departure of US military forces. The final section, which is most explicitly environmental, rejects the privatization of natural resources, resists megaprojects that affect natural resources, requests the strengthening of the Ministry of the Environment, and moratoria on new extractive concessions, bioprospecting, and genetically modified organisms, among other demands. The declaration is a broad critique of the political-economic process. It is much more encompassing than statements made by individual environmental organizations, with the exception of the "radical" Acción Ecológica. Parts of the declaration would eventually make their way into the new 2008 Constitution. With the legitimacy of the state in question, the voices of "the movement" that had a more radical critique of the neoliberal model of development, along with grassroots social-environmental groups, were heard by a national audience. Their ideologies and demands were not constrained by international donors. For mainstream national level organizations, much of what was happening on the ground for them—scurrying for limited contracts and funds—did not match this rhetoric. Cuts to national groups, which weakened them and had them searching for resources, coupled with the new voices and demands being articulated, created an overall shift in demands and the political agenda. In this time of relative scarcity, groups with overlapping themes worked to merge missions and generated a political plan.[123]

Four simultaneous processes enabled this more radical expression of environmentalism and a broad critique of the political economy. First, underlying all of the actions was the state's neoliberal shift, notably in this case, the move toward decentralizing its services. Second was the reduction of international resources. In 2001, when the transnational funding sources dried up, the large national NGOs were left scrambling for funds. They were distracted by their internal maintenance. Third, this allowed other voices, the social-environmental voices, to he heard. Small local groups had arisen in specific locations, concurrent with the state's decentralization and its resource extractivism, and had adopted radical positions. Finally, the political crisis of the state, which was the impetus for ANA, created an opportunity for many groups to speak out. Broader participation by the social groups tapped the radical ideology that already existed within the environmental movement. It is ironic that international neoliberal agents promoted decentralization of the state and that its success is one of the sources of the strengthened local democracy that contributed to the creation of the radical propositions that emerged from ANA and offered a critique of neoliberal development.

Reflecting on the relative power of the state and NGOs with regard to the environment and development, an Ecuadorian who had experiences with numerous national NGOs and INGOs noted:

If there were a strong government that was aware of environmental problems and could solve poverty, we wouldn't need NGOs. They should disappear. Civil society can arrange self-management. There are two ways to go about this. For example, in Venezuela there is a strong government and they give money to the people. The second way is for people to organize and self-manage. There is either a strong government or strong grassroots and then you don't need NGOs. I hope it will happen. [TLL: Which way?] We need social capacity to reduce poverty, be more equitable, end impunity, raise environmental issues as a priority. Personally, I think this will be some sort of socialism ....[124]

His comments reflected what would come.

Ecoentrepreneurs: Pragmatically Protecting Local Environments within the System

Two new groups with noteworthy funding strategies also emerged in this era that were not part of ANA: Fund for the Protection of Water (Fondo para la Protección del Agua, FONAG) and Corporation for Environmental Health of Quito—Life for Quito (Corporación de Salud Ambiental de Quito—Vida Para Quito). They attempted to create local- and national-level funding strategies so that they would not be solely reliant on transnational organizations. Their organizational models sought to overcome resource dependency on foreigners and were timely, given the resource constraints of the era. These groups were rare. Ecoentrepreneur groups differ from the ecoresisters in a few key ways: (1) they were not responding to a local crisis, (2) they did not resist the dominant form of development, and (3) they were not trying to create an alternative to the system. They were seeking innovative ways to deal with recurrent local problems within the system. They wanted to institutionalize solutions and improve communities' quality of life by addressing issues such as access to clean water and green spaces. Elsewhere I have called these groups eco-independent sustainability organizations, as their missions are to improve local sustainability.[125] A big part of doing this work required generating sustainable funding streams from within Ecuador.

FONAG was founded by the City of Quito in 2000 to provide financing to protect the sources of water for the growing city. It is not registered as an NGO with the government; it is registered as a trust (*fideicomiso*) and regulated under the Securities Market Law. The idea for FONAG originated with the national NGO Fundación Antisana, which pitched the idea to the city of Quito in 1995. It took the city a long time to be convinced that watershed protection was necessary and in its interest. But in 1998 Roque Sevilla, one of the original founders of Fundación Natura, became mayor and he helped move the project forward.[126]

FONAG's initial funding included $1,000 from The Nature Conservancy and a major contribution from an Ecuadorian source: the city's water company (Empresa Pública Metropolitana de Agua Potable y Saneamiento, EMAAP-Q), whose initial contribution was $20,000. Eventually other partners were added, including the Ecuadorian electric company (Empresa Eléctrica Quito, EEQ), an Ecuadorian brewing company (Cervecería Nacional), the Swiss Agency for Development, and an Ecuadorian water bottling company (Tesalia). USAID also provided some support but was not a legal partner in the trust. The water company agreed to contribute one percent of its water sales, and the electric utility agreed to pay $45,000 a year. FONAG initially generated a fund of $21,000 in 2000, and the base investment grew as partners were added to almost $2.7 million by the end of 2005. The fund was invested, and the proceeds are used to manage the watershed through a variety of projects including reforestation, environmental education, monitoring, and other community-based conservation efforts. According to its own documentation, the yields for use in conservation projects in 2000 were just under $6,000; in 2005 they were over $221,000.[127] FONAG differentiates between specific, time-bound projects, and processes that it is engaged in. The organization is interested in the *largo plaza* (long term) and it funds its processes for twenty years.

The people who work at FONAG consider it an environmental organization in that they "take responsibility to protect the water, part of the environment."[128] However, they don't associate with other environmental NGOs. It is not linked into networks of environmental NGOs or social movement activists. It works with local communities to protect the watershed through education, reforestation, and training and hiring of park guards, who are highly regarded in local communities.

The organization is local in that it is only dealing with the watersheds affecting Quito; however, other communities are emulating the model throughout Ecuador in the watersheds of Tungurahua, Chimborazo, Paute, Zamora, and Loja. There are also examples growing throughout Latin America and the Caribbean, including in Colombia, the Dominican Republic, among others. At FONAG, they proudly call these FONAGcitos (little FONAGs).

FONAG has been written about by a number of analysts, and by most accounts, is considered a success. The following conclusion is representative of the literature:

The growing number of water trust funds in Ecuador and beyond suggests these funds offer many advantages for financing watershed conservation. The independence, contractual arrangement, sustainable revenue stream, and long-term horizon provide a level of political and financial security lacking in other payment for environmental services schemes. In addition, water funds provide institutional spaces linking a wide variety of stakeholders (both upstream and downstream), which facilitates collaborative decision-making and project implementation. Finally, water trust funds are easily adapted to fit different local socio-cultural and political conditions, including those that oppose the commodification of natural resources. As such, they provide an innovative model for providing sustainable financing for watershed conservation in places like Ecuador where privatization is not possible for either legal or cultural reasons.[129]

FONAG is a public–private partnership with local, national, and international partners focusing on an issue—clean water for city residents—that doesn't have a singular international donor. The local government (via the water and electricity companies) contributed funds to ensure that citizens and consumers/users continue to have access. Corporate donors (beer and bottled water) are self-interested because they depend on the water resource for their profits. FONAG uses market mechanisms to receive payment for environmental services (PES). FONAG preserves the watershed (the ecosystem) and receives payments from its users (residential water users and companies). Because its funds are invested, it also relies on the market for the generation of profits. In this way a growing economy is good for FONAG. From a treadmill of production perspective, this is problematic because a growing economy typically means more withdrawals from the ecosystem and more negative additions to it. The speeding up of the treadmill, creating more social and environmental disruptions, provides more funds for environmental protection.

Vida Para Quito is a private organization also created by the municipality of Quito and EMAAP-Q to do "works that improve environmental health and the quality of life of the city and its inhabitants."[130] Though it was private, its aims were public, as was its funding source. Vida Para Quito led a number of programs, including work on urban parks, urban reforestation, recycling, environmental education, river recuperation, and more. Its projects were geographically focused, and the amenities it promoted had the potential to help a wide swath of Quiteños, not just tourists visiting the eco-reserves. For example, the Ciclo-Q bikeway project provides a way for people to use their bikes as a safe means of transportation in an automobile-centric city. This reduces air pollution, increases public safety and provides an inexpensive means of transportation.

Vida Para Quito was fairly well known among Quiteños because of its funding structure: it was funded by voluntary tax contributions of up to 25 percent of local taxes. When Quito's residents filled out their tax forms, they could check a box indicating they would like a portion of their taxes to go to Vida Para Quito. Its budget in 2006 was $53 thousand dollars. Residents had more positive views of the organization than they had of environmental organizations, in general. This is due to in part to the perception that NGO leaders are among a higher class and average Ecuadorians do not know how or where the NGOs spend their money. Vida para Quito, by contrast, was required to report data publically, since it was subject to the "transparency law." Its budget and the salaries of its staff could be found online. In 2006 half of a percent of its funding was spent on staff costs and 98 percent of its budget was spent on investment in construction and services.[131] An environmental professional remarked that groups funded independently like Vida para Quito, "will be around for fifty years." This is a long life in a sector where groups come and go, year to year. That professional was wrong, though; the organization was dissolved in 2009 and its works were incorporated into the tasks of the city (see figures 6.7 and 6.8 on public transportation eventually implemented by the city).[132]

Ecoentrepreneurs are noteworthy because (1) they used creative mechanisms to fund their operations in a culture in which philanthropy is not common; (2) they addressed problems without international sponsors, namely local urban environmental issues; (3) they had an agenda that was locally driven; and thus (4) they were able to make choices that benefited local citizens rather than transnational donors. They were vulnerable to other things: market volatility and changes in the state's priorities.

Figure 6.7
Bikeshare in Quito

The State Practices Economic Synthesis while the Movement Seeks Ecological Synthesis

In the bust period, transnational funding declined (table 6.1). That drop altered the environmental organization sector: ecodependent groups lost strength and groups that were not dependent on external funding for their work—ecoresisters—gained a larger share of the political space. Ecodependent groups struggled, searching for ways to survive, and competed with each other for the limited resources. Nationally, a more radical ideology was expressed by the environmental sector, one that questioned the dominant development discourse and the state's role in extraction.

Figure 6.8
Public transportation in Quito

Table 6.1
Summary of Bust Era

	Origins 1978–1987	Boom 1987–2000	Bust 2000–2006	Revolution 2006–2015
Transnational funding			Public and private resources dwindle	
Environmental sector			Ecodependents lose influence; ecoresisters gain ground; social issues integrated into agenda	
State characteristics			Weak, unstable, indebted, resource dependence	
Environment and development policies			Weak institutions and enforcement; continued extractive development and exploration of new resources to mine	
Schnaiberg's synthesis			In practice, state shift toward economic synthesis and in ideology, movement shift toward ecological synthesis	

Ecoentrepreneurs—the other type of group that was free from transnational economic dependence—were like ecoresisters in that they were more autonomous in their agenda setting, and they too sought to protect their environments for local communities. They were a smaller force and did not have an explicit stance on the development trajectory.

The state was politically and economically unstable during this period. It did not enforce its own environmental laws (as in the mangroves), and its proactive work in conjunction with the World Bank sought to prepare the laws and inventories for further extractive development (as in mining). Turning its head away from environmentalism and toward increased extraction suggests that the state was shifting back toward an economic synthesis. This was not the direction that environmentalists hoped to move in. For environmentalists, in ideology, at least, there was a shift in vision from managed scarcity toward ecological syntheses. Alternative economic arrangements being put on the ground by groups like DECOIN and C-CONDEM attempted to reconcile the relationship between local social needs and ecological limits. In the next era the ideology of *buen vivir/sumak kawsay*/good living would be articulated in the new constitution, thus integrating the ecoresisters' alternative vision of development into the state's rules.

The lessened influence of transnational funders created space for alternative development visions. Just as economic globalization made states dependent on and beholden to international financial institutions like the World Bank, transnational funding for the environment made environmental organization dependent on and beholden to transnational funders. Environmental organizations altered their structures and agendas to align with transnational funders. When that bond was weakened and ecodependent groups were weakened, local groups with local organizational structures and agendas emerged with alternative, independent ideas about the future, and with a radical critique of the dominant development model. The key argument of "world polity theory" is that globalization creates similar political institutions and structures around the world. A study by David Frank, Ann Hironaka, and Evan Schofer (2000) shows this to be the case for governments' creations of environmental protection agencies and for the establishment of environmental policies. Extended to look at environmental movement organizations, the case of Ecuador shows that transnational environmentalists are also agents of dispersing global environmental norms. By this logic, nongovernmental organizations that are connected to transnational environmentalists around the world will share similarities in terms of their structures, policies, and practices. What this case also shows is that the declining significance of transnational actors enables local "culture" and local institutions to have more space. Decoupling from transnational/globalizing forces creates more possibilities, more alternatives, less homogeneity. When the transnational linkages are weakened, there's more diversity. Organizational types (species) thrive and adapt when they can grow in local conditions.

The end of this period is marked by the presidential election of the populist, socialist, Rafael Correa, who claimed to lead a "citizens' revolution." Correa listened to ideas from activist organizations, such as Acción Ecológica, and he incorporated their ideas into his initiatives, such as the Yasuní-ITT proposal, and into laws, as would happen with the changes to the 2008 Constitution. The convergence of the state's leftward shift and the radical agenda rising from the ANA created hope for a new development trajectory leading toward an ecological synthesis.

7 Citizens' Revolution, 2006 to 2015: The Rise of the Paradoxical State

We cannot be beggars sitting on a sack of gold.

—President of Ecuador, Rafael Correa

In this chapter I examine the sweeping changes that have taken place since President Rafael Correa came to power, and how the state has been transformed from a weak and incapacitated agent into a strong and effective actor. As the state has gained power, the environmental sector has been altered in a number of ways. First, international agents, such as USAID, have decreased their involvement in some cases, and others, such as Conservation International, have shifted their target partners from *ecodependents* to the state. Because the state now has capacity and resources, environmental leaders have moved from the nonprofit sector into the government. In general, *ecodependents* are weaker than in previous periods. Some prominent *ecodependent groups* have closed due to fiscal limits, and others are in precarious positions. For *ecoresisters*, the results of a stronger state have been mixed. On the one hand, many of their ideas have been incorporated into the state, such as constitutional rights for nature and the Yasuní-ITT Initiative. On the other hand, the state continues to be resource dependent; its logic still relies on legitimation and accumulation. As the state has gained strength and promised to lift its people out of poverty, struggles that had been formerly waged between *ecoresisters* and resource extractors (mostly transnational corporations) are being played out between activists and the state. The state has used its power to limit the civil liberties of groups that have spoken out against its actions. This leads back to the theoretical discussion regarding the treadmill of production. This final case chapter looks at the role of various types of civil society groups in altering (or not altering) the state's choices, and discusses the potential for democratic practices to slow the treadmill of production.

From Neoliberalism to 21st-Century Socialism

The Washington Consensus that dictated neoliberalism as the route to "development" prevailed in Latin America and the Caribbean during the 1990s. But around the turn of the millennium the increasingly obvious failure of that path led citizens to take to the streets, question neoliberal policies and make political changes throughout the region. Citizens of Latin America elected left-leaning governments that promised development for the people. Big changes were underway in Venezuela and Bolivia, and to lesser extents Brazil and Argentina.

Ecuador's citizenry shifted with this tide. Rafael Correa was elected President of Ecuador in 2006 and took office in 2007 with the support of social movements, including the environmental movement and the indigenous movement, especially the powerful indigenous confederation CONAIE. Alianza PAIS (Country Alliance/Proud and Sovereign Fatherland), the political party that Correa founded, promised to create a new 21st-century socialism (figure 7.1). In the 2006 election Correa's party won a majority of

Figure 7.1
Billboard in Quito: "All to vote. Elections 2006. Guarantee of the Democracy." The photo is of two indigenous people from the Amazon.

seats in the national assembly (73 out of 130). That election started a period of relative political stability. From 1984 until 2005, Ecuador had nine presidents, including three who were ousted due to social protests. To date (2015), President Correa is the longest continuously serving president in Ecuador, presently serving his third term.[1]

Commentators have analyzed these regional changes seeking to determine what, if anything, is new about this political period, and what, if anything, is a carryover from the neoliberal period. There are lengthy debates about how these nations should be characterized. Venezuela, Ecuador, and Bolivia proclaim to be creating a "21st-century socialism."[2] Analysts have described the shift to the left as Latin America's Pink Tide (it is not quite "Red"), and have assessed to what extent the new era should be characterized as "post-neoliberal,"[3] "post-developmental,"[4] "neo-developmental"[5] and/or "progressive neo-extractivism."[6] My purpose here is not to delve into the intricacies of those debates. However, what can be taken away from these analyses is that a shift has definitely occurred and these countries have altered their paths. There are at least five elements that describe this arguably new era: (1) states have taken on a role of responsibility for social welfare that differs from their laissez faire approach during the neoliberal era, (2) economic development gains have been translated into social goods such as health care and education and are being distributed to "the people," not just to elites, (3) there are efforts for broader social inclusion and the deepening of participatory democracy, (4) economic gains from natural resource extraction have shifted away from private actors (e.g., multinational corporations and national elites) toward the state and have been an important source of funding for states' social welfare programs, and (5) through the establishment of new regional institutions, nations in the region have consciously attempted to shift the nexus of power away from the United States toward Latin America and the Caribbean.

Changing Responsibility

Moving away from the laissez faire state perpetuated by neoliberalism, Venezuelan President Hugo Chávez brought the state back in to play a strong role in the economy. His election to President, as a member of the United Socialist Party of Venezuela, was part of a series of events that began roughly around 1999 and started Latin America's leftward tilt. Over the next decade other leftists were elected to serve as presidents, including in Brazil (Luiz Inácio Lula da Silva, the founder of the Workers Party in 2003), Bolivia (Evo Morales, unionist and indigenous *Aymara* in 2006), Argentina (Cristina

Kirchner in 2007), and Ecuador (Rafael Correa in 2007). Chávez led this movement by enacting redistributive policies nationally and creating regional structures internationally, such as ALBA (the Bolivian Alliance for the Peoples of Our America).

In his inaugural speech, President Correa remarked, "Latin America and Ecuador are not going through an epoch of changes, but through a genuine change of epoch."[7] Escobar explains this shift in approach: "The state is back as far as a main actor in the management of the economy, particularly through redistributive policies ...."[8] Grugel and Riggirozzi argue that the goal of rebuilding states is to "'make the state public' and ensure that it is better able to defend the public interest."[9] These new states have increased social spending, and created and implemented policies that provide the public with free education, health programs, subsidized food, cash transfer programs, and titled lands to indigenous groups. Large gains have gone to the poor who had suffered disproportionately under neoliberal structural adjustment policies. Correa's oft-cited wish is "to end the long and sad night of neoliberalism."[10]

Gains for the People

Data from the Economic Commission for Latin America and the Caribbean (ECLAC) show that the increases in funding for social welfare programs have made a difference for the poorest in Latin America.[11] In 2002 over 221 million people (44 percent) in the region were poor; these numbers declined to 180 million (23 percent) in 2010. The numbers for extreme poverty over the same period declined from 97 million (19 percent) people to 72 million (13 percent). In contrast to the neoliberal era of the 1980s and 1990s, during this period, Ecuador and the region also recorded rising GDP, and a lower percentage of public debt to GDP, while they received less official development assistance from abroad.[12]

In Ecuador, President Correa implemented a number of redistributive policies shortly after taking office, including doubling cash payments to the poor (bono) to $30 per month and subsidizing electricity.[13] Rather than calling this "redistribution," an Ecuadorian explained to me that they consider this the non-aggregation of wealth; in other words, it distributes wealth to the people who create it rather than aggregating it to elites at the top unjustly. These policies have been tremendously popular and contribute to high approval rates for the president. De la Torre reports that just prior to Correa's election in 2006, Ecuador's poverty rate was 37 percent and by 2011 it had declined to 29 percent. The Gini index over that same time span showed signs that income redistribution was beginning to create more equality; the figure moved from 50.4 to 47.0 (with 100 being total inequality and 0 being total equality).[14] While campaigning for his third term in 2012, one of Correa's challengers, a banker, promised to raise the *bono* to $50 per month if elected. Voters did not need to wait. Correa made the increase immediately. "In classic Correa style he also announced that he would finance the increase through a tax on banking transactions ...."[15]

Deepening Democracy

Alongside changes in policies affecting citizen's economic situations, analysts, such as Steve Ellner, argue that Venezuela, Bolivia, and Ecuador have moved toward practicing radical democracy. He notes: "One distinctive characteristic is the frequency of electoral contests, including party primaries, recall elections, and national referendums, which have been marked by high levels of voter turnout."[16] Catherine Conaghan (2008) noted this style early on and calls Correa a "plebiscitary" president; in other words, calling on the electorate for their assessment of proposals. Indeed, in one of his first actions, President Correa called for a referendum to elect a constituent assembly that would rewrite the constitution. The constitution, in turn, was approved by referendum. That sort of process—attaining a majority of votes on key issues—legitimizes politicians and provides them with a mandate. In Ecuador, all voting age citizens are required to vote. In addition to expanding the number of issues that were voted on, the new states looked for ways to engage more citizens in participatory democracy through a bottom up approach. In Venezuela, for instance, Chávez instituted communal councils that focus on local development at the neighborhood level. In Ecuador, the 2008 constitution is noteworthy in its incorporation of the Confederation of Indigenous Nationalities of Ecuador's (CONAIE's) long-standing vision for a plurinational country, in which historically excluded groups, are recognized and guaranteed rights.[17]

Primary Resource Dependency

Latin America has exported natural resources to North America for centuries,[18] and in this era it continued to do so at increasing rates. Grugel and Riggirozzi report, "Between 2000 and 2008 the volume of regional exports rose by a remarkable 42.4 per cent."[19] The key break with the past is that in this era the benefits of extraction are going to the many rather than the few because states have increased the proportion of the revenues that they collect from extractors and are moving those funds into social welfare programs. This has perhaps been most pronounced in Venezuela where they have vast petroleum resources and have been able to use these resources not just at home but to assist their allies and strengthen relationships with other like-minded nations, such as Cuba. Likewise Bolivia has increased the public benefit from tin extraction. In using their natural resources in this way, these states prioritized poverty reduction over environmental protection. In Ecuador, doing this was more complicated because of Correa's political base and the environmental elements in the new constitution.

In Ecuador, the increase in primary exports has disappointed social movement actors, especially environmentalists and indigenous, who were hopeful that President Correa would lead the country away from the extractivist development model. Clashes in the past that took place between anti-drilling and anti-mining activists and multinational extraction corporations are now taking place between those activists and the state, and will be elaborated on later in the chapter. As the environmental activists face off against the state, they are also armed with the 2008 Constitution in which the state provides rights to nature. But the environmental promises that were made in the constitution are not being realized. Correa used state-led extraction to pay for the citizen's revolution. Even though profits were for the people, the profits were fueled by environmental damage. Critics of Correa ask to what degree this form of development is any kind of real break with the past especially since resource depletion and resource dependency ultimately limits the future of Ecuador.

Shifting Power

A regional coalition with a "people's" agenda was being strengthened in this era, complete with the creation of regional institutions including ALBA (Bolivarian Alliance for the Peoples of Our America, created in 2004), Banco del Sur (Bank of the South established in 2009), and UNASUR (Union of South American Nations, created in 2004).[20] These institutions were designed to de-link Latin America from the United States' heavy influence.[21] The start of this realignment can be traced to the Argentinian fiscal crisis beginning in 1999, which signaled a failure of neoliberalism. Chávez's opposition to the Free Trade Areas of the Americas at the 2000 meetings in Quebec, was the beginning of state-level led resistance to neoliberal trade policies. After defeating that Northern-inspired institution of free trade, Chávez built an alternative. Beginning with Cuba in 2004, Venezuela formed a regional integration framework: ALBA. Observers have called this a "strategic de-linking from international trade and finance systems."[22] The creation of this and other regional structures minimized the power of US markets and politics over Latin America. Chávez had the power to do this because Venezuela is a resource-rich nation. Fred Rosen notes: "Chávez used the great fortune of the country's petro dollars to help create and/or strengthen institutions that could credibly complete with, and to a certain extent even replace the U.S.-dominated institutions of politics and trade within the Americas."[23] Stephanie Pearce argues that the regional cooperation institutions "have lessened both the dependence on, and influence of, the United States in the region, protecting countries' ability to act autonomously and not follow the dictates of Washington."[24] At the time Washington had its eyes and its resource concerns turned in a different direction—the Middle East—making the effort to de-link easier for countries like Ecuador.

Up until the Correa administration, Ecuador had a strong relationship with the United States. Ecuador hosted a US military base, the countries were regular trading partners, had long-standing diplomatic relationships, and the US Agency for International Development had been providing official development assistance almost fifty years. When President Correa came to office, things changed. Like other nations of the Bolivarian revolution, Ecuador withdrew from a number of these relationships in an attempt to de-link from neoliberalism and Washington's domination, and joined the regional institutions such as ALBA. When President Rafael Correa took office in 2007, he took a series of steps to decouple the Ecuadorian dependency on US influence. While still "dollarized," and thus intimately linked to the US economy, the state limited what it claimed as its debt responsibility. It still needed to repay debt, and still required foreign income, especially because of dollarization. Ecuador shifted its debts toward China, with whom it could also trade oil. The Correa administration also took a series of political steps, some symbolic and others with very concrete ramifications that indicated that Ecuador was not going to play the role of the United States' little brother. For instance, in 2009, Correa did not renew the treaty that would have allowed the United States to keep its air base in Manta. In 2011, the US ambassador was expelled, though later ties were reestablished. In 2013, with the Wikileaks scandal, Ecuador invited Edward Snowden into the country, but he never ended up going because he was unable to leave Russia. These actions strained Ecuador's relationship with the United States.

In sum, Correa's Citizens' Revolution delivered the goods to the people, but it did so while increasing resource extraction. The state rechanneled profits away from transnational corporations and into the state and the people and the country's infrastructure. It is hard to overestimate some of the changes that have happened since Correa took office. An environmentalist I interviewed in 2013 sums it up well: "There are a lot of interesting things going on in Ecuador. It is a completely different country than it was seven years ago."[25]

A Strong State and a Diminishing Role of Transnational Funding for the Environmental Movement

Transnational funding for the environment to Ecuador remained low during this period. An INGO representative noted: "It's pretty challenging to raise funds …. There's just less money."[26] In 2014 USAID ended its program in Ecuador altogether after President Correa sent a letter to the Embassy informing them not to initiate new activity.[27] The impending global recession did not increase global flows, nor did Correa's attempts to de-link from the United States. State actions made transnational corporations, bilateral donors and international nonprofit funders reluctant to continue investing in Ecuador.

In this era the state became far stronger and more effective than it had been in any other era since the military government ceded rule in 1978. The power of the state grew in terms of resources and political power. The state could pass and enforce new laws. It could take on the environmental management roles that had been ceded to NGOs under neoliberal regimes. It could enforce the laws it had on the books regarding foreign agents, which is just what it did with Conservation International. In 2011 the government temporarily closed Conservation International's doors for not having filed the appropriate paperwork with the Ministry of Foreign Relations and the Secretariat of International Technical Cooperation (Secretaría Técnica de Cooperación Internacional).[28] This act signaled that the government sought to make it more difficult for foreign agents— public and private—to have an influence on Ecuador's environment. An Ecuadorian commentator noted, "The departure of CI signifies retrieving national sovereignty in the management of environmental programs and policies."[29]

Through the Ministry of Environment, the state increased attempts to protect the environment, with a higher budget for the ministry and more funds going to protected areas. In the beginning, environmentalists saw this as good news, with progress on areas that had long been neglected. For example, the Correa administration created a Subsecretaría de Cambio Climático (Undersecretary for Climate Change) within the Ministry of the Environment. An environmentalist described the government in 2013 as "much more present and they regulate much more."[30] In 2013 interviewees from *ecoimperialist* and *ecodependent* groups took some care in describing government's actions, calling the state "more independent" and "autonomous" while lamenting that it has become more difficult for NGOs to get a seat at the table.

The shift in social structure—the simultaneous strengthening of the state and weakening of international influence—debilitated national *ecodependent* NGOs, such as Fundación Natura and Jatun Sacha in two ways. First, there was a brain drain from the NGOs into the state as government agencies grew and poached staff from the leading environmental organizations. An interviewee explains: "NGOs are suffering a lot on the one hand because of funding issues; on the other hand a lot of key people from NGOs have gone to the government."[31] The environmental intelligentsia was incorporated into the state. While there were problems related to this, many environmentalists saw it as positive. Workers in the government were described as well prepared, fresh, enthusiastic, hardworking, and motivated. This is in sharp contrast to the boom-and-bust period when government workers were described in opposite terms.

The second way that this shift hurt ecodependent groups was that transnational partnerships and funding that had formerly gone to ecodependents were being shifted to the state. One example is a partnership with Conservation International (CI), which was reinstated in Ecuador after some legal maneuvering. Prior to Correa's election, CI had piloted a project that had the dual goals of protecting land and alleviating poverty. Conservation International shifted their strategy significantly from its beginnings in Ecuador when it was focused singly on biodiversity to a new emphasis on the connection between ecosystem and human well-being. The pilot project started with support of the German development agencies. Conservation International worked on the ground to broker deals with indigenous Chachi communities in Esmeraldas. The Chachi communities entered a voluntary agreement to conserve 7,200 hectares of tropical humid forests, part of the Chocó biodiversity hotspot, in return for annual payments to be managed by the communities. "The local community centers decided to invest those resources in piped drinking water, medical supplies, education, creation of micro-enterprises, a community emergency fund, and salaries for community forest rangers."[32] In 2008 the Ministry of Environment decided to take the pilot program to the national level through what is now called Socio Bosque (Forest Partner). Socio Bosque promotes conservation agreements in which landowners commit to conserving part of their land in exchange for a financial incentive. The land cannot be logged or burned, but subsistence hunting and collection of nontimber forests products is permitted.[33] Incentives can go to individuals or to communities. The contracts are for twenty years. In the past Socio Bosque most likely would have been implemented through an INGO-NGO (ecoimperialist-ecodepdendent) partnership. However, presently the government provides the funding for incentives and CI assists with technical advice and strategic funding (about $100,000 in 2012) for special topics, such as train the trainer sessions on how to create a community plan. In the first two years of Socio Bosque, the government paid out $8.5 million in incentives.[34] According to the government website, in 2014 it had 2,748 agreements with 173,233 beneficiaries, protecting 1,434,061 hectares (5 percent of national territory; 5,537 square miles—just six square miles smaller than Connecticut), and the government provided $10,011,899 in investment incentives.[35]

In the past, groups like CI worked with ecodependent organizations, not the state. An employee of an international NGO noted the shift since Correa came to office:

There has been a shift towards supporting governments. I think one reason is because the government has changed a lot over the last seven years .... They are much more influential. So in order to obtain impact, we need to be working with them; not only with them, but they are of course a very main actor at the moment. They were more hands-off in the past and now they are very hands-on.[36]

Unlike the relationships that the INGOs had with NGOs in prior eras, the INGOs do not have financial relationships with the government. "They don't pay us and we don't pay them .... We just finance activities in collaboration with them .... We never charge fees to the government. That's not our role. I mean, we are not the consulting firm."[37] When INGOs worked with NGOs, INGOs (ecoimperialists) were the dominant partner; now that INGOs work with the state, they are the junior partner.

A poignant example of the devastating effect that the change in social structure had on ecodependent groups is what happened to Fundación Natura in this era. Prior to the start of the Correa administration, Fundación Natura had created a new entity, a for profit subsidiary—Fundación Natura, Inc.—a mechanism it could use to make up for the loss in international funds. It was diversifying by creating a fee-for-service consultancy that focused on trash and recycling. On October 11, 2012, Ecuador's daily paper *El Comerio* reported: *"Fundación Natura pone fin a 35 años de trabajo en Ecuador"* (Fundación Natura puts end to 35 years of work in Ecuador). I thought my Spanish must be getting pretty rusty because there was no way that could be true. But it was true. Fundación Natura, the seed organization for the environmental movement in Ecuador, internationally renowned for its policy work and for executing the first debt-for-nature swap, the nurturer of environmentalists and environmental groups, was done. Natura was just the most prominent example of what was happening to other NGOs. Other *ecodependent* organizations were suffering, if not closing up shop. In 2013 a former leader told me, "We [ecodependent NGOs] are a dying species."[38] A former board member of Natura said, "Environmental nonprofits are pretty much dead."[39] The most obvious problem was that international funding had ceased. The boom-and-bust of international funding had finally taken its toll in Ecuador. The global recession forced funders to dump Ecuador. A longtime environmental leader spoke of his discouragement and explained ecodependents' demise as the result of a perfect storm: the decrease in international funding, government maneuvering, and distrust between the government and NGOs. He added that to survive, it would be best for the environmental movement to be a low profile movement. This was not a call to arms.

Other groups have had less dramatic changes, but changes nonetheless. For instance, a leading group in conservation, Fundación Jatun Sacha, owned and managed nine biological research stations during the boom period. In 2013 this had declined to four. A member of that organization explained to me that after the global financial crash of 2007 to 2008, it was hard to get external funding, and despite applying for numerous grants, the organization was not receiving them. Volunteers who paid to work at the stations remained a critical source of funding and labor for the stations, including working in the agroforestry programs at the station at the coast near Muisne at the Congal Research Station (figure 7.2).

The shift in social structure significantly altered the influence of the transnational actors that remained in Ecuador. Ecoimperialists did not have the clout that they had in the past. Take, for example, what this foreign environmentalist explained to me:

If seven years ago, we put for example half a million on the table, that would really make a difference. But because of the incredible rising budget of the government institutions, half a million is just okay. 'Yeah, that's interesting.' That doesn't really make them smile .... It's not bad to put half a million on the table, but it's not that relevant anymore, so I think there is a different role for us. ...We like to consider ourselves as trusted advisors. ... Our financial support is not as relevant as it used to be.[40]

Now that the government has the upper hand with resources, they can control the process of protection. Foreign actors cannot dictate

Figure 7.2
Entrance to Jatun Sacha's biological station Congal in Muisne. Note at the bottom of the sign how this area is managed: "Area of conservation and integrated management of natural resources." The site includes organic shrimp ponds and agro-forestry.

environmentalism. Again, a transnational actor notes: "There is a limitation [to being involved]. The limitation is that the government is much more autonomous than it used to be, so it was easier in the past to say, 'Well, I don't Agree. We should do it differently.' I think at that time it was easier to convince people that things should be done differently. Now, it's a different ball game."[41] Transnational actors can no longer run the show. Structural changes led to the declining influence of foreigners on both Ecuador's political economy and its environmentalism. Many of the INGOs formerly had influence with NGOs and the state via their roles in transferring resources from the Global North to the Global South. With their funds limited by the slowed global economy, ecoimperialists' influence also became limited.

Ecoentrepreneurial groups were also affected by the macro-level changes. For instance, Vida para Quito, which I described as quasi-governmental because it was a private organization that was publicly funded to do public works, has been incorporated into the state. The work of Vida para Quito, such as maintaining bike paths and planting trees in urban areas, is still done, but it is done by state agencies. The value of incorporation is that "brown" environmental problems, such as who will collect the trash and plant trees in parks, has now been made public with municipalities taking over routine activities such as maintaining bike paths, collecting trash, and recycling household materials. In the previous eras the municipalities had outsourced their activities to groups like Vida para Quito, which had become known as the "Tree people"—they took care of the city's trees and other groups did other things. Vida para Quito was an outgrowth of the neoliberalization and outsourcing of government; now their duties were being moved back into the state.

Finally, ecoresisters weathered the storm better than ecodependents in this era. In fact, at the beginning of Correa's term, they were quite hopeful because Correa supported a number of their proposals. Moreover these social movement actors were not internationally reliant, and thus the decrease in international funding did not disrupt their work, much of which has focused at the local level. However, as will be discussed below, over time Correa's shine lost its luster, and ecoresisters who had been fighting multinational extraction corporations found that Correa's administration was the new extractor. Local problems continued to cause grievances, which motivated the volunteer base. An interesting twist was that Correa's success at eliminating poverty revived longstanding debates in local communities. Ecoresisters debated with their neighbors the costs of environmental protection versus modernization and roads, the trade-offs of development. This has pitted brother against brother, as the state attempts to build roads and purchase lands in resource-rich areas. In other areas it has only strengthened ecoresisters' resolve.

Thus the weakening of foreign roles and the strengthening of the national state had mixed effects on the various types of environmentalists: ecodependents were drained, ecoimperialists lost influence, ecoentrepreneurs were in incorporated into the state, and ecoresisters continued to fight, though their enemy shifted from foreign capitalists to the socialist state.

The State Legitimates: Incorporation of Environmentalism via the 2008 Constitution and the Yasuní-ITT Initiative

The state has the dual task of protecting citizens and the natural environment (making it legitimate in the eyes of the people) and accumulating resources to carry out its tasks of protecting citizens and the environment. The tasks of legitimacy and accumulation compete, even under the banner of "21st-century socialism." It isn't only a neoliberal development model that creates this conflict. While the socialist state may prioritize social welfare, that does not decrease its role in accumulation; in fact it can increase the need for accumulation. The state needs revenues to pay for its policies.

In regard to the environment, this creates a paradox: to protect the environment, the state needs to make money from the environment. The socialist state has two primary means of doing this. First, it can get a bigger piece of the pie than the neoliberal state did by altering the percentage of revenues it receives from resource extracting multinational corporations, as has been done in Bolivia under Morales with minerals.[42] Second, it can increase and intensify resource extraction, as Chávez did in Venezuela with petroleum. Ecuador used both tactics. Ecuador increased the windfall taxes on petroleum resources (from 13 to 87 percent)[43] and renegotiated a greater share of revenues from foreign oil companies. Ecuador also took over oil fields after Occidental Petroleum's contract expired, and it expanded the possibility of increasing mining by making changes to its mining law and expanding mining operations, especially in the south. The revenue increasing strategies were not met with resistance, but intensifying and increasing extraction were.

As I explained in the beginning of the chapter, the state was successful in gaining the public's approval and thus legitimating itself at a general level through social welfare policies that improved people's well-being. In terms of the subset of environmentalists that helped bring Correa and his party to office, there were more specific initiatives that the state incorporated so that environmentalists (and indigenous rights activists) would view Alianza PAIS as the legitimate holder of power and defender of the environment. The two most prominent legitimizing acts were (1) incorporation of environmental protections into the new constitution and (2) the promotion of the Yasuní-ITT proposal.

The 2008 Constitution

The Asamblea Nacional Ambiental (ANA—National Environmental Assembly) Declaration of 2005 was used as the basis for a proposal that ANA participants presented to the Constituent Assembly (CA) during 2007 and 2008 when the CA was rewriting the nation's constitution.[44] Language from those documents made it into the constitution, which was approved on September 28, 2008, by referendum (by 64 percent of voters), and included constitutional rights for nature. Title II, Chapter 7, article 71 of the constitution states, "Nature, or Pacha Mama, where life is reproduced and occurs, has the right to integral respect for its existence and for the maintenance and regeneration of its life cycles, structure, functions and evolutionary processes."[45] This was the first time that nature had these rights, anywhere. Bolivia would adopt a similar change to their constitution in 2011. Indigenous and environmental coalitions were key in this constitutional development. Participants in ANA say that the approved constitution contained more than thirty articles formulated by the alliance that gathered at ANA. This was a promising sign for environmentalists. In addition to the rights of nature, the constitution gives every individual and community the right to demand that the state uphold the rights of nature; it also protects water rights, prohibits genetically modified organisms, and promotes *buen vivir/sumak kawsay*. These are key examples of how radical environmentalists' proposals were integrated into the new government.

The 2008 constitution included language, written in Spanish and Kichwa, expressing the right to *buen vivir, sumak kawsay*—a right to living well. It also invoked *"pacha mama"* (mother earth), an indigenous concept that views humans as part of nature/earth and nature as having intrinsic rights. The section of the constitution on development (Title VI, Chapter 1, article 275) states, "The development structure is the organized, sustainable and dynamic group of economic, political, sociocultural and environmental systems which underpin the achievement of the good way of living (sumak kawsay)."[46] This is a paradigmatic shift.[47] There is a rich and growing literature explaining and parsing the concepts of *buen vivir/sumak kawsay*.[48] Eduardo Gudynas provides a summary of the *buen vivir* concept:

The richness of the term is difficult to translate into English. It includes the classical ideas of quality of life, but with the specific idea that well-being is only possible within a community. Furthermore, in most approaches the community concept is understood in an expanded sense, to include Nature. Buen Vivir therefore embraces the broad notion of well-being and cohabitation with others and Nature. In this regard, the concept is also plural, as there are many different interpretations depending on cultural, historical and ecological setting.[49]

Many observers believe that these changes create an opening necessary for an alternative development model—an alternative to extractivist neoliberal globalization—that incorporates nature.[50] Escobar refers to Alberto Acosta's work that makes the argument of the new constitution, "This makes possible a novel ethics of development, one which subordinates economic objectives to ecological criteria, human dignity, and social justice and the collective well-being of the people."[51] Gudynas (2013) further argues that rather than being a "development alternative," *buen vivir* is in fact an "alternative to development." He summarizes:

[Buen vivir] moves away from the classical views of development as perpetual economic growth, linear progress, and anthropocentric, to focus on people's well-being in a broad sense that also includes their emotions and beliefs. The break with anthropocentrism makes it possible to recognise values intrinsic to the environment, do away with the society/nature duality and reconfigure communities of political and moral agents.[52]

The Pachamama Alliance, an organization that works with indigenous peoples in the Amazon and is based in San Francisco (with a sister foundation in Ecuador), summarizes aspects of the indigenous conception of *sumak kawsay* that relate specifically to development:

Sumak kawsay values people over profit. It is also a new way of viewing 'developing nations' because it expresses a relationship with nature and surroundings that epitomizes the opposite of profit and commodification. A key piece is how development is defined: it calls for a decreased emphasis on economic and product development, and an increased focus on human development—not in population, but an enrichment of core values, spirituality, ethics, and a deepening of our own connection with pachamama [mother earth].[53]

In sum, *buen vivir* and the new constitution value quality of life, community, nature over economy, human dignity and well-being, social justice, ethical living, and spirituality.

President Correa's administration created the Secretaría Nacional de Planificación y Desarrollo (SENPLADES, the National Secretary for Planning and Development) as the name suggests, to develop the national development plan for *sumak kawsay/buen vivir*.[54] This organization was described to me as the "most powerful institution in the country." Environmentalists think this organization has good ideas, such as using green accounting, and considering the nation's global footprint in planning. SENPLADES created the inaugural Plan Nacional para el Buen Vivir, 2009–2013 (National Plan for Good Living) in President Correa's first term, which rejects the dominant development paradigm and embraces the alternative: *buen vivir/sumak kawsay*. Literally, the plan calls for a moratorium on the term "development":

... The prevailing concept of development has remained immune to questioning. It has "resisted" feminist, environmental and cultural attacks and criticisms. Its detractors have been unable to institutionalize their alternative proposals. This is the reason why, today, more than ever, the South needs to put forward proposals which [sic] to re-think social, cultural, economic and environmental relations. By following the new social contract set forth in the 2008 Constitution, this Plan proposes a moratorium of the word "development" and the incorporation of the concept of Good Living in the debate.[55]

The plan begins the creative project of crafting an alternative. It is still largely defining the future in terms of "not" the development of the past. But it is also forging new ground in its affirmation of *buen vivir*.[56] It rejects anthropocentrism and measures that value quantity over quality. It favors nature, social sustainability, diversity, and human development.[57] This, too, gave environmentalists and ecoresisters, in particular, hope that Ecuador could craft a future that was radically different from the US view of development.

The concept of *buen vivir* was supported on the ground by ecoresisters. For instance, anti-mining activist Carlos Zorrilla has emphasized how "development" created the "poor" in Ecuador. "People didn't know they were poor! They were rich in community, but made to feel poor because they didn't have cars."[58] He has also argued that traditional development focuses on economic wealth, but other forms of wealth, such as cultural, environmental, and social, are also critically important. Zorrilla believes mining will destroy that other wealth. "And enough people have got that message. And they don't want to destroy the social wealth in the community. To them, it's important."[59] Similarly an ecoresister from the coast points out what *buen vivir* can look like:

Where an ecosystem is alive, where there is life, with a nice beach, sun, good food, good hammock, good home ... the people are good. ... What more do you want? We are good with this life." He goes on to draw a distinction between that rural life and what people in the city want: They want another life, they want the car, the telephone ....[60]

Presumably those in the city have been marred by the northern concept of what it means to be "rich" and "developed." Thus the promotion of *buen vivir* in the constitution and the state agency created to promote it resonated with ecoresisters and suggested that their values and vision were being incorporated into the government's plans for Ecuador's future.

An important piece that did not make its way into the constitution was communities' rights to decide how their land should be used. In the previous chapter's discussion, I explained Acción Ecológica's stance that sovereignty was part of sustainability and local people should have power to decide about how their lands are used. The constitution trumps local sovereignty with national priorities in two ways. First, there is a clause that gives the state power over "strategic sectors." Title VI, Chapter 5, article 313 states: "The State reserves the right to administer, regulate, monitor and manage strategic sectors .... The following are considered strategic sectors: energy in all its forms, telecommunications, nonrenewable natural resources, oil and gas transport and refining, biodiversity and genetic heritage, the radio spectrum, water and others as established by law."[61] What this means, in national parks, for instance, is that the interests of the state can override the clause that oil cannot be extracted in parks. The second way the state limits local sovereignty is that the constitution only requires consultation of the people in taking such action on their lands, not consent. Title II, Chapter 4, article 57(7) of the constitution provides the right to all people "To free prior informed *consultation*, within a reasonable period of time, on the plans and programs for prospecting, producing and marketing nonrenewable resources located on their lands and which could have an environmental or cultural impact on them ...." (my italics). This is in contrast with the UN Declaration on the Rights of Indigenous People, of which Ecuador is a signatory, which requires free, prior, and informed *consent* (FPIC), not simply consultation. Activists in Intag (DECOIN) and on the coast (C-CONDEM) believe they would be winning their struggles against mineral extraction and shrimp farming, respectively, if the national government respected communities' decisions. Thus, despite incorporating many items that activists deemed desirable, the constitution lacked this critical component of local control.

The Yasuní-ITT Initiative

In addition to the constitution and its promotion of the potential for a new development path via *buen vivir*, the state proposed a second major initiative that gave it legitimacy in the eyes of environmentalists: the Yasuní-ITT Initiative. In 2007 President Correa presented a concrete proposal, seemingly influenced by *sumak kawsay*: the Ishpingo, Tambococha, and Tiputini (ITT) Initiative to leave the oil in the soil in Yasuní National Park.[62] This would be a tremendous feat environmentally and socially and could shift the course of "development." Yasuní National Park, Ecuador's largest national park, is a biologically important area, considered to be one of the most diverse areas on Earth, home to 173 mammal species and 40 percent of Ecuador's bird species.[63] It is also the home to indigenous Huorani and two uncontacted groups that live in voluntary isolation (the Tagaeri and Taromenane). It is of particular interest because it contains 20 percent of the country's known oil reserves, some 850 million barrels.[64] The Yasuní-ITT idea originated with the radical environmental group Acción Ecológia and was presented to Alberto Acosta (who at that time was the environmentally sympathetic director of the Ministry of Energy and Mines), who then presented the idea to President Correa.[65] The President took the Initiative to the United Nations in 2007 with the basic plan that the state would not grant oil concessions in the oil corridor that runs through Yasuní National Park if the international community could compensate Ecuador for half of the revenue that they would have earned over a ten-year period (i.e., asking for $3.6 billion in donations in lieu of $7.2 billion in profits). A fund was set up at the UN Development Program for countries to contribute to. The argument was that the plan would protect one of the most biodiverse places on earth *and* protect indigenous people living on those lands *and* reduce greenhouse gas emissions. It was later framed as a climate change initiative. Private and public organizations promoted the project and solicited funding. If they would not be able to secure the funding, they would likely resort to Plan B: drill.[66]

The ITT proposal was not Correa's idea; it originated with ecoresisters—individuals from Acción Ecológica and Oilwatch, including Alberto Acosta.[67] They successfully moved the concept "up" to the highest level in the national government and then higher up to the United Nations. They took advantage of the opportunity of the world's attention being focused on climate change to address a long-standing concern of radical, Ecuadorian environmentalist: the destruction that oil drilling causes the environment and communities, and the inequalities that it creates within nations. Acción Ecológica has even broader goals. The group is attempting to scale the idea up to create a "post-oil society." Their slogans go beyond oil to link to other climate change-producing fossil fuels: "Keep the oil in the soil, the coal in the hole, and the tar sand in the land." A leader of AE, Ivonne Yanez, explained that this movement is internationalizing beyond Yasuní and Ecuador.

We have groups in Brazil that want also to leave oil in the soil in Acre region. There are people in Peru that want to leave oil in the soil in one province, for example, in Loreto. There are people in Bolivian Amazon that want also to leave oil in the soil, the gas in the soil, in this case, and they are proposing *Amazonía sin Petróleo* [Amazon without petroleum]. And there are other groups, for example, in Nigeria, that are making a statement for the government that it's a better deal, in terms of economics, for Nigeria to leave the oil in the soil than to sell it internationally, because of the damages, because of the corruption linked with that, because of all the oil that has been stolen by the corrupted people there. So they are also asking to leave oil in the soil in the Niger Delta.[68]

By November 2012, Ecuador had only received promises totaling approximately $200 million. Despite the deadline for pledges being extended several times, Ecuador was not able to secure funding, and in August 2013,

Correa signed the documents that ended the experiment and would allow the area to be exploited for oil. The problems of oil extraction in the Amazon are well known because they have been well documented by the Ecuadorian government, the UN, and even Texaco.[69] Ecuador's 1993 case against Texaco (now Chevron) by the homegrown Frente de Defensa de la Amazon, is ongoing. There is a high level of consciousness regarding the environmental and human health costs to oil development.[70] Nonetheless, while President Correa is outspoken against Texaco, he remains open to the potential of drilling for the people. Although the constitution forbids extraction of nonrenewable resources in protected areas (article 407), it contains a clause that these resources can be accessed at the request of the president if there is the support of the national assembly, which he received in October of that same year. As analyst Rochlin puts it, "Correa's is not a green government, it is a populist one."[71]

In response to Correa's actions leading toward Plan B, a coalition of environmentalists, social activists, and indigenous groups formed the YAS-unidos (a creative combination of YAS from Yasuní and unidos, which can be translated as joined or united). They describe themselves as a youth movement seeking to save Yasuní and to keep the Yasuní-ITT Initiative alive.[72] They collected over 757,000 signatures to put the issue on a refer-endum and delivered them to the state in April 2014, but the National Election Commission (CNE in Spanish) claims they failed to get the requi-site 580,000 signatures, a claim the Yasunidos contest. At the time of this writing (January 2015), this conflict is ongoing, and the YASunidos are taking their case to the Inter-American Commission on Human Rights.[73] Thus, even though the Yasuní-ITT was used as a legitimating tool to keep environmentalists on board with the Correa administration and a poten-tial concrete alternative to development project in the spirit of *buen vivir*, it has so far failed. At this moment it symbolizes Correa turning his back on environmentalists.

The State Accumulates: Resource Extraction and the Suppression of Resistance

The state needs to accumulate resources for its social spending. Despite hopes for alternatives, the state has continued to do so through extractive practices. Unlike prior eras, the gains of extraction have gone to the poor. The people love Correa because they have jobs, roads, schools, and health care. There is a more equitable distribution of profits. However, the basis of this wealth—extraction—has undercut Correa's early support from indigenous groups and environmentalist. An ecoresister complains, "It is the same model: extraction, extraction, extraction."[74] While Correa's social policies have appeased the general public, his extractive policies have inflamed supporters. They feel betrayed and under attack.

According to the Bank of Ecuador, government earnings based on petroleum exports rose from $3,235 million in 2006 to $11,443 million in 2013. However, the tons of crude exported in those two years was roughly identical. The state increased revenue without increasing production. In mining, though, things were different. Over the same period, the amount of minerals increased exponentially: exports of gold and silver increased from 91 to 19,505 tons (an increase of over 213-fold) Similarly exports of copper and lead almost doubled from 5,903 to 10,376 tons. Over this time span the United States remained the main destination for exports.[75]

A stronger state has a double-edged effect. An interviewee explains:

The Ministry of the Environment is completely different than what it used to be. It's way more active. It has a lot more funding and it's doing a lot more, a lot of positive things. The risk is not what's happening within the Ministry of Environment, the problem is that there are other ministries that are also really active. ... So if you have one ministry that implements a really interesting program ... and is strengthening the protected area system ... and at the same time, you see that most of the Amazon is under [oil] concessions ... then we have a contradiction.[76]

The stronger presence of the state is not just in the Ministry of the Environment, it is also in the Ministry of Energy and Mines. "The government is not just one homogeneous group."[77] A former minister and strong supporter of Correa's government suggested that environmental conflicts, especially related to mining, were and would be a large problem for the government. The minister noted that the Canadian (and then Chinese) mining companies announce each year that they "produce" X amount of gold. Bewildered, the minister replied, "It is not 'produced,' it's 'extracted.'"[78]

Members of Correa's original administration have left the government over disputes between ministries. Of note in the environmental realm was the departure of Alberto Acosta, who was the president of the Constituent Assembly that rewrote the constitution in 2008 and then became Correa's Minister of Energy and Mines. Acosta did not believe that Correa's extraction plans were consistent with *sumak kawsay/buen vivir*. In an interview after leaving the ministry, he noted of Correa's administration, "In view of the fact that this government wants to expand the oil frontier and force the 'mega mining,' rather than speaking of 'socialism of the XXI Century,' what we should be talking about is 'extractive 21st century.'"[79] In 2013, Acosta ran for President against Correa. He was backed by a group of leftist parties including the Pachakutik (the party that had been founded by the indigenous group CONAIE), but he only won 3 percent of the vote.

President Correa routinely says, "We cannot be beggars sitting on a bag of gold." Geographer Anthony Bebbington describes this position as "resource nationalist environmentalism."[80] Correa is willing to trade off small pockets of Ecuador's environment for the good of the nation. This view is in contrast to ideologies embraced by ecoresisters who focus on local sovereignty and alternative conceptions of wealth, as expressed by Carlos Zorrilla above. Like Acosta, ecoresisters believe that Correa is taking the wrong path. For instance, another ecoresister pointed out the incompatibility of the government's development model:

The State is doing capitalist development. It is making major investments in a model that is already sold in the world. That is, it is the same [as the] European model, the same American model: big roads, big machines, large airports, large refineries. All of that is great. We all want to be best in the world, but that is not development for a country like Ecuador that is a diverse country. That's the difference. In a little space we have everything, but we are running out. We are exploiting it very quickly and the government is doing so without consultation. If we want to change from the oil country we are now to a mining country, we need debate. But there is no debate; now tell me if it is good, if it's bad, what I'll gain .... It is the same as imposing capitalism.[81]

The majority of Ecuadorians have been very happy with Correa's actions. But some of Correa's administration and the social movements that had supported him were parting ways as he indicated that he was willing to make trade-offs that they were not.

In addition to the concern about the nature of extractive development, activists worry about the process of development: "there is no debate." Opponents believe that Correa is actively limiting the role of civil society and in this way differs from other Bolivarian nations that have truly deepened democracy. Correa has limited the role of the public in a few ways. One way is informal: he's mocked resisters to his plans, with a focus on anti-mining resisters. A second way, more difficult to track back to the government, is through repressive actions that have been taken to subdue activists. A third way is by using the legal system and by making specific changes to the legal system. Some examples follow.

First, with the passage of a new mining law in 2009 and the support of the World Bank, Ecuador's fastest growing extractive industry became mining. With its rise, socioenvironmental resistance to it escalated.[82] Correa promotes what he calls socially responsible mining, but his critics point out that the law allows for mineral exploration on communal and indigenous lands, and is at odds with rights set out in the 2008 Constitution. When the mining law was passed, the anti-mining movement mobilized thousands of people throughout the country in a "Day of Mobilization for Life" and blocked a major highway in the south.[83] President Correa spoke out against the organizations that were coordinating the protests, including the indigenous confederation, CONAIE, which had initially supported him. Correa stated:

I think they [CONAIE] are going to lose more credibility with these extreme positions, which often do not come from them, but from foreign NGOs. These people have nothing to lose, and work to convince indigenous leaders with their ideas. These "childish" radical positions are camouflaged in indigenousness or environmentalism.[84]

Correa has also called anti-mining opponents "nobodies," "allies of the right," "attempting to destabliz[e] progressive governments."[85] Members of the *ecoresisting* DECOIN were targets of these claims. After years of successful resistance preventing Japanese and then Canadian corporations from mining copper in the cloud forests of the Intag valley, they found themselves confronting the national mining company, ENAMI, which proposed to mine copper at the same site.

In addition to being verbally chastised by the president they elected, protesters have been harassed. Not all of these events can necessarily be traced back to the government (presumably they could have come at the hands of corporations or others); nevertheless, the number of suspicious activities and accidents that have occurred around ecoresisters is on the rise. For instance, in the Intag Valley, local protests against mining companies have been met with paramilitary forces.[86] Police have searched activists' homes without just causes. The state has charged activists using its laws against terrorism, much as the US government did with "ecoterrorists" following the 9/11 attacks. As I write (February 2015), Javier Ramirez, president of the community of Junín in the Intag Valley, awaits his court date for terrorism, having been incarcerated since April 2014. A global letter writing campaign has been launched to encourage Correa to free him. His supporters argue that the accusations against him are false: he was at home in Junín, which is many hours away from Quito by bus, where and when the alleged crime was committed; moreover they argue that he is being charged because he has defended nature, which is not a crime.[87] The state is criminalizing protest, and it appears as if it is targeting critics of its extractive practices. In an article that warns of Correa's authoritarian drift, De la Torre argues "Adversaries, especially from the left, have been transformed into 'enemies of the revolution.'"[88]

Similar activities are happening in the south of the country in *la Cordillera de Condor*, in Shuar territory along the Peruvian border, where anti-mining protesters are fighting against the Mirador mine. In March 2012, the government signed an agreement with Ecuacorrientes, a Chinese-funded company, to do large-scale mining for copper, gold, and silver.[89] Activists responded with protests, including a fifteen-day, 600-kilometer march led by CONAIE, called the Plurinational March for Life, Water, and Dignity of the Peoples.[90] An attempt to use the constitution to stop the Mirador mine was dismissed because the mine was in the national interest.[91] There was local resistance, with residents refusing to leave their lands to make way for the mine. Ecuacorrientes filed suits, including one against the indigenous leader and anti-mining activist José Isidro Tendetza Antún. In December 2014, he was found dead, reportedly terrorized and killed. He was to be part of a "climate caravan" of activists headed to Lima, Peru, for the COP20 (United Nations Climate Change Conference, Conference of the Parties) discussions. Following his death, the activists on the caravan were harassed—repeatedly stopped by police and eventually their bus was confiscated. According to a report in the *Guardian*: "Luis Corral, an advisor to Ecuador's Assembly of the People of the South, an umbrella group for indigenous federations in southern Ecuador, said that if Tendetza had been able to travel to the COP20 it would have put in 'grave doubt the honorability and the image of the Ecuadorean government as a guarantor of the rights of nature.'"[92] According to a group that maps environmental justice cases worldwide, José Tendetza was a high profile target:

He was one of the plaintiffs in the action of violation of the Rights of Nature given by the Ecuadorian state Constitution and brought before the National Authorities in January 2013. He was one of the plaintiffs, as affected, to the IACHR (Inter-American Commission on Human Rights) in January 2014. He was one of the signers of questions put to six Chinese banks financing the Mirador Project in February 2014. On 5 December 2014, José Tendetza was expected to file a complaint against the company [Ecua]Corriente before the International Tribunal Court for the Rights of Nature, in the Peoples' Summit in Lima Peru.[93]

The dangers of harassment, imprisonment, and/or death have made it far riskier for ecoresisters to act against the state. One of them noted: "Before, we didn't think twice about blocking the roads. Now people are saying, you know, we can't really do this anymore. What do we do now?"[94] At the same time people are committed to what is right. An ecoresister recounted to me what an indigenous leader said at a gathering: "If we fight, we may lose. If we don't fight, we're lost." The ecoresister added, "Obviously we need to fight, if for nothing else, to set a precedent that you don't need to put up with so much injustice and to show how the state is violating the constitution, outrageously violating the constitution."[95]

Alberto Acosta suggests that what is happening in Ecuador is common among states with abundant resources. He writes:

We cannot conclude our reflections without mentioning another feature of these countries trapped by the curse of plenty: violence, which seems to go hand in hand with a model that damages democracy. This violence may be practised by the state itself, even with governments considered progressive, as they criminalise popular protest against the extractivist activities with the sole purpose of keeping them going.[96]

Finally, the government has also used legal tools to limit protest and created new legal hurdles for civil society groups. For instance, in March 2009 the government shut down Acción Ecológica, which had helped organize and lead the protests against mining, based on legal technicalities related to AE's charter. This caused an international uproar, and the government altered its decision, stating that the organization simply needed to have their registration switched to the Ministry of Environment, which did not exist when they were established.[97] A year earlier, President Correa made an Executive Decree (982), which, according to The International Center for Not-for-Profit Law (ICNL):

... tightened Ecuador's already restrictive law governing NGOs. Among other restrictions, the decree authorized the Government to dissolve an NGO on discretionary grounds such as 'compromising the interests of the state;' to demand virtually unlimited information from an NGO; and to post the names of every member of all registered NGOs on a publicly accessible website.[98]

A few years later, in 2011, Correa altered an existing Executive Decree (812) that affects International NGOs. According to the ICNL:

Decree 812 amends existing law to prohibit international NGOs registered with the Ecuadoran Government from 'intermediating, implementing, or executing plans, programs or projects' that are funded with resources from bilateral or multilateral cooperation entities. Moreover, international NGOs that already hold agreements to operate in Ecuador must sign new agreements that conform to the Constitution and guidelines of the national development plans.[99]

This decree can be read as either a state crack down on civil society, in general, or as an attack against foreign intrusions into Ecuador. That year, sixteen international NGOs were expelled from Ecuador, including Conservation International, and in 2012, twenty-six were asked to leave. Correa said of the groups ousted in 2011: "They are extreme right-wing NGOs that seek to replace governments to impose their policies, and if they cannot, they destabilize governments."[100] Venezuela took similar actions in 2010. Both nations pointed to USAID as a problem. Groups like Conservation International that have returned to work in Ecuador have gone to great pains to avoid being perceived as gringo, imperialist, and capitalist.

In 2013 President Correa enacted another key legal action that limited civil society organizations: Decree 16. The twenty-five page decree, which included 51 articles, dictated new procedures for NGOs to register with the state, including new paperwork requirements, a centralized system that would collect data from all of the groups, and actions that the state could take to intervene in groups' activities, including justifications for dissolving organizations. The decree was heavily criticized by international organizations, such as Human Rights Watch. A former government official noted, "The nonprofit industry is under heavy scrutiny .... The government wants control. Period."[101]

The state used the decree to shut down the environmental organization Fundación Pachamama, a group that works in the Amazon with indigenous groups to defend their territories and cultures from the perils of oil development. The International Center for Not-for-Profit Law reported:

On December 5, 2013, the government shut down ... Pachamama, for violating the provisions of Presidential Decree No. 16. The official justification for the dissolution was that Pachamama was "interfering with public policies that undermine internal or external State security that might affect public peace." This action followed President Rafael Correa's criticism of Pachamama ... on his weekend radio program. On February 12, 2014, the Ministry of Environment turned down Pachamama's appeal .... It also blamed Pachamama for a "violent demonstration" in November 2013. In light of the dissolution of Pachamama, representatives of the organization attended the IACHR [Inter-American Court on Human Rights] hearing titled "Situation of the Right to Freedom of Association and Environmental Defenders in Ecuador" on March 28, 2014, in Washington, DC. On July 17, 2014, three foreign advisers to Pachamama were detained by Ecuadorian police in Quito ...."[102]

State actions to limit civil society put environmentalists in a defensive position and people were scared. A long-time environmental leader told me that the government was using the various regulations to systematically threaten and harass NGOs.[103] The government could walk into a NGOs office at any moment and demand information, and the NGOs were obliged to provide it or be shut down. Other national organizations, not just environmental, but civil society groups, were discouraged, frustrated, and distrustful of what was happening with Correa's administration. For environmentalists, at least, the attack on them created a moment for them to regroup under the banner of CEDENMA. CEDENMA convened meetings immediately after the decree was announced and produced a collective statement that argued that the decree violated the rights that they had under the law.[104]

Groups believed that the state was intentionally trying to tamp down their critical edge and put the brakes on democracy. Both national and international groups expressed this. A representative from an international NGO noted: "We are NGOs, we are not government agencies. We are not an extension of the government. So personally, my personal feeling is of course we should support the government on issues that we think make sense. But we shouldn't lose our critical position of also saying, 'Okay, this is what we think.' Because we are a civil society. We are not a government agency .... It's a bit more challenging [in this era] to be critical."[105]

Ecoresisters believed it was their duty to speak out: "We are a social movement and we need to maintain our independence and be critical, to be purposeful. We maintain some independence so that we can say what we think when we think it is necessary."[106] They lamented that some groups and individuals lost their willingness to speak up. For instance, with many environmentalists going to work within the government, there's been a mixed result. On the one hand, there are environmentalists within the government who can promote environmentalism. On the other hand, they aren't listening to the ecoresisters because they fear the repercussions of siding with them. Another ecoresister expressed disgust about this:

Whatever the president says, all the ministries have to go ahead with it. There is no independent power—you probably heard that before .... All the ministries, they have to do exactly what Correa orders, exactly. There is no commitment to do their job. It's just what Correa needs to do .... I would be embarrassed if I was in administration and I was expected to say yes to everything he comes up with. There's no dignity. You know, if you were to be put as a minister of environment and they want you to violate the principles of the ministry, you quit. You denounce the jackass who's opening up the country to mining and you quit. [But] nobody does that here.[107]

Another leader confirms this: "One of the issues that worries of course everybody in civil society is to have the freedom to have an opinion. That's become more challenging."[108]

A related concern is that the government no longer welcomes the input of civil society. While the government is regarded as having a high level of human capital and greater funding (more capacity), its "autonomy" and "independence" makes it such that decisions are made within the government institutions without civil society's perspective. When there is input, the inclusion of civil society appears arbitrary: "One day you can be at the table, and the next day you're not .... Sometimes you win and sometimes you lose."[109]

Ultimately activists are concerned that democracy is being eroded.

Correa's not democratic, no matter what people say .... Many people are afraid to confront Correa .... A lot of people are fearful, and you lose if you're ruled by fear .... People are their worst self censors. The press is now doing it. NGOs are afraid to speak out. The hell with it. That's sad how you change, giving in to that fear.[110]

The environmental and indigenous rights movements had long sought to institute nature and indigenism into the state. Correa promised to help do this, they supported him, and their ideas were incorporated into the 2008 Constitution. However, the state's need for accumulation and President Correa's focus on extraction deviated from those principals. Environmental and indigenous rights activists resisted. Their priorities had been subsumed under Correa's development agenda. Dosh and Kligerman summarize:

These decades of organizing have resulted in at least a partial shift toward reorganizing the state apparatus to show greater respect for natural resources. Correa has not been at the forefront of these movements, however, and natural resource protections granted in the Constitution stem more from the grassroots than from the National Palace. This tension is likely to foster continued conflict in the months and years ahead.[111]

On Correa's side are the people. Ecoresisters, ecodependents, and ecoentrepreneurs all remarked that the governments' policies have made people happier, more hopeful and better off economically. People in places like Bunche along the coast, near Muisne, home to C-CONDEM, like Correa (see figure 7.3). The roads and schools and health care centers he has built make peoples' lives easier and improve their quality of life. Ecuadorians in towns like Muisne can turn the other cheek to environmental disruptions and limits to civil liberties when their commutes to market, school, and health care are reduced by hours. It is hard to overestimate how big a change this is in peoples' daily lives. The downside, critics like De la Torre argue, is that "Citizens are being turned into passive and grateful recipients of the leader's benevolent and technocratically engineered redistributive

Figure 7.3
Road in the town of Bunche, near Muisne. People in the town are glad that traditional development (e.g., paving of roads) is happening.

policies."[112] Acosta agrees that this sort of "fiscal pacification" is taking place. Further he argues: "The government's large revenues enable it to prevent the formation of opposition or independent groups or powerful factions that would be able to demand political and other rights (human rights, justice, shared government, etc.), by displacing them from power."[113] This is indeed what activists have been facing. While they have achieved some institutionalization of their goals, it appears as if the state wants to be completely in charge. As the state consolidates economic and political power, the political opportunity structure for national NGOs shrinks.

The Paradoxical State

A radical environmental leader summed up the paradox of this period, "The government dedicated a little more to exploit more resources because it needs money to stay in power, because without money, there isn't a government on the left or on the right."[114] The nature of the state is that it needs to be seen as legitimate in the eyes of the citizens, and a key mechanism to do so, is to distribute social benefits. To afford those benefits, the state engages in activities to accumulate wealth, such as resource extraction. Whether to the left or right, *"el estado es el estado"* (the state is the state).[115]

In complete contrast to the origin and boom eras, transnational funding for the environment played a negligible role in this period. Also, in stark contrast to those periods, Correa's state was strong and capable. These sharp differences are ideal for teasing out the relative importance of these various factors in seeking to understand what configurations of possibilities provide the greatest hope for generating a balance between the social system and the ecosystem, or in Schaiberg's terms, ecological synthesis (see table 7.1).

While the state was the weakest agent in previous periods, trailing transnational funders and the environmental sector, in this period the state was by far the dominant actor. Through the state's incorporation of nature and *buen vivir/sumak kawsay* into the constitution and its planning efforts, and its championing of the Yasuní-ITT Initiative, it has shown through words,

Table 7.1
Summary of Citizens' Revolution era

	Origins 1978–1987	Boom 1987–2000	Bust 2000–2006	Revolution 2006–2015
Transnational funding				Limited funds, especially public ones; private funds directed to the state
Environmental sector				Ecodependent organizations continue to be weak; ecoresisters are vocal and active
State characteristics				Strong, populist, socialist
Environment and development policies				Big environmental and development alternatives proposed but not executed; new constitution recognizes nature; resource extraction "for the people"
Schnaiberg's synthesis				Managed scarcity in practice with rhetorical calls for ecological synthesis

at least, that environmentalists' concerns are the state's concerns. However, this may simply be a form of greenwashing. The state's actions related to the environment and development have communicated otherwise. The Correa administration promotes resource extraction for the people. In word, we hear an ecological synthesis, but in deed, the state practices managed scarcity.[116]

Environmentalists made gains in this era. Environmentalism became institutionalized within state structures. Environmentalists' actions and ideas altered the constitution and the state's plans for development. The ideas that were incorporated were not themes from North American ecoimperialists; they came from the radical Ecuadorian ecoresisters. The global recession, which caused the Global North to restrict international environmental funding, weakened the mainstream ecodependent groups. They played a smaller role in civil society, and many individuals from these groups entered the state bureaucracy. Ecodependents' influence rose and fell with their transnational funding. Ecoresister organizations, which drew support from local volunteers, were fueled by increased resource extraction, especially mining. They also had overlapping concerns with indigenous groups that were mobilized against extraction. In prior eras, ecoresisters and indigenous groups fought transnational corporations; in this era, they fought the newest extractor: the state. State-led extraction replaced foreign-led extraction. Ecoresisters and indigenous people defended their lands from the state's developmentalist agenda and the state pushed back. Ecoresisters' strength was independent from international funding. Their influence depended on local and national grievances. In this way the ecoresisters were much more aligned with "the people"; however the people, in general, were more attuned to economics than ecology.

If the premise of this history is that Ecuadorians are going to destroy the environment by extracting resources from it, then getting the biggest bang for the buck is the way to do it. In the neoliberal era, corporations, politicians, and other elites benefited from extraction, but "the people" did not. In Correa's Citizens' Revolution, the revenues from extraction have been more equitably distributed. People can buy into tapping that bag of gold. At this point the benefits of extraction are now going to the country that bears the costs; and for most Ecuadorians, the benefits outweigh the costs. But this varies geographically and those closest to the extraction sites argue the opposite. With Ecuador's new constitution, the people (and largely the people forming the environmental and indigenous movements) have attempted to change the premise of Ecuador's history. *Buen vivir/sumak kawsay* alters the premise and forces the politicians and the people to ask, how can we live richer lives and protect the environment? Acosta underscores the challenge: "One of the most complex tasks is therefore to design and implement a strategy that will lead to a post-extractivist economy."[117]

Buen vivir/sumak kawsay and even sustainable development presume that people should have the right to decide their fates. There should be sovereignty. However, this chapter has underscored the relationship between national sovereignty and sovereignty on a smaller scale, such as bioregion or community. In the case of Ecuador, the constitution allows the state to make such decisions for the nation and the state is less concerned with each bioregion or community.

The treadmill of production model assumes that civil society can influence the state. "Civil society" in the form of environmental NGOs (ecodependents) has largely promoted foreigners' concerns with the environment. "Civil society" in the form of grassroots environmentalists (ecoresisters) has largely promoted the interests of small communities, albeit with an ideology based in *buen vivir* and the good of the nation. In theory, in a democratic country, especially one with universal suffrage, elections are an arguably good measure of "civil society"—the people's will. In Ecuador, the people have repeatedly elected President Correa. They have chosen his form of "development"—which prioritizes the broad distribution of economic gains at the cost of the environment, while also planning for *buen vivir/sumak kawsay*. They have chosen good roads, good schools, good health care, and good talk about the environment. Whether this changes may depend on whether state repression becomes too intense and visible or environmental destruction becomes too widespread. For now, at least, Ecuador is prioritizing the economic and social pillars of sustainability but not the environmental one. Presumably electoral democracy provides a mechanism for altering the calculus. If state repression and manipulation are too powerful, ironically, movements may need to look for transnational partners to shine a light back on Ecuador. In August 2015, uprisings led by CONAIE contesting state policies, especially extractivism, are coinciding with labor strikes, also opposing government policy, and demonstrate that civil society continues to voice the peoples' will. This is the contested nature of *buen vivir.*

8 Hypotheses from Ecuador

From 1978 until 2015 the Ecuadorian environmental movement changed immensely. The movement grew, diversified, struggled, and radicalized. During the same period the state expanded its conception of development beyond simply economic goals to include social and environmental goals too. The impetus for these shifts came from social actors working within Ecuador, but they were heavily influenced by international funders.

The four case studies of a single country over time show how the interplay of transnational funders, civil society, and states affected development paths (what Schnaiberg calls the resolution to the socioenvironmental dialectic). Because there were changes in the strength and emphases of the key actors over time, we can assess which configurations of actors are most likely to produce a balance for the nature–society dialectic: Schnaiberg's ecological synthesis. This is crucial to the future of Ecuador and for the future of the planet and of humanity.

Historical Review

Each period is summarized below with an emphasis on the relationships among the actors—transnational funders, movement actors, the state—and the development outcome. The thematic focus is on (1) the role that transnational funding played in the Ecuadorian environmental movement, (2) how the movement changed over time, and (3) the consequences the movement has had on the state's development trajectory. Table 8.1 provides a comparative summary of the eras.

Era 1: Origins, 1978 to 1987

The international context was critically important to the development of the environmental movement in Ecuador. Economically Ecuador was already tied to global structures through its natural resources; exports of oil,

Table 8.1
Summary of eras

	Origins 1978–1987	Neoliberal boom 1987–2000	Neoliberal bust 2000–2006	Citizens' Revolution 2006–2015
Transnational funding	Seed funds for new organizations and projects	Multiple funders and large amounts of funds for NGOs	Public and private resources dwindle	Limited public funds; private funds directed to the state
Environmental sector	Bifurcated into ecodependent and ecoresistent	Many new ecodependents with ecoimperialists' goals; ecoresisters building support for social-ecological issues	Ecodependents lose influence; ecoresisters gain ground; social issues integrated into agenda	Ecoresisters are vocal and active; ecodependents weakened
State characteristics	Weak, indebted, resource dependent	Weak, indebted, following neoliberal model	Weak, unstable, indebted, resource dependent	Strong, populist, socialist
Environment and development policies	Environmental policies not implemented nor existing ones enforced; export-led development based on petroleum	New environmental ministry and environmental laws; continued resource dependence	Weak institutions and enforcement; continued resource dependence and exploration of new resources to mine	Big alternatives proposed but not executed; new constitution recognizes nature; resource extraction "for the people"
Schnaiberg's synthesis	Economic synthesis	Slight shift toward managed scarcity in laws but not deeds	In practice, state shift back toward economic synthesis and movement shift toward ecological synthesis	Managed scarcity in practice with rhetorical calls for ecological synthesis

bananas, and shrimp; and eventually its debt relationships. The transnational environmental community, which was interested in Ecuador because of its high biodiversity, increased the country's international connections when it reached in to offer environmental aid. As transnational conservationists saw it, Ecuador's natural resources could be sold or they could be protected. Major conservation groups such as The Nature Conservancy and the World Wide Fund for Nature wanted them protected, and they were willing to pay for conservation by funding nongovernmental organizations.

Ecuadorian environmentalists had already created Fundación Natura when transnational funding for the environment became available. While transnational environmentalists influenced Ecuador's environmental movement, they did not create the movement. Ecuador did not need international agents to establish its movement. The nation's universities produced a cadre of scientists concerned about their environment and dedicated to action. They took advantage of the opportunities presented by transnational organizations like USAID to expand their work and grow the movement. As the number of professionals working within Natura grew, they created new organizations, such as EcoCiencia, which specialized in research.

During most of this history the state was weak and limited by the burden of external debt. The environmental movement was able to pass some laws and expand the protected area system. On paper, this provided the appearance of a pro-environmental state; however, the state could not implement its laws. Extractive oil development was largely unregulated and symbolized an economic synthesis, unresponsive to environmental concerns.

Era 2: Neoliberal Boom, 1987 to 2000

Transnational funding for the environment grew during the boom era, exemplified by debt-for-nature swaps. Foreign influence was heightened by the UN Earth Summit in 1992 that focused attention on environment and development. Aspiring nations like Ecuador prepared for, participated in, and used the summit to garner resources. Global governance structures validated local movement actors, and facilitated getting "the environment" on the nation's agenda. Neoliberal agents advanced efforts to fund private actors rather than the state to conduct environmental work.

Two distinct types of environmentalism grew during this period in Ecuador. The first type—the *ambientalistas*—took a path of compromise; the other form—the *ecologistas*—took a path of resistance. In both cases, local actors emerged independently from international interests, but the local and the transnational soon intertwined. *Ambientalistas* connected globally to bilateral aid agencies, such as USAID and to I-NGOs, such as World Wildlife Fund (the groups I call *ecoimperialists*). They became the sponsored organizations that I call *ecodependent*. Like their international counterparts, the *ecodependents* primarily focused on the environmental pillar of sustainability, and when sustainable development became a buzz-word, they expanded to include the economic pillar of sustainability to their portfolio. The strong transnational actor/weak national state combination supported organizations that were project-based and dependent on foreign funds.

The weak national state/extractive economy generated social movement activists that responded to state-permitted transnational corporate destruction. From the start, *ecologistas* connected their analysis to the global political-economy and resisted neoliberal forces while teaching local communities how to resist. These actors that I call *ecoresisters* did not rely on foreign funds. Their vision focused on the environmental and social pillars of sustainable development. Organizations proliferated along these two lines. *Ecodependents* chased the funds of transnational donors, and their agendas shifted over time in line with funders' concerns. *Ecoresisters* organized around local grievances that were specifically tied to the quality of the environment. They mobilized workers and communities against extraction. Transnational funding exacerbated the organic bifurcation of the movement.

With the help of transnational funding, *ecodependents* exerted their political power and created numerous changes in the state, including new institutions dedicated to the environment and national conferences that focused on how to achieve sustainability. Because the state was weak, transnational funders were able to influence it significantly via the *ecodependents*. The *ecoimperialists* focused on conservation and protected areas, and they improved the way the state dealt with those concerns. However, the concerns of *ecoresisters*, which focused on the nature of development, notably the state's neoliberal commitment to resource extraction that generated funds for debt repayments and foreign corporate gain, were largely ignored by the state. Some novel organizational experiments (*ecoentrepreneurs*) were also created at this time to deal with persistent problems. For instance, FONAG was established to address concerns about the water supply in Quito. It was structured not as an NGO, but as a fiduciary trust. Overall, incorporation of some environmental policies into the state's agenda signaled a small move toward a managed scarcity synthesis.

Era 3: Neoliberal Bust, 2000 to 2006

Transnational funding shrank in this period, and in conjunction with that contraction, *ecodependents* lost a symbolic fight against the construction of the OCP pipeline through fragile environments. In the prior era, the power of *ecodependent* groups had risen with transnational resources; in this era, their power fell with the decline in transnational funding. *Ecodependents* were not able to respond independently or collectively to the state's moves to expand the infrastructure for resource extraction. The power of *ecoresisters*, on the other hand, was independent from foreign influence. They could maintain themselves. They waged grassroots, local campaigns against extraction that raised awareness and led communities to seek alternatives to extraction. C-CONDEM fought industrial shrimp farming on the coast, DECOIN battled against foreign copper mining corporations in the Andes, and indigenous groups in conjunction with *Acción Ecológica* sought reparation for the human and environmental damages left by Texaco's petroleum extraction in the Amazon. These efforts taught neighbors how to organize and fight not just one development scheme but others that would come. Affected communities changed how they lived as they sought to create *propia economia* (their own economy) and a set up demonstration projects for agroforestry, ecotourism, sustainable harvesting, and nature-based crafts.

The relative power of environmentalism during this time shifted to the *ecoresisters*. Since the *ecodependents* were literally dependent on the transnational funding that had declined precipitously, they descended while the *ecoresisters* cultivated their power. When this crisis-ridden era climaxed in 2005 and created a political opportunity, *ecoresisters* stepped in to voice their radical stance toward the state's development plans.

Ecoresisters organized and dominated the National Environmental Assembly (Asamblea Nacional Ambiental—ANA). The collective effort, which included the participation of *ecodependents,* resulted in generating a set of themes that would eventually be incorporated into the next government's plans. It also set the stage for these groups to scale up, to create international change through the Yasuní-ITT Initiative, a new mechanism aimed at combating climate change. Though the environmental movement's strongest voices at the time argued for an ecological synthesis, the state's weakness and political instability kept it on a weak managed scarcity trajectory, at best. Its addition of the OCP pipeline, among other actions, suggested a shift back toward an economic synthesis.

Era 4: Citizens' Revolution, 2006 to 2015

With President Correa's election and his subsequent re-elections, Ecuador enjoyed a period of political stability. Elected for the people, explicitly to break with international economic relationships believed to weaken Ecuador, and to forge relationships with other left-leaning states in Latin America, the state's role was strengthened. In its more powerful position, the state committed to lift its people out of poverty. While candidate Correa had championed environmental protection, President Correa's efforts to increase citizens' quality of life was achieved by state-led resource extraction, which was odds with environmental sustainability.

Coinciding with Correa's election, a global recession caused transnational funders to restrict funding for the environment, thus further limiting the influence of *ecodependent* organizations. *Ecoresisters* gained more ground with the incorporation of some of their proposals, such as the Yasuní-ITT proposal, and the rights of nature into the constitution. *Buen vivir/sumak kawsay* became the cornerstone for the state's plan for Ecuador's future. However, the state demonstrated contradictory tendencies—one to protect the environment; the other to drill for oil and extract minerals as its socioeconomic needs demanded. When environmentalists resisted, the state suppressed environmental protest.

Neoliberal capitalism can lead states toward extractive economies, but so can "21st-century socialism." If *sustainable development protects the environment, facilitates economic well-being, and enables people to have the capacity to make their own choices about resource use,* extraction weakens the environmental pillar of sustainability. The advantage of socialism for Ecuador was in the economic pillar: public sector spending rose (from 22 percent of GDP in 2006 to 44 percent in 2013) while rates of poverty and extreme poverty declined (poverty from 37.6 percent in 2006 to 24.5 percent in 2014, and extreme poverty over the same time from 16.9 to 8 percent).[1] While voters continue to elect Correa, activists argue that Correa's edicts have hampered democracy (the social pillar). Ecuadorians debate to what degree this development trajectory is in line with *buen vivir/sumak kawsay*. By the fact that the state had adopted *buen vivir* as its official planning strategy, in word if not deed, this era comes closest to an ecological synthesis.

To sum up, I return to the three country-specific questions asked at the beginning of this book. First, what role has transnational funding played for Ecuador's environmental movement? Transnational funding had an enormous influence on Ecuador's environmental movement. It aided its growth and diversification, and it affected the goals of the movement. It also helped the movement create laws and institutions within the state that mirrored those in the Global North. Prior to funding, environmental organizations had split into two streams: *ambientalistas* and *ecologistas*. Transnational funding supported the ambientalistas whose goals were more aligned with transnational conservationists. The *ecologistas* were not funded. They took a more radical stance toward globalization and the state's development schemes.

Second, how did the movement change over time? The power of the mainstream element (*ambientalistas/ecodependents*) of the movement rose and fell with transnational funding, and movement goals shifted with changes in funding. Like their funders, *ecodependents* prioritized conservation and then sustainable development. In the absence of transnational funding, *ecologistas'/ecoresisters'* goals and strategies triumphed. Their concerns focused on quality of life issues, such as local land use and public health concerns linked to pollution. These groups more closely represented the interests of Ecuadorians.

Third, how has the environmental movement's relationship to transnational funders ultimately affected the state's environment and development policies? The movement has played an important role in Ecuador's environment and development trajectories. When the state was weak, the *ecodependents* positioned themselves to establish internationally normed laws and institutions. Under a stronger state and weaker transnational influence, the *ecoresisters* in conjunction with indigenous groups developed alternative practices and alternative visions that have been incorporated into the nation's constitution and development planning. Despite these changes, the state's logic regarding accumulation continues to dominate Ecuador's approach to the human-environment interface.

Transnational Environmentalism beyond Ecuador

In the first three eras of this history Ecuador was an example of a nation from the Global South that was democratic, weak, indebted, and had homegrown environmental organizations. It is likely that other nations in these circumstances that engage with transnational environmental funding have or will experience similar processes with their environmental movement. Under these conditions transnational actors wield considerable power. The following hypotheses apply to similar nations:

1. Transnational environmental funders (*ecoimperialists*) will target environmental movement organizations (*ecodependents*) rather than states to meet the transnational funders' goals.
2. Environmental movement organizations (*ecodependents*) will affect laws in weak states.
3. Weak states will not have the capacity to effectively implement laws.
4. Environmental movement organizations (*ecodependents*) will manage public environments with transnational (*ecoimperialist)* funding.
5. Environmental movement organizations (*ecodependents*) will compete with each other over funding, thus weakening the movement.
6. Funded (*ecodependents*) and unfunded (*ecoresisters*) environmental organizations will diverge on goals and tactics.
7. The dominant goals of the environmental movement will vary with transnational funding; when transnational funding is high, the goals of *ecoimperialists* will dominate, and when transnational funding is low, the goals of *ecoresisters* will dominate.
8. The development trajectory will remain unchanged as long as transnational funders (*ecoimperialists)* are engaged in the movement.

Some of these predictions potentially contribute to an improved environment, but others counterbalance them. There is no obvious net gain or loss for the environment at the macro level. In the case of Ecuador, transnational funding brought gains (more laws, more land protected) and losses (a piecemeal approach due to internal competition, lack of internal goals setting, maintenance of status quo in the development trajectory).

In the most recent era of this history Ecuador is an example of a nation taking a turn to the left, with an emphasis on populism and socialist redistribution. Many environmental organizations have persisted, though transnational funding has been limited. Other nations like this, including nations in the Pink Tide (Venezuela, Bolivia, Brazil, Argentina, Uruguay), will likely follow similar paths. In this configuration, power is focused in the state. In such circumstances the following hypotheses apply:

1. Strong socialist/populist states will increase resource extraction to fund socioeconomic goals.
2. The moment of radical transition will create an opening for *ecoresisters'* ideas to be incorporated into the new state ideology.
3. Increased resource extraction will lead to increased environmental disruptions.

4. Increased environmental disruptions will lead to increased environmental movement resistance by *ecoresisters*.

5. The state will limit environmental movement activity of both *ecodependents* and *ecoresisters*.

6. The state will make it more difficult for transnational funders (*ecoimperialists*) to affect the environmental movement and the state.

7. *Ecoresisters* will seek transnational networks, not for funding per se but for information sharing and to shine a light on the state's repressive actions.[2]

8. *Ecoresisters* have the potential to shift the state toward an alternative trajectory, but that possibility depends on the degree to which the state limits or empowers them. Without limits, they have the greatest likelihood of alternatives being expressed and enacted.

Transnational Movements beyond Environmentalism

For social movement scholars, the case of Ecuador shows how the international political economic opportunity structure affects states and social movements over time. "Economic" is added to the social movement concept of political opportunity structure in view of the fact that international *economic* conditions contribute to creating political openings.[3] In the neoliberal periods, the state was weakened by the international economic structure due to its debt burden. A weak state enabled transnational movement funders to alter state-level policies via national organizations. Funding streams were a clear way to trace the lines of influence: from transnational funder to national organization to state change. In the process of distributing their resources, transnational actors also altered social movement industries' agendas (making them more like their funders), altered organizations' level of professionalization and their likelihood for survival, and influenced inter-organizational dynamics. In the "post-neoliberal" period, the absence of strong transnational funders coupled with a strong state made it possible for the state to repress social movement actors.

The findings from this case can be used to generate theory by assessing to what degree the transnational processes related to environmentalism apply to other transnational movements, such as labor, human rights, women's rights, indigenous rights, peace, religious, anti-GMO, HIV/AIDs prevention, and anti-globalization movements. Regarding other transnational social movement funders and policy, in general, the following hypotheses can be assessed:

1. Transnational movement funders (movement imperialists) influence policy in weak states by working through national social movement actors (dependents), thus having their goals enacted at the state level.
2. Transnational funders (movement imperialists) bifurcate national social movements and empower the side of the movement that most shares its goals (dependents), while marginalizing more radical goals (resisters).
3. Transnational funders (movement imperialists) create tensions and competition among national groups (dependents) that otherwise might form a more coherent and successful movement.
4. Transnational funders (movement imperialists) are most powerful in nations with weak states.
5. Strong states will limit transnational funders' (movement imperialists) influence.
6. Transnational funders (movement imperialists) are agents of global hegemony and perpetuate the status quo.

Neoliberalism versus the Bolivarian Revolution

For development sociologists the case of Ecuador demonstrates how neoliberalism weakened the state, increased transnational funders' influence on the state, and de-movementized the environmental movement. Neoliberalism perpetuated extractive development/economic synthesis. Neoliberalism mixed with a global ideology of "sustainable development," shifted Ecuador toward managed scarcity. At the turn of the millennium, the regional shift to the left empowered states, weakened transnational funders' influence, radicalized the movement, and expanded the discourse related to "development." When Ecuador retreated from the global hegemony of neoliberalism, the alternative ideologies of *buen vivir/sumak kawsay*/ecological synthesis came to the fore, though the state materially engaged in extractivism. This is the closest Ecuador, or perhaps any state for that matter, had come to an ecological synthesis. While close, though, the country was not balancing what the earth could bear with what humans extracted. The state's words of *buen vivir/sumak kawsay* greenwashed state-led extraction, and at best amounted to a managed scarcity synthesis in practice.

The global political economy affects the strength of states through the forces of trade, aid, and debt. It also structures transnational environmental funding, which affects national movements. Indebted states are more vulnerable to national movements, and because national movements are heavily guided by transnational actors via funding, indebted states are generally more vulnerable to transnational movement desires (ecoimperialism). Weak states with high levels of transnational movement funders are most vulnerable to having their development path dictated by outsiders, and vice versa. Weak states, which neoliberalism produced and reproduced, enabled outside forces to have a strong role in states' development paths.

This flow was broken around the year 2000 when the United States shifted its resources away from Latin America to the Middle East, decreasing both environmental funding and aid. At that same time there were massive protests in Latin America against the Free Trade Area of the Americas (FTAA), which would have extended the North American Free Trade Agreement (NAFTA) to the Americas. Agreement on the FTAA has not been reached, thus thwarting increased economic policy harmonization and financial linkages between North and South America.

Sustained resistance to these economic connections is likely the only way that South American actors can create an "alternative to development," short of the intentions of economic globalization changing radically. On its current trajectory, connections with the Global North propel the Global South toward extractive development/economic synthesis at worst, and a weak form of managed scarcity at best. *Ecodependent* environmentalists are captured by the international funding structure because they are dependent on it. Their relationship to funders is parallel to the way that states are dependent on global actors in relationship to debt, trade, and aid. "Radical," "social" *ecoresister* environmentalists that are independent from the constraints of the financial lure of the Global North are the potential sources of resistance to an extractivist model and can be the proponents of alternatives. Limits to resources "from above" allow actors "from below" to flourish and have a louder voice. Similarly, when states de-link, as Correa has done, they can also act more independently.[4]

What are the implications for this? Essentially, for alternatives to development to take place, there needs to be diversity. The global political economy, if one takes the world polity stance, is hegemonic and homogenizing. As operationalized here, the global political economy makes its influence felt through financial transactions. More global financial transactions (economic globalization) create more homogeneity and more resource extraction. Globalization limits alternative voices. Less economic globalization leads to more difference and makes alternatives to development possible. There are a number of scenarios in which this could take place: with global recession, intentional state isolationism and protectionism, and with the formation of regional alliances, all of which we've seen in this book.

Is Another Ecuador Possible?

Early formulations of the treadmill of production were criticized for not offering mechanisms by which change could occur. However, Schnaiberg (1980) did in fact lay out specific policy changes that could be made to slow the treadmill.[5] He argues that to meet social and ecological goals: "The task is a monumental technical and political one. We must first estimate a biospherically and geopolitically feasible sustainable production level for the society. And then we must decide how to allocate the production options and the fruits of such production. Neither the state nor the market currently perform all these functions in any system—socialist or capitalist."[6] Schnaiberg outlines seven policies that include incentives and taxes to encourage "the *disaccumulation* of physical capital that is committed today to high-energy, low-labor production."[7] The program includes taxes for materials and energy and incentives for employment and recycling. These have the effect of requiring less fossil fuel extracted from the earth and more renewable human labor.

Later formulations of the treadmill incorporate the "global era" and look to global mechanisms for slowing the treadmill.[8] Transnational social movements are considered an important element for movement toward an ecological synthesis. "Because the treadmill of production is a global phenomenon, challenges to this system must also operate globally, while building strength at the local level."[9] This analysis contributes to that assessment by showing that the type of transnational linkages among global movement actors matters. Movements that are tied by resources may actually impede progress toward ecological synthesis, while movements tied by information sharing, such as those in the mangrove network started by C-CONDEM, may help. These South–South information sharing networks are much more like the TANs described by Keck and Sikkink. In Ecuador's case, groups that engaged in South–South networks were decoupled from dominant ideologies and were most likely to slow the treadmill and to make inroads toward ecological synthesis; whereas the organizations that were tied by resources reproduced global power arrangements and ideologies. In addition to the networks discussed in the preceding chapters, others such as the Network for GMO–Free Latin America (RALLT—Red por una América Latina Libre de Transgénicos) show promise in slowing the treadmill. RALLT was formed in 1999 after a workshop in Quito attended by individuals representing civil society organizations around Latin America concerned about the negative effects of GMOs on the region's food sovereignty and the corporate control of food (figure 8.1). [10]

Treadmill theorists have also noted that "the erosion of the Washington Consensus and direct challenges to U.S. hegemony, especially among the states of Latin America" is a process that in conjunction with other

Figure 8.1
Sign hung by activists outside of government ministry offices: "Monsanto Sows Death"

shifts, support the possibility of an alternative development trajectory.[11] Again, the on-the-ground alternatives being developed by ecoresisters like DECOIN and C-CONDEM are essential. Treadmill theorists note that alternative models are "in fact concrete, achievable, and eminently doable. *Defeating* the treadmill may be much more difficult than establishing its *alternatives,* but that alternatives are readily available substantially lowers the social costs and risks associated with its dismantling. It also provides activists and ordinary denizens of the planet with the psychological satisfaction of knowing that the neoliberal model is no longer the 'only game in town.'"[12] This is why the work of C-CONDEM and DECOIN is so important. The efforts by DECOIN and C-CONDEM to create real alternatives to extractive development (including coffee cooperatives and sustainable fish harvests discussed in chapter 6) are examples of efforts occurring in other regions as well.[13] For instance, the Landless Peasant Movement (MST) in Brazil is "imagining an alternative socio-economic and political order through worker-led, worker-run farming cooperatives that sell products to urbanites. MST communities in Brazil are beginning to think about wind-powered settlements, training young people across Latin America in agroecology and alternative forms of medicine."[14] If these experiments are successful, the lessons learned can be shared in South–South networks, and *strut by strut* a new local and then regional economy can be built. Regional affiliations with like-minded countries, such as Bolivia, which shares a similar indigenous worldview, may provide the best route toward *buen vivir.*[15]

As noted throughout the book, there are similar stories in both Venezuela and Bolivia, two key countries that are part of the Latin American Pink Tide that shifted regional politics to the left during the 2000s. In both cases new states promised "21st-century socialism" to create better lives for their citizens. A key difference between these nations is that Venezuela did not promise the protection of nature in conjunction with improving the lot of its people. Bolivia is more like Ecuador on this count. Its indigenous president Evo Morales embraced a form of *buen vivir* (the aymara concept of *suma qamaña*) and Bolivia was the second nation, after Ecuador, to give constitutional rights to nature in 2009.[16] The leftward shift in Venezuela and Bolivia has led to the redistribution of income and bringing up the poorest of the poor.[17] However, it has come at the cost of some plunder of the earth and some suppression of social movement activists. As in Ecuador, their economic growth is based in mineral extraction. While the states' ideologies and distribution of profits have shifted, the material bases of the countries' wealth remain natural resources. In Venezuela, President Chávez at least did not greenwash his people. He built his "21st-century socialism" explicitly on oil revenues. However, Bolivia, like Ecuador, forged a more complicated route, since its ideological changes were linked to indigenous conceptions of balance with nature but its economic means of achieving a higher standard of living relied on resource extraction. Bolivia's experience more closely resembles Ecuador's because of this complication. In Venezuela, the state is criticized for repression of social movement actors who opposed Chávez, and after his death, his party, on broad ideological grounds. In Bolivia, environmental and indigenous social movement actors who once backed Presidents Morales are those who are claiming to be suppressed, which is precisely the case in Ecuador.[18] For instance, activists have been repressed during protests against the construction of a highway through Tipnis, a national park and the ancestral homeland of indigenous groups.[19] A similar controversy is being played out where regional destruction is being traded with national goals.[20] There's also been an eerily similar criticism of and expulsion of social movement organizations that once backed the Morales regime, as occurred in Ecuador.[21] The processes related to the shift away from neoliberalism to "21st-century socialism" in Latin America appear to be similar with regard to states' relationships to extractivism and consequential environmental change and social movement suppression.

For environmental sociologists, Ecuador illustrates the trade-offs inherent in generating sustainable development/ecological synthesis/*buen vivir*. In Ecuador's early environmentalism, the dominant environmentalism was willing to trade off social sustainability for environmental sustainability. In the most recent era, even though the state's proclaimed policies can be interpreted as promoting sustainable development/ecological synthesis/*buen vivir*, such policies serve to greenwash the state's actual practices, which trade off environmental sustainability for economic benefit. Indeed it is unlikely that a "win-win-win" for environmental, economic, and social goals is ever possible.[22] Given that, it is critical that the choices of what are being traded have some relationship to the people that the choices are affecting. In Correa's era, questions of scale became paramount: does the country as a whole decide by means of the elected legislature, or do local communities affected by local actions, such as mining, decide?

Traditional "development" as we have known it has only sped up the treadmill of production. Ecuador's plan for *buen vivir* rewrites the goals for development and offers some hope for an ecological synthesis of the human–nature dynamic, but only if the ecological withdrawals are contained within natural resource limits. Community-led on-the-ground experiments in which ecological withdrawals are in balance with natural regeneration provide some hope. However, scale again is key, and these efforts must be attentive to the costs of scaling up; indeed the benefits of sharing information and knowledge horizontally across regions looks far more sustainable than selling commodities or products outside of the region.

Neoliberalism supported a worldview that was not conducive to ecological synthesis. If there is more ideological and economic diversity in this world, there can be more varied local trials that value forms of *buen vivir* and attempt to sustainably integrate the natural and social systems. This increases the likelihood that some community can find the balance and others can replicate it. Ideally these paths will be chosen by sovereign communities and sovereign states. Links to a "globalized" world can have positive impacts for the environment. However, without a deep analysis of the fundamental contradictions of economic growth—the central driving logic of the treadmill of production—in both capitalist and socialist economies, globalization of economies do more to speed the treadmill. Thus for many nations the degradation caused by a globalized economy outweigh the protection generated by globalized environmental norms.

Figure 8.2
Buen vivir on the coast at Same

At what point will Ecuador's economic development be "enough"? Is there enough *pachamama* (mother nature) for all Ecuadorians to have enough? In part, that will depend on whether their goals are matched with those espoused by the rest of the world or if their goals are more home grown, and like the *ecoresister* said, "Where an ecosystem is alive, where there is life, with a nice beach, sun, good food, good hammock, good home … the people are good…. What more do you want? We are good with this life" (figure 8.2). Not just in Ecuador but around the world, individuals, communities, and governing bodies need to figure out how much we can take from the earth, and at what point we can be satisfied if we want nature and humanity to coexist.

Notes

Chapter 1

1. In 2013 the estimated GDP per capita was $10,600. See p. 5 of *The World Factbook*. Nd. Central Intelligence Agency. Accessed August 10, 2015. https://www.cia.gov/library/publications/the-world-factbook/geos/print/country/countrypdf_ec.pdf.

2. See "'Keeping the Oil in the Soil': Ecuador Seeks Money to Keep Untapped Oil Resources Underground." 2007. Accessed 16 June 2013. http://www.sosyasuni.org/en/index.php?option=com_content&view=article&id=136%3Akeep-the-oil-in-the-soil-ecuador-seeks-money-to-keep-untapped-oil-resources-underground&catid=15%3Acampaign&Itemid=27. See also Martin (2011).

3. See Multi Partner Trust Fund, "Ecuador Yasuní ITT Trust Fund—Fact Sheet." Accessed 30 July 2013. http://mptf.undp.org/yasuni.

4. See the Movimiento Alianza Pais website: http://www.alianzapais.com.ec.

5. See p. 5 of *The World Factbook*. Nd. Central Intelligence Agency. Accessed August 10, 2015. https://www.cia.gov/library/publications/the-world-factbook/geos/print/country/countrypdf_ec.pdf.

6. The decision to drill needed the approval of Congress, which was granted in October 2013.

7. The focus in this work is environmental movements. Organizations in the movement often work in alliance with indigenous groups and other civil society groups, and those key moments are noted throughout. Key works on indigenous movements in Ecuador include Martin (2003), Sawyer (2004), and Becker (2011).

8. World Commission on Environment and Development (1987).

9. I use the terms "sustainability" and "sustainable development" interchangeably.

10. Humphrey, Lewis, and Buttel (2000: 179); for an excellent discussion of the various environmental ideologies of environmental organizations in the United States, see Brulle (2000).

11. For a summary of some of these, see Gould and Lewis (2015).

12. For instance, see McMichael (2010). I use Acosta's (2013b: 62) definition of extractivism: "those activities which remove large quantities of natural resources that are not processed (or processed only to a limited decree), especially for export."

13. Karl (1997); Humphreys, Sachs, and Stiglitz (2007).

14. McMichael (2010).

15. International development agencies have drawn plans for how to extract sustainably, or at least create better outcomes than we've seen in the past. For instance, the United Nations Development Programme (UNDP) argues that the resource curse can be overcome. The UNDP has developed a "Strategy for Supporting Sustainable and Equitable Management of the Extractive Sector for Human Development," in which the negative outcomes of resource extraction "can be tackled through effective strategies, legal frameworks and policies." This program seeks to address the problems of traditional extractive development schemes and lead toward some form of sustainable development. The UN's work is reformist in that it works within current structures to produce better outcomes and overcome the resource curse (United Nations Development Programme 2013a).

16. In general, development strategies have not succeeded in the Global South. Philip McMichael (2010: 1) summarizes some of the consequences:

At a time when the promise of development is increasingly in question, with dwindling social gains, the vision of modernity is losing its certainty. Financial meltdown, arctic thaw, imploding states, diminishing resources, global migrations of economic and environmental refugees, and the resurgence of slavery are a few of the dramatic changes that are now part of the social and natural landscape. By and large, these represent particularly visible and broad reversals in the narrative of progress.

"Development as we know it," McMichael continues, "is measured monetarily, and the vehicle for development is the market." In the traditions of Karl Marx and Karl Polanyi, he argues that we are unable to "imagine alternatives to development as we know it" (p. 3).

Post-development theorists have made similar arguments. In his book *Encountering Development*, Arturo Escobar examines the hegemonic "development discourse" that agents of development spread around the globe, including sustainable development (1995: 192). He argues, "The tasks of articulating alternative productive strategies – autonomous, culturally grounded, and democratic—is difficult. Worldwide, there is no clarity about what those alternatives might look like, even if some general principles have been put forward" (Escobar 1995: 205). *Sumak kawsay/buen vivir* is an articulation of one alternative.

17. National Plan for Good Living (2009), Change of Paradigm: From Development to Good Living. http://plan2009.senplades.gob.ec/web/en/change-of-paradigm. English translation by the Ecuadorian government.

18. National Plan for Good Living (2009), Presentation. http://plan2009.senplades. gob.ec/web/en/presentation.

19. Schnaiberg (1980); Schnaiberg and Gould (1994); Gould, Schnaiberg, and Weinberg (1996); Gould, Pellow, and Schnaiberg (2004, 2008); Pellow (2007).

20. Another way that corporations are classified in the theory are as shareholders: investors and managers. Another way that citizen-workers are classified are as stakeholders: workers and community residents (Gould, Pellow, and Schnaiberg 2004: 297). The 2004 article has perhaps the most succinct explanation of the "treadmill" concept: "The treadmill of production was thus, primarily an economic change theory, but one that had direct implications for natural resource extraction as well as for the opportunity structure for workers. In essence, the 'treadmill' component recognized that the nature of capital investment led to higher and higher levels of demand for natural resources for a given level of social welfare (including wages and social expenditures). Each round of investment weakened the employment situation for production workers and worsened environmental conditions, but it increased profits. For workers, this treadmill implied that increasing investment was needed to employ each production worker. For ecosystems, each level of resource extraction became commodified into new profits and new investments, which led to still more rapid increases in demand for ecosystem elements."

21. In theory, pressure from citizen-workers can force corporations to change practices and policies, but more frequently, corporations make changes based on state regulations.

22. Rodrigues (2004:6–7) outlines the problems of discussing "NGOs," including the myriad of definitions and the overinclusiveness of the definitions. In her work on transnational advocacy organizations, she separates NGOs and grassroots actors along much of the same lines as I have separated NGOs and SMAs. My division also parallels Alvarez's (1999: 185–86) distinction between NGOs and "the movement" (she focuses on the feminist movement), though she also argues that there is a hybrid character to most feminist NGOs.

23. Keck and Sikkink (1998: 2).

24. "This model is more complex and substantially more heterogeneous than the other two. It essentially recognizes that economic activity generates both ecological disorganization, and exchange and social use values. Dialectical tensions between economic growth and ecological protection are most overt in this model" (Schnaiberg 2007: 12). Schnaiberg goes on to explain what this might look like in practice: "State regulation may thus exist through rationing by price, if surcharges

or fines are used, or by direct command-and-control policies, where outright access to resource is controlled or simply prohibited (as in many conservation policies), or through the more recent cap-and-trade marketing of environmental degradation rights." (15).

25. Schnaiberg (2007:17).

26. Gould, Pellow, and Schnaiberg (2004: 305). Researchers have examined the interactions of actors in the treadmill of production to show how different choices lead to different syntheses at smaller scales (e.g., communities) and at moments in time (e.g., Gould, Schnaiberg, and Weinberg 1996).

27. Schnaiberg (1980: 429).

28. Schnaiberg (1980: 440).

29. "Non elite treadmill participants alter the nature of social system–ecosystem interactions through pressuring private capital and/or state decision makers to make more proenvironmental decisions in production processes" (Gould, Pellow, and Schnaiberg 2004: 302).

30. Gould, Pellow, and Schnaiberg (2004: 305).

31. Gould, Pellow, and Schnaiberg (2004: 305–306).

32. Treadmill theorists argue, "Transnationally, the Southern debt crises of the 1980s disabled many alternative development strategies adopted by developing nations. This crushed most treadmill-alternative pilot projects" (Gould, Pellow, and Schnaiberg 2004: 311).

33. Gould, Pellow, and Schnaiberg (2008: ch. 8).

34. Buttel (2003: 335).

35. Buttel (2003: 336).

36. Lewis (1996).

37. It could also have been labor unions, but the labor movement in Ecuador has been small and weak (Corkill and Cubitt 1988: 39).

38. This was a worldwide trend. See Brechin et al. (2003).

39. Lewis (2000).

40. An excellent example is Kathyrn Hochstetler and Margaret E. Keck's (2007) *Greening Brazil.*

41. Some view sponsorship as beneficial to the growth and professionalization of movements (McCarthy and Zald 1977; Walker 1991) while others, critical of the benefits of external support, argue that elites offer assistance as a means to moderate

grassroots efforts (McAdam 1982; Brulle 2000). Other suggests that there is a middle ground: support aids professionalization and success while at the same time narrowing organizations' choices, thus "channeling" them (Jenkins and Eckert 1986; McCarthy, Britt, and Wolfson 1991; Jenkins and Hacli 1999). These researchers have looked primarily to the effects of support from national foundations to local movement actors within national boundaries. This work also contributes to questions of interorganizational competition (Minkoff 2002).

42. A rich literature has expanded the questions of elite sponsorship beyond national borders to addresses the processes and outcomes of transnational movements (e.g., Smith, Chatfield, and Pagnucco 1997; Keck and Sikkink 1998; Waterman 2001; Khagram, Riker, and Sikkink 2002; Smith and Johnson 2002; Bandy and Smith 2005; della Porta and Tarrow 2005; Tarrow 2005; Pellow 2007; Smith 2008). Studies have analyzed aspects of the anti-sweatshop movement (Armbruster-Sandoval 2005), the human and indigenous rights movements (Brysk 1993; Martin 2003), the women's movement (Naples and Desai 2002), and the environmental movement (Wapner 1996; Lewis 2000; Carmin and Hicks 2002; Rodrigues 2003; Hicks 2004; Murphy 2005).

43. The construction of environmental problems must be understood as part of power relationships, especially when resources are being deployed to solve problems. Environmental sociologists and anthropologists have looked at who defines the "environment" and its problems, which can range from local problems such as water and air pollution to global problems such as ozone depletion, deforestation, and climate change. Anthropologists have shown how different conceptions have generated conflicts between groups in the Global North and the Global South (Escobar 1995). Others writing about "green imperialism" and "ecoimperialism" suggest that environmentalists from the Global North, conservationists in particular, have ignored the needs of indigenous people by focusing on the environment that is separate from humans whereas those who rely on nature for their livelihoods see themselves as part of the environment (Guha and Martinez-Alier 1997). The conventional wisdom is that in rich nations environmentalists want to preserve biodiversity for biodiversity's sake and by contrast, in poor nations, environmentalists seek to maintain the environment for the sake of the people whose livelihoods are dependent on it (Humphrey, Lewis, and Buttel 2002). A number of studies compare environmentalists in the Global North and the Global South in terms of patterns of beliefs, interests and strategies (Brechin and Kempton 1994; Guha and Martinez-Alier 1997; Cristen et al. 1998; Redclift and Sage 1998; Pfaff, Barelli, Chaudhuri 2004; Doyle 2005; Dunlap and York 2008). In short, these studies find high levels of concern for environmental quality in both the North and the South though the expression of this concern varies widely.

44. Numerous collections highlight the link between Latin American social movements and the global context. See, for example, Escobar and Alvarez (1992),

Johnston and Almeida (2006), Stahler-Sholk, Vanden, and Kuecker (2008), de la Barra and Dello Buono (2009), and Stahler-Sholk, Vanden, and Becker (2014).

45. See Roberts and Hite (2000); Goldman (2005); McMichael (2012). In the development literature, there are a range of understandings about the benefits of interactions between the Global North and the Global South. Some argue that international interactions create the growth of a "world culture" (Boli and Thomas 1999; Frank, Hironaka and Schofer 2000); on the other end of the spectrum are those who highlight resistance in the Global South to the Global North's neoliberal agenda (e.g., Gedicks 1993; Taylor et al. 1993; Taylor 1995; Collinson 1996; Gedicks 2001; Carruthers 2008).

Chapter 2

1. World Bank. Accessed January 22, 2014. data.worldbank.org/sites/default/files/wdi06.pdf.

2. Ecuador Data Profile and Latin America and Caribbean Data Profile. Accessed August 20, 2015. data.worldbank.org/country/Ecuador.

3. World Bank. Accessed January 22, 2014. http://povertydata.worldbank.org/poverty/region/LAC.

4. United Nations Development Programme. Human Development Report. 2013b. http://hdr.undp.org/sites/default/files/reports/14/hdr2013_en_complete.pdf., pp. 145–55.

5. World Bank, Data, GINI Index. Accessed March 19, 2015. http://data.worldbank.org/indicator/SI.POV.GINI/.

6. World Bank, World DataBank, Poverty and Inequality Database. Accessed March 19, 2015. http://databank.worldbank.org/data.

7. Crude Oil Exports, barrels per day. CIA World Factbook. Accessed March 17, 2014. https://www.cia.gov/redirects/ciaredirect.html?countryname=Brazil&countrycode=br&regionCode=soa&rank=21.

8. Calculated using World Bank data: total external debt stock divided by GDP in current millions.

9. World Factbook. Accessed January 22, 2014. https://www.cia.gov/library/publications/resources/the-world-factbook/index.html.

10. CIA Factbook (2006).

11. Corkill and Cubitt (1988).

12. Freedom House, Freedom in the World 2014. Accessed April 4, 2014. https://freedomhouse.org/report-types/freedom-world#.

13. Manosalvas et al. (2002).

14. California Department of Fish and Game (2003).

15. New York Flora Atlas, New York Flora Association. Accessed on April 4, 2014 at http://newyork.plantatlas.usf.edu.

16. Myers (1988).

17. Mittermeier (1988).

18. Lewis (2014).

19. Myers (1988: 187).

20. Myers (1988: 187).

21. Rudel (1993).

22. Myers (1988: 196).

23. Mittermeier (1988).

24. Mittermeier (1988: 145).

25. Mittermeier (1988: 152).

26. There are 17 megadiverse nations, most in the Americas: Brazil, Colombia, Ecuador, United States, Mexico, Peru, and Venezuela. Five are in Asia: Philippines, India, Indonesia, Malaysia, and China. Three are in Africa: Madagascar, Democratic Republic of the Congo, and South Africa. Oceania has two: Australia and Papua New Guinea. Accessed April 10, 2014. http://www.biodiversitya-z.org/content/megadiverse-countries. Ecuador's funding structures differ considerably from the countries in the Global North on this list, and likewise from those large countries with large economies, such as Brazil, Mexico, India, and China. It is more like Colombia, Peru, Venezuela, Madagascar, Congo, and Papua New Guinea in terms of its relative power and resources.

27. McNeely (1991).

28. Brooks et al. (2006: 58–61).

29. Conservation International (2011).

30. Abramovitz (1994).

31. This study also ranked ten countries according to total aid received over the same period. Ecuador was not on this list. Presumably this is because it is a small country and the figures were in total aid received, not per capita aid. The list included a number of large countries: India, Brazil, China, Mexico, and Indonesia (Miller, Agrawal, and Roberts 2012).

32. Castro et al. (2000). Hicks et al. (2008) analyzed 1,267 biodiversity projects funded from 1980 to 1999 globally and found that a total of $2.35 billion was allocated for such projects. A conservative estimate that uses just the 1990 to 1997 funding total for Ecuador ($96 million), shows that though Ecuador's total land area is just 0.02 percent of the total world land area, it received (at least) 4 percent of biodiversity funding for that period.

33. Compared to other environmental problems, such as water pollution, the cost of protecting biodiversity is relatively low: "the estimated cost in Agenda 21 of global biodiversity conservation seems low: roughly $1.75 billion annually from the international community.... By contrast ... measure to reduce carbon emissions ... were estimated in Agenda 21 to require $20 billion annually (in 1993 dollars) in foreign assistance" (Hicks et al. 2008: 47–48).

34. The nations that have had high levels of biodiversity funding from abroad over the period of interest include Costa Rica, Mexico, Brazil, Madagascar, and Kenya. Others on the high end include India, China, Indonesia, Colombia, Philippines, and Tanzania. Many of these are large, which explains their high level of assistance (Miller, Agrawal, and Roberts 2013).

35. Gould (1999) argues that until ecotourism dollars can match resource extraction revenues that ecotourism will not be a viable option for development.

36. See various years of the CIA Factbook for Ecuador: https://www.cia.gov/library/publications/the-world-factbook/geos/ec.html.

37. 2013 OPEC Annual Statistical Bulletin. Table 3-6 Daily crude oil production (average) in OPEC members (1,000 b). Accessed November 15, 2013. http://www.opec.org/opec_web/static_files_project/media/downloads/publications/ASB2013.pdf.

38. US Energy Information Administration. 2014. "Ecuador."

39. US Energy Information Administration. 2014. "Ecuador."

40. Calculations based on 2013 *OPEC Annual Statistical Bulletin*. Table 3-6 Daily crude oil production (average) in OPEC members (1,000 b). Accessed November 15, 2013.

41. Banco Central del Ecuador. 2013. Boletín Anuario 35. 3.2.2 Export. Accessed on March 23, 2014. http://www.bce.fin.ec.

42. Food and Agriculture Organization of the United Nations (2014).

43. World Tourism Organization (2013).

44. "Ecuador designated 2015 as the year of touristic quality" (March 31, 2015). Accessed at http://www.andes.info.ec/en/news/ecuador-designated-2015-year-touristic-quality.html.

45. Jochnick et al. (1994: 16).

46. Quoted in Anderson (1990: 35).

47. Anderson (1990: 36).

48. Anderson (1990: 38).

49. For popular accounts written for a general public about the early period of drilling, see Judith Kimerling (1991), *Amazon Crude*. Natural Resources Defense Council and Joe Kane's 1995 *Savages*. For a later documentary, see Crude (2009).

50. Fundación Natura (1991: 31–32).

51. Jiménez (1994: 44).

52. Rudel (1993).

53. Fundación Natura (1993: 44).

54. Jochnick et al. (1994: 15).

55. Hey and Klak (1999).

56. Escribano (2012).

57. http://www.eia.gov/beta/international/?fips=ec. Accessed March 28, 2014.

58. Escribano (2012) and Widener (2011: 272).

59. Schneyer and Medina Mora Perez (2013).

60. Ecuador is not unique in its strategy. For instance, this is also true in the US–Alaskan wilderness areas where the United States continues to consider oil exploration and extraction (Lewis 1996).

61. ITTO (2011: 301).

62. ITTO (2011: 299).

63. Little Green Data Book, World Bank (2006). For 2012 data, Little Green Data Book (2013). https://openknowledge.worldbank.org/bitstream/handle/10986/14396/9780821398142.pdf.

64. World Bank (2004).

65. The Little Green Data Book (2013). https://openknowledge.worldbank.org/bitstream/handle/10986/14396/9780821398142.pdf.

66. The Little Green Data Book (2013). https://openknowledge.worldbank.org/bitstream/handle/10986/14396/9780821398142.pdf.

67. Southgate et al. (1995).

68. Little Green Data Book (2013). https://openknowledge.worldbank.org/bitstream/handle/10986/14396/9780821398142.pdf.

Chapter 3

1. This typology builds on my prior analysis (Lewis 2011a).

2. Brulle (2000).

3. Dowie (1995: 115). R. C. Mitchell et al. (1992) also look to organizations' budgets and to their numbers of paying members.

4. Other ways environmental organizations can be classified is by the origins of their grievances, ideology, constituency, their size, budget and other resource amounts, degree of influence, issue area, geographic focus, mission, goals, tactics and strategies, type of staff, and survival/longevity.

5. See Gedicks (1993, 2001); Taylor (1995); Collinson (1996).

6. See Brechin and Kempton (1994); Guha and Martinez (1997); Redclift and Sage (1998); Doyle (2005).

7. To give a sense of the prevalence of such organizations in a moment of time, in an online organizational survey of environmental groups in Ecuador that I conducted (the 2007 Ecuadorian Environmental Organization Survey), 15 percent identified as "international NGOs" (ecoimperialist) and 54 percent identified as national-level NGOs (the others were "local" or "other"). Over three-quarters of the responding groups received funding through donors. The most commons sources of funding were foreign sources (foundations, international NGOs, and foreign governments). Fifty percent of responding groups received at least half of their funding from foreign sources, including foreign foundations, international NGOs, and foreign governments. Of the population of 176 organizations, 45 percent responded to the survey ($n = 80$). The sampling frame excluded a number of social movement actors (in particular, if they did not have an email address or any web presence). Thus these percentages likely overestimate the percentage of environmental organizations that received foreign funding. In terms of organizations' budgets, at the top, more than 10 percent of organizations had budgets of US$1 million and just under 10 percent of the groups had budgets of zero. Ninety percent of the organizations working on environmental issues in Ecuador believe that international funding is "somewhat" to "very important" in resolving the environmental problems that they are working on."

8. The Nature Conservancy, "Our History." Accessed April 15, 2014. http://www.nature.org/about-us/vision-mission/history/.

9. "Parks in Peril: History." Accessed April 15, 2014. http://expomaquinarias.com/aboutus/history/index.html.

10. "Parks in Peril: About Us." Accessed April 15, 2014. http://expomaquinarias. com/aboutus/index.html. During the last phase of the program, a novel approach to watershed management was developed in the Condor Bioreserve, and launched an ecoentrepreneur organization, FONAG, that was also successful and used as a model for watershed management in the region.

11. Fundación Natura (nd, c. 1993). "Proyectos en Marcha: Areas Protegidas."

12. Lewis (2011b: 321).

13. UN-REDD Programme. Accessed April 14, 2014. http://www.un-redd.org/ aboutredd/tabid/102614/default.aspx.

14. There are organizations that fall in the middle of the types. The ideal types are conceptual. For example, there are mission-driven actors that use a combination of local and international resources to meet their goals. Fundación Maquipucuna is a good example of such a group. Their goal is to preserve lands for animal habitats; they have purchased lands in the sierra, garnered resources from abroad, and sought to generate local funds through ecotourism. They are a combination of types, as are other organizations.

15. The dynamics at play among the types of environmentalists in Ecuador can be seen in other contexts, as well, such as the domestic US movement, and the relationship among foundations, "Big 10" groups, and environmental justice groups.

Chapter 4

1. An earlier group—Sociedad Ecuatoriana Francisco Campo de Amigos de la Naturaleza—appears to have been founded in Quito 1975, but must have folded. They were identified by CEDENMA in the 1995 opening speech to the *II Congreso,* and they published a *Lista de Aves de Ecuador* (list of birds of Ecuador) in 1975.

2. Interview NGO 22 (2007).

3. Interview NGO 22 (2007).

4. Teodoro Bustamante cited in Tamayo, Eduardo. 1996. "La Riqueza de la Diversidad," p. 2. Author's translation.

5. Interview NGO 22 (2007).

6. USAID (1993).

7. Acción Ecológica. "Historia." Accessed April 30, 2014. http://www .accionecologica.org/iquienes-somos/nuestra-historia/140-historia.

8. Tamayo (1996: 2).

9. Esperanza Martínez cited in Tamayo (1996: 3). Author's translation.

10. Acción Ecológica. "Petroléo." Accessed April 30, 2014. http://www.accionecologica.org/petroleo.

11. This contrast between environmentalists and social ecologists is apparent in other nations' movements, too.

12. Interview NGO 28 (2007).

13. Interview NGO 22 (2007).

14. Cited in Tamayo (1996: 5).

15. Cited in Tamayo (1996: 5).

16. Varea et al. (1993). Author's translation.

17. CEDENMA (1995a: 5).

18. CEDENMA (1995a: 7–8).

19. CEDENMA (1995b: 4).

20. Esperanza Martínez cited in Tamayo (1996:3). Author's translation.

21. WWF (2003).

22. Lewis (1996).

23. WWF (2003).

24. For examples, see Mahony (1992); Jakobeit (1996); Lewis (2000); Didia (2001).

25. Corkill and Cubitt (1988).

26. Larrea and North (1997: 925).

27. For elsewhere in Latin America, see Hipsher (1998); Sawyer (2004); Johnston and Almeida (2006); Sholk, Vanden, and Kueker (2008).

28. Larrea and North (1997: 920–21).

29. Corkill and Cubitt (1988: 58).

30. EIU (1993: 36–37).

31. Corkill and Cubitt (1988: 52).

32. Corkill and Cubitt (1988: 80).

33. Hey and Klak (2002).

34. Hey and Klak (1993).

35. Corkill and Cubitt (1988: 52).

36. Corkill and Cubitt (1988: 78).

37. Hey (1993: 544).

38. Hey (1993: 553–54).

39. Corkill and Cubitt (1988: 2, 77).

40. Corkill and Cubitt (1988: 84).

41. Corkill and Cubitt (1988: 95).

42. Cardoso and Faletto (1979).

43. Sawyer (2004: 15).

44. Political opportunity structure (POS) is a core concept in this work that helps explain the conditions under which social movement actors mobilize forces and influence their targets. The basic argument is that it is necessary to understand the political conditions that a social movement faces to determine if it will mobilize and if it will succeed. Studies using this rubric have looked to how elements of the POS, such as degree of political openness, level of political stability, existence of alliances, and degree of elite divisions, have correlated with social movement emergence and outcomes at the national level (e.g., see Kitschelt 1986). Doug McAdam has noted, "Social movement scholars have, to date, grossly undervalued the impact of global political and economic processes in structuring the domestic possibility for successful collective action" (1996: 36). David Pellow's work (2007) on the transnational toxics movement suggest that economic conditions are an important element to understanding transnational social movements' entry into national struggles, which is in line with this analysis.

45. CEDENMA (1995a: 5).

46. CEDENMA (1995a: 5).

47. Walton and Ragin (1990).

48. Polít cited in Tamayo (1996: 4).

Chapter 5

1. See https://www.iucn.org/about/union/secretariat/offices/iucnmed/iucn_med _programme/species/invasive_species/.

2. See http://www.necis.net/intro-to-invasive-species/what-we-know/.

3. WCED (1987: 43).

4. WRI (1994).

5. United Nations (1992).

6. Interview NGO 28 (2007).

7. CAAM also received support from the World Bank, Inter-American Development Bank, the European Commission, the UNDP, GEF, the Netherlands, Belgium, and Germany. Over 18 months, it received almost $32 million. (CAAM 1995: 22–23).

8. CAAM (nd).

9. Myers (1988).

10. CNN (1998), Ecuador Oks protections for Galapagos Islands. Accessed July 7, 2014. http://www.cnn.com/EARTH/9803/12/galapagos/.

11. Interview CEDENMA (1995).

12. Interview GTZ (1995).

13. Interview CECIA (1995).

14. World Bank (1994).

15. USAID (1994: 1).

16. USAID (1994: 3).

17. USAID (1994: 117).

18. USAID (1994).

19. Interviews Bi/Multilateral Donor 3 & 4 (2007).

20. Interview Bi/Multilateral Donor 3 (2007).

21. USAID (2003: 33–34).

22. Interview CEDENMA (1995).

23. Interview NGO 16 (2007).

24. Interview NGO 22 (2007).

25. Ecuadorian Environmental Organization Survey (2007).

26. Interview NGO 17 (2006).

27. Interview Peace Corp (1995).

28. Interview USAID (1995).

29. Interview NGO (2007).

30. Interview INGO (2007).

31. Interview NGO (2007).

32. Interview NGO (2007).

33. Interview NGO (2007).

34. Interview NGO (2007).

35. Interview former NGO/government (2007).

36. Interview former NGO/government (2007).

37. Bräutigam and Segarra (2007: 171), in an analysis of NGOs in general in Ecuador (not just environmental ones), found, "[I]mprovements in the level of professionalism among NGOs (in particular) were conducive to helping partnerships form. This shared professionalism may have made NGOs better and more feasible partners for the 'social technocrats' in the government. Many of the people interviewed during this research had moved from NGOs to government or from either to donor agencies, and thus had retained their contacts and legitimacy among their former colleagues." Thus the professionalization provided legitimacy for working with government agencies. It also created a connection that would later play out in personnel changes within the government in the environmental sector.

38. Interview NGO (2007).

39. Interview INGO (2007).

40. Interview NGO (2007).

41. Interview Bi/Multilateral Donor (2007).

42. Interview Bi/Multilateral Donor (2007).

43. Interview Bi/Multilateral Donor (2007).

44. Interview NGO (2007).

45. Interview NGO (2007).

46. Interview NGO (2007).

47. Zald and Ash (1966: 327); see also Staggenborg (1988).

48. I have written about this elsewhere: Lewis (2003, 2011b).

49. However, when asked in open-ended questions what the most severe problems faced by the country, "environmental problems" ranked sixteenth out of twenty-four types of responses given, with just 0.3 percent of the responses. The top response was economic problems (44 percent) followed by poverty (13 percent)

and unemployment (12 percent). When asked the same question regarding their municipality, "lack of environmental care" ranked ten out of fifteen, receiving 1.8 percent of the responses, with bad administration (15 percent), road maintenance (14 percent), and lack of security, delinquency (13 percent) in the top positions. The open-ended question suggests that though people are concerned, economic priorities outweigh environmental ones (Seligson 2003).

50. Southgate et al. (1995).

51. Guha (2000). It is also worth noting that many Ecuadorians express a view of humans in nature, rather than as separate from nature, especially indigenous communities.

52. Interview INGO 12 (2007).

53. Interview INGO 11 (2007).

54. Interview NGO 19 (2007).

55. Interview INGO (2007).

56. In 2007 TNC continued to be very clear about its goals, which included eight clearly articulated strategies for South America, including working to consolidate the National Protected Area Systems and working with indigenous in the Amazon to create a network of indigenous territories.

57. Interview INGO (2007).

58. Interview Bi/Multilateral Donor 4 (2007).

59. Interview INGO (2007).

60. Interview INGO (2007).

61. Interview INGO (2007).

62. Interview INGO (2007).

63. Interview Bi/Multilateral Donor 1 (2007).

64. Interview NGO 18 (2007).

65. Interview NGO 16 (2007).

66. Interview NGO 21 (2007).

67. Ecuadorian Environmental Organization Survey (2007).

68. It may also be that these issues are not framed as "environmental." This was certainly true in urban sanitation movement in US cities. Though today we might consider such activities as part of the environmental justice movement, they weren't labeled as such in the early 1900s (see Taylor 2009). Some interna-

tional funding for urban issues had moved through multilateral banks to work with government on large capital, infrastructure projects, such as sewers. The banks do not hire NGOs to do this work; they hire international consultants to build these projects. These are public projects that borrow internationally and hire internationally.

69. Selig (2001).

70. Lewis (2011).

71. Interview NGO 14 (2007).

72. Interview NGO (2007). In addition to the dearth of international funding for urban issues, there are a few other reasons that urban issues are not addressed. One is that in the educational system the "environment" is considered to be *bosques* (forests) that are "out there" in "nature." This separation of "nature" from "humans" is more evident in the cities than in the countryside. Many of the indigenous who live in the Amazon are very much one with nature. I am reminded of a colleague's (Chuck Bergman's) photo taken in the Amazon region of a boy with parrots around his neck—what he called a living necklace. However, city residents differ. They have expressed a concept of nature "over there" and people "here in the city."

73. Interview NGO 17 (2007).

74. Ecuadorian Environmental Organization Survey (2007).

75. Social movement theorists would call this cognitive liberation.

76. Ecuadorian Environmental Organization Survey (2007).

77. In 1987 Unesco named Yasuní a Biosphere Reserve.

78. Interview CEDENMA (1995).

79. CETUR (nd: 35, 39).

80. Gould and Lewis (2015).

81. USAID (2010).

82. Smith (1995).

83. Alvarez (1999); see also Alvarez (1998, 2009) and Díez (2008).

84. Interview MAG (1995).

85. Lewis (2000).

86. Interview Bi/Multilateral Donor (1995).

87. Lewis (2000).

88. Hey and Klak (1999: 67).

89. McMichael (2008: 341).

90. Kauneckis and Andersson (2009).

91. Keese and Argudo (2006: 114).

92. The effectiveness of this approach has been mixed. See Willis et al. (1999); Faust et al. (2008); Kauneckis and Andersson (2009).

93. Derber (2000).

94. Regarding the World Bank, see Bräutigam and Segarra (2007).

95. Bräutigam and Segarra (2007: 149). One of the reasons that the World Band tried to incorporate NGOs was because in the 1980s, the Bank had been the target of a campaign by international environmental NGOs over environmental and humanitarian damages of some of the Bank's large projects in Brazil and India. As a result they created an NGO-Bank committee.

96. Keese and Argudo (2006).

97. These processes were informally promoted in this era and codified in projects in the next era; see Faust et al. (2008).

98. USAID (2006).

99. Keese and Argudo (2006: 117).

100. Andolina (2003).

101. Hey and Klak (1999).

102. See, for example, Sawers (2005).

103. McMichael defines the Washington Consensus as "a set of neoliberal economic policies (trade and financial liberalization, privatization, and macro-stability of the world economy) uniting multilaterial institutions, representatives of the US state, and associated G-7 countries that enable corporate globalization" (2012: 346). Gould et al. (2008: 105) note: "The so-called Washington Consensus among global economic elites is that neoliberal globalization benefits everyone and represents the only viable global development trajectory."

104. Hey and Klak (1999: 84).

105. Ironically, the "dependency theory" perspective, which originated in Latin America, and argues that economically dependent states essentially surrender power to stronger states that hold the purse strings, was lost in this discussion. Hey and Klak point out this paradox: "Whereas the dependency theory ... held that Latin America was structurally disadvantaged in its trade relationship with the United

States, the new [neoliberal] viewpoint calls for higher levels of trade with the United States" (Hey and Klak: 1999: 84).

106. "Ecuador Set to Leave OPEC." 9/18/92. *New York Times*. Accessed July 1, 2014. http://www.nytimes.com/1992/09/18/business/ecuador-set-to-leave-opec.html.

107. Hey and Klak (1999: 79).

108. Keese and Argudo (2006: 115).

109. Keese and Argudo (2006: 124).

110. Alvarez (1999: 183); Petras (1997); Díez (2008).

111. McAdam (1982).

112. McCarthy, Britt, and Wolfson (1991); Jenkins and Eckert (1986); Jenkins and Halcli (1999).

113. Petras (1997).

114. See Alvarez (1999).

115. Bräutigam and Segarra (2007: 145).

116. Lewis (2000). Transnational corporations also took the tact of working with NGOs as a means of addressing corporate social responsibility, and in meeting the social and environmental goals of sustainable development. For instance, in oil extraction in the Amazon, "Indigenous peoples, already increasingly exposed to the unfamiliar logic of transnational extractive industries ... are now faced with a new challenge: they are expected to become 'stakeholders' asked by the 'private sector' to take part in sustainable economic development" (Rival 1997: 1).

117. Alvarez (1999: 181). An early analysis of environmental NGOs in Ecuador by Meyer (1993) highlights some of these themes.

118. Interview NGO 16 (2007).

119. Interview NGO 22 (2007).

120. Interview INGO 11 (2007).

121. CEDENMA (1995a).

122. Interview INGO 11 (2007).

123. Interview NGO 27 (2007).

124. Interview former NGO/government 33 (2006).

125. Interview NGO (2006).

126. The same question, asked of the municipal government and the central government, yielded similar results, with the municipal government appearing to

do the most (14 percent "a lot," 56 percent "a little," 30 percent nothing) and the central government the least (6 percent "a lot," 54 percent "a little," 39 percent nothing) (Seligson 2001).

127. Interview 17, 2006.

128. James Petras (1997) has argued that this happens across sectors with the rise of neoliberalism and NGOs: "The net effect is a proliferation of NGOs that fragment poor communities into sectoral and sub-sectoral groupings unable to see the larger social picture that afflicts them and even less able to unite in struggle against the system."

129. Interview Bi/Multilateral Donor 1 (2007).

130. Interview Bi/Multilateral Donor 3 (2007).

131. Interview Bi/Multilateral Donor 1 (2007).

132. Interview Bi/Multilateral Donor 1 (2007).

133. President Correa later expelled a Sea Shepherd member who pointed out that fishermen were breaking the law regarding shark fins. Correa eventually reversed his decision because the Sea Shepherd member was married to an Ecuadorian. With the Correa administration, the state had also incorporated an anti-foreign environmental stance.

134. "Movimiento Ambientalista" (2007: 7). Accessed online. Author's translation.

135. CEDENMA (1995a: 13).

136. CEDENMA (1995a: 23).

137. Acción Ecológica website: http://www.accionecologica.org/iquienes-somos/nuestros-lineamientos/475-lineamientos-ecologia-sustentable. Accessed February 2, 2007.

138. Andolino (2003).

139. Andolino (2003: 739) notes that in November 1997, Pachakutik won 10 percent of the seats and was the third largest group in Ecuador's official constitutional assembly. A January 1999 newspaper poll ranked "CONAIE to be the third most trusted institution in Ecuador."

140. Rochlin (2011: 22).

141. Rochlin (2011: 22).

142. See https://www.iucn.org/about/union/secretariat/offices/iucnmed/iucn_med_programme/species/invasive_species/.

143. Interview NGO 17 (2007).

Chapter 6

1. See, for example, Frank, Hironaka, and Schofer (2000).

2. Interview NGO 15 (2007).

3. Interview NGO 16 (2007).

4. Interview NGO 15 (2007).

5. Interview NGO 15 (2007).

6. Widener (2011).

7. Interview INGO 12 (2007).

8. Interview NGO 21 (2007).

9. Interview NGO 21 (2007).

10. Interview NGO (2007).

11. Widener (2011: 67).

12. Widener (2011: 105).

13. Interview INGO 13 (2007).

14. Finer et al. (2009: 12).

15. Arsel (2012: 159).

16. Interview NGO 19 (2007).

17. Interview NGO 17 (2007).

18. Interview NGO 19 (2007).

19. Interview NGO 14 (2007). This was also noted of other bilateral programs. When funding ended, so did the practice: "For instance, the USAID/EDNAT program, when the funding for education was over, that's it. The program stopped" (Interview former NGO/government 33, 2007). There was no "sustainability."

20. Interview Bi/Multilateral Donor 9 (2007).

21. Interview NGO 27 (2007).

22. Interview INGO 10 (2007).

23. Interview former NGO/government 33 (2007).

24. The population consists of organizations with offices in Ecuador working on environmental issues with valid e-mail addresses; see Lewis (2011b).

25. Keese and Argudo (2006: 125) found projects to be unsustainable: "In terms of sustainability, past experience in the study region demonstrated that the local people rarely took ownership of NGO projects. The ideas, and frequently the funds, originated from the NGOs. The beneficiaries generally accepted the projects because they did not want to lose the financing. However, once the assistance stopped, project work usually stopped as well."

26. Pfeffer and Salancik (1978).

27. Interview NGO 17 (2007).

28. Interview NGO 27 (2007).

29. Interview NGO 17 (2007).

30. Interview NGO 19 (2007).

31. Interview NGO 17 (2007).

32. Interview NGO 26 (2007).

33. Interview NGO 17 (2007).

34. Interview NGO 27 (2007).

35. Interview INGO 13 (2007).

36. Interview NGO 21 (2007).

37. Interview INGO (2007).

38. Interview INGO 11 (2007).

39. Interview former NGO/government 33 (2007).

40. Interview Bi/Multilateral Donor 2 (2007).

41. Interview NGO 19 (2007).

42. Interview Bi/Multilateral Donor 4 (2007).

43. Interview NGO 15 (2007).

44. Interview NGO 18 (2007).

45. Interview INGO 11 (2007).

46. Interview NGO 22 (2007).

47. Ecuadorian Environmental Organizational Survey (2007).

48. Interview NGO 18 (2007).

49. Interview INGO 11 (2007).

50. Interview INGO 11 (2007).

51. Interview INGO 13 (2007).

52. Interview NGO (2007).

53. Interview Bi/Multilateral Donor (2007).

54. Interview NGO 17 (2007).

55. Interview INGO 13 (2007).

56. Interview INGO 12 (2007).

57. Interview NGO 16 (2007).

58. Interview Bi/Multilateral Donor 5 (2007).

59. Interview NGO (2007).

60. Interview INGO (2007).

61. Interview 12 INGO (2007).

62. Interview 15 NGO (2007).

63. Interview 12 INGO (2007).

64. Interview INGO (2007).

65. Interview NGO 15 (2007).

66. Interview NGO (2006).

67. Fundación Maquipucuna (nd.b). "Proyectos y Logros," p. 1.

68. Interview NGO (2007).

69. Interview NGO (2007).

70. Fundación Maquipucuna (nd.c). "Institutional CV."

71. Fundación Maquipucuna (nd.a.). "Maquipucuna, de la mano con la conservación."

72. Interview NGO 26 (2007).

73. Interview INGO 11 (2007).

74. Interview INGO 13 (2007).

75. Varea et al. (1997).

76. Interview INGO 11 (2007).

77. Interview INGO 11 (2007).

78. Interview NGO (2007).

79. Interview NGO (2007).

80. Similar comments are made among US environmentalists, with mainstream groups calling the Sea Shepherds and Earth First! both radical and necessary.

81. Interview NGO 18 (2007).

82. Interview INGO 12 (2007).

83. Interview Bi/Multilateral Donor 2 (2007).

84. Interview NGO 26 (2007).

85. Ecuadorian Environmental Organizational Survey (2007).

86. Interview NGO (2007).

87. Interview NGO 23 (2007).

88. Ecuadorian Environmental Organizational Survey (2007).

89. Interview NGO (2007).

90. Bebbington et al. (2008a).

91. See http://www.theguardian.com/science/2013/aug/15/teddy-bear-olinguito-ecuador-carnivore.Accessed on November 5, 2014.

92. Interview SMA 41 (2013).

93. Interview SMA 41 (2013).

94. Interview SMA 41 (2013).

95. Interview SMA 41 (2013).

96. Cited in Kuecker (2007: 96).

97. This chronology of events relies heavily on Carlos Zorrilla's presentation at Brooklyn College, "Clash of Visions and Intag's Resistance to Extractivism," September 2013 and the documentary *Under Rich Earth*.

98. Interview SMA 41 (2013).

99. Interview SMA 41 (2013).

100. Interview SMA 41 (2013).

101. Interview SMA 41 (2013).

102. Interview SMA 41 (2013).

103. Beitl (2012: 94).

104. Beitl (2012: 98).

105. CLIRSEN-PMRC (2007).

106. Acción Ecológica (1996).

107. Interview SMA 42 (2013).

108. See http://www.ccondem.org.ec/tempccon.php?c=43. Accessed on October 27, 2011.

109. Interview SMA 42 (2013).

110. For information on REDMANGLAR, see "Acerca de Nosotros." http://redmanglar.org/sitio/index.php?option=com_content&view=article&id=46&Ite mid=27. Accessed on October 27, 2014.

111. Interview SMA 42 (2013).

112. Martínez (2000: 113). This view resonates with Ramachanda Guha's observation that in the North, environmentalists are concerned with other species, while in the South, the concern begins with the human species.

113. Martínez (2000: 111).

114. Bebbington et al. (2008a: 15).

115. Bebbington et al. (2008b: 2891).

116. Earlier groups were also founded as a response to perceived crisis. For example, Fundación Arcoiris, located in the southern province of Loja, was founded in 1990 to address issues around mining and the protection of Podocarpus National Park. Arcoiris responded to small-scale gold miners, whereas the two examples here were in response to the state's development approach encroaching on their lands.

117. Conahan (2008).

118. ANA (2008).

119. Ecuadorian Environmental Organizational Survey (2007).

120. Interview NGO 23 (2007).

121. Interview NGO 20 (2007).

122. Declaratoria de la Asamblea Nacional de Ambiental (2005).

123. This was not altogether new. In the 1990s the sustainable development trend coupled environment and development themes. Human rights themes (in Ecuador played out in indigenous movements) had already started coming together with the environmental theme (e.g., see Brysk 1996). As was noted in the survey, it was also related to shifting funding streams: "In light of the reduction of funds for development, development NGOs have converted into environmental NGOs."

124. Interview INGO (2007).

125. Lewis (2011a).

126. Interview Ecoentrepreneur 36 (2013).

127. El FONAG en Cifras (nd).

128. Interview Ecoentrepreneur 36 (2013).

129. Kaufmann (2014: 48).

130. Vida Para Quito website, translated, accessed December 2008 at vidaparaquito. com. This website is no longer available.

131. These data were accessed in 2008 online, but are no longer accessible.

132. I had difficulty ascertaining what actually happened with this organization. The best that I can tell, the city chose to continue the duties of the group, but under the larger city umbrella. Some environmentalists that I interviewed believed this was positive because the city was taking on the tasks of environmental protection for the people.

Chapter 7

1. In 2009, Correa won 52 percent of the popular vote; in 2013, he won 57 percent, suggesting what was clear on the ground: there was widespread support for his presidency. In 2013, his party also won 100 of the 131 seats in the national assembly (some argue that new voting rules rigged the election to favor the ruling party). De la Torre notes of this political period: "When Rafael Correa won his third presidential election with a commanding 57 percent of the vote on 17 February 2013, Ecuador went from being a country that seemingly could not keep a chief executive in office—there had been no fewer than seven of them during the decade before Correa's first win in 2006—to being one with a stable president" (2013: 33).

2. "... Twenty-first-century socialism claims to build on the mistakes of both neoliberalism and twentieth-century socialism, seeking to increase state regulation and power, but in a democratic manner that allocates resources more efficiently and does not stifle innovation or personal choice .... Unlike Marxism–Leninism, then, twenty-first-century socialism does not completely reject capitalism; instead, this new model rejects market policies imposed by any foreign source, seeking instead to incorporate capitalism within a humanitarian rubric. To that end, the state also assumes control over critical natural resources, and redistributes the revenue" (Kennemore and Weeks 2011: 267–68).

3. "[W]e understand it [post-neoliberalism] to embody a different conceptualization of the state from that which reigned in the high period of neoliberalism, based on a view that states have a moral responsibility to respect and deliver the inalienable (that is, not market-dependent) rights of their citizens, alongside growth ... [and] ... Postneoliberalism is, then, an evolving attempt to develop political economies that are attuned to the social responsibilities of the state whilst remaining responsive to the demands of 'positioning' national economies in a rapidly changing global political economy" (Grugel and Riggirozzi 2012: 3–4).

4. "By post-development, I mean the opening of a social space where these premises [of the development discourse] can be challenged, as some social movements are doing" (Escobar 2010: 20).

5. "By neo-developmentalism I mean forms of development, understanding, and practice that do not question the fundamental premises of the development discourse of the last five decades, even if introducing a series of important changes" (Escobar 2010: 20).

6. Progressive neoextractivism "promotes and legitimises mining or oil industry projects as necessary to sustain welfare benefits or cash payments to the poorest sectors of society" (Gudynas 2013: 25). See also Acosta (2013b).

7. Correa cited in Escobar (2010: 5).

8. Escobar (2010: 8).

9. Grugel and Riggirozzi (2012: 15).

10. This remark has been widely quoted. See, for example, Monte Hayes, December 2, 2006, "Ecuador Leader Eyes Wealth Distribution." Associated Press. Accessed January 7, 2015. http://www.washingtonpost.com/wp-dyn/content/article/2006/12/02/AR2006120200590_pf.html.

11. Data reported in Grugel and Riggirozzi (2012: 10).

12. See chapter 2, table 2.1.

13. Conaghan (2008).

14. De la Torre (2013: 40).

15. Rathke and Gomez (2013: 20).

16. Ellner (2012: 98).

17. CONAIE, "The Plurinational State." www.conaie.org/accessed on January 15, 2015.

18. Acosta (2013a).

19. Grugel and Riggirozzi (2012: 6).

20. The purpose here is not to give a detailed history of these ongoing changes but to provide some context. For a fuller discussion, including case studies of five countries, see Burbach, Fox, and Fuentes (2013).

21. Ellner (2012) notes that this strategy is reminiscent of what the Non-Aligned Movement of the 1960s attempted to do.

22. Pearce (2013: 44).

23. Rosen (2013: 24). Pearce adds: "Chavez's time in office saw an unequivocal reassertion of the state as economic actor throughout the region. This dynamic was particularly felt in the crucial energy sector" (p. 43).

24. Pearce (2013: 44).

25. Interview INGO 40 (2013).

26. Interview INGO 40 (2013).

27. AP Exclusive: USAID's Days Counted in Ecuador, May 9, 2014. Accessed January 27, 2015. http://www.nytimes.com/aponline/2014/05/09/world/americas/ap-lt-ecuador-usaid.html.

28. Tamayo (2011: 1).

29. Tamayo (2011: 2).

30. Interview INGO 40 (2013).

31. Interview INGO 40 (2013).

32. De Konig et al. (2011: 533).

33. De Konig et al. (2011: 537).

34. De Konig et al. (2011: 539).

35. Ministerio del Ambiente (2014), "Resultados de Socio Bosque." Accessed January 27, 2015. http://sociobosque.ambiente.gob.ec/node/44. See also Conservation International (2014). "Economic Incentives to Protect Ecuador's Forests." Accessed January 19, 2015. http://www.conservation.org/projects/Pages/Economic-Incentives-to-Protect-Ecuadors-Forests-socio-bosque.aspx. There is something ironic about the "socialist" government using this sort of payment for ecosystem services in which market-based mechanisms are used to protect the environment. Rather than asking communities simply to protect environments, they are paid to do so. Within the literature, there is parsing over whether this should be called "market based" or simply a direct payment for conservation. De Konig et al. (2011: 532) lay out some of the associated literature on this issue. This type of project is in line with the Yasuní-ITT Initiatives and also with REDD+ strategies, which fall under the new Undersecretary of Climate Change. This is not totally different from other approaches to

resources in the "21st-century socialism." Ecuador and other Bolivarian nations have not nationalized resources; instead, they have exerted more control over resources and increased their takes while using the expertise, skills, and capital of multinational corporations to do the extraction.

36. Interview INGO 40 (2013).

37. Interview INGO 40 (2013).

38. Interview former NGO/government 43 (2013).

39. Interview former NGO/government (2013).

40. Interview INGO 40 (2013).

41. Interview INGO 40 (2013).

42. Kaup (2013: ch. 7).

43. Becker (2013: 47).

44. Asamblea Nacional Ambiental (2008), "Hacia Una Sociedad Equitativa y Sostenible." Enero. Accessed 6 July 2011. http://www.ccondem.org.ec/imagesFTP/2905. libro_ana.pdf .

45. Republic of Ecuador Constitution of 2008. Last updated January 31, 2011. http://pdba.georgetown.edu/Constitutions/Ecuador/english08.html.

46. Republic of Ecuador Constitution of 2008.

47. Larrea Maldonado (2012).

48. See, for example, Gudynas (2011), Radcliff (2012), and Acosta (2013).

49. Gudynas (2011: 1).

50. Davalos (2009).

51. Escobar (2010: 23). Escobar's own summary of the concept is especially useful (2010: 23): "In relation to dominant conceptions [of development], the notion of development as buen vivir (a) questions the prevailing 'maldevelopment'..., highlighting the undesirability of a model based on growth and material progress as the sole guiding principles; (b) displaces the idea of development as an end in itself, emphasizing that development is a process of qualitative change; (c) it enables, in principle, strategies that go beyond the export of primary products, going against the 'reprimarization' of the economy in vogue in the continent; (d) it broaches the question of the sustainability of the model; (e) it has made possible the discussion on other knowledges and cultural practices (e.g. indigenous and Afro) at the national level."

52. Gudynas (2013: 35).

53. The Pachamama Alliance (2012).

54. The plan's definition of good living was laid out in chapter 1 and is repeated here:

... Covering needs, achieving a dignified quality of life and death; loving and being loved; the healthy flourishing of all individuals in peace and harmony with nature; and achieving an indefinite reproduction perpetuation of human cultures. Good Living implies having free time for contemplation and personal emancipation; enabling the expansion and flourishing of people's liberties, opportunities, capabilities and potentialities so as to simultaneously allow society, specific territories, different collective identities, and each individual, understood both in universal and relative terms, to achieve their objectives in life (without causing any kind of material or subjective dominance over any other individual). Our concept of Good Living compels us to rebuild the public sphere in order to recognize, understand and value ourselves as diverse but equal individuals, and in order to advance reciprocity and mutual recognition, enable self-advancement, and build a shared social future .... (National Plan for Good Living, 2009 Presentation. http://plan2009.senplades.gob.ec/web/en/presentation).

55. National Plan for Good Living (2009), Change of Paradigm: From Development to Good Living. http://plan2009.senplades.gob.ec/web/en/change-of-paradigm.

56. Quotes on "Good Living" from: National Plan for Good Living (2009). Presentation. http://plan2009.senplades.gob.ec/web/en/presentation.

57. The Plan makes it clear that good living cannot be created nor measured using old economic tools:

Good Living is based on a vision that surpasses the narrow confines of quantitative economicism and challenges the notion of material, mechanic and endless accumulation of goods. Instead, the new paradigm promotes an inclusive, sustainable, and democratic economic strategy; one that incorporates actors historically excluded from the capitalist, market-driven logic of accumulation and redistribution.

Moreover the Plan critiques the economistic manner in which development is measured:

Development as modernization and economic growth tends to be measured through the variations of the Gross Domestic Product (GDP). Industrial development is what society should expect development and the culmination of the modernization process. Underdevelopment is attributed to the backwardness of society; which ignores the importance of external factors and the nature of the capitalist accumulation process.

It rejects the dominant Northern worldview of nature:

... Good Living revises and reinterprets the relation between nature and human beings, and proposes a shift from the current prevailing anthropocentrism to what we may call bio-pluralism .... Good Living posits that humans should use natural resources in a way that allows their natural generation (or regeneration).

And it addresses social sustainability:

... Good Living also relies on social equality and justice, and gives importance to dialogue with— and acknowledgment and value of—diverse peoples, cultures, forms of knowledge, and ways of life.

The Plan critiques development as a hegemonic model that ignores diversity:

The hegemonic ideas of progress and development have generated a monoculture that invisibilizes the historic experience of the diverse peoples that compose our societies. A linear vision of time supports the concept of progress, modernization, and development in which history has only one purpose and one direction: developed countries are ahead and are the "model" all societies should follow. Whatever falls outside these ideas is considered savage, primitive, obsolete, pre-modern ....

Finally, it presents an alternative definition of development, focused on people's needs and quality of life, which are in line with the UN Development Program:

In contrast, the concept of "human development" defends the idea of development based on human beings, and not merely on markets or production. What must be measured, therefore, is not GDP but the living standards of people through indicators related to the satisfaction of their human needs. The concept of human development emphasizes quality of life, human opportunities, and capabilities that must be encouraged in order to cover different types of needs, such as livelihood, affect, participation, freedom, identity, creativity, etc. Quality of life is understood as living a long and healthy life, the capacity to acquire knowledge, and having access to the resources required for a decent level of life (UNDP 1997: 20). The emphasis is on what people can "do and be," based on their potentialities, ways of thinking, needs, cultural values and patterns of organization.

The Plan also adds an element of sustainability to a definition of development that is not environmental sustainability:

In addition to covering needs and expanding current human capabilities, it is clear that human development must be sustainable. This is not viable without respecting historic and cultural diversity, the very basis on which the necessary unity of the people is constructed. For this purpose, it is vital to grant equal rights and opportunities to women and men, to peoples and nationalities, to boys, girls, youngsters, and adults. This also implies unrestricted citizen participation in the exercise of democracy.

58. Zorrilla, Carlos. Personal communication. September 25, 2013.

59. Zorrilla, Carlos. Personal communication. September 25, 2013.

60. Interview SMA 42 (2013).

61. Republic of Ecuador Constitution of 2008.

62. See Martin (2011).

63. Data cited in Arsel and Angel (2012: 213).

64. Finer et al. (2009: 12).

65. Democracy Now (2009).

66. Acosta et al. (2009).

67. Arsel and Angel (2012: 214). In this regard, Arsel and Angel (2012: 221) argue that the Ecuadorian state has started to colonize civil society.

68. Democracy Now (2009).

69. See Rochlin (2011).

70. Within Ecuador the proposal has created debates and analyses regarding the relationship between human rights and nature's rights, what collective rights mean, how equity gets translated at both the national and international level, and how the 2008 Constitution should be interpreted. See, for example, Narváez, De Marchi, and Pappalardo (2013).

71. Rochlin (2011: 35).

72. YASunidos. Accessed January 29, 2015. http://sitio.yasunidos.org/en/.

73. El Universo (2014), "YASunidos Buscará Respuesta de la CIDH a Dos Solicitudes." Accessed December 29, 2014. http://www.eluniverso.com/noticias/2014/12/29/nota/4385116/yasunidos-buscara-respuesta-cidh-dos-solicitudes.

74. Interview SMA 42 (2013).

75. Banco Central de Ecuador (2014), Boletín Anuario N° 36. Tables 2.1, 3.2.2, 3.2.3. Accessed January 29, 2015. http://www.bce.fin.ec/index.php/component/k2/item/327-ver-bolet%C3%ADn-anuario-por-años.

76. Interview INGO 40 (2013).

77. Interview INGO 40 (2013).

78. Interview former NGO/government (2013).

79. "Interview with Alberto Acosta: The 'Citizen Revolution,' The Extractive Model and the Left Critiques. February 19. Upside Down World. http://upsidedownworld.org/main/news-briefs-archives-68/4139-interview-with-alberto-acosta-the-qcitizen-revolutionq-the-extractive-model-and-the-left-critiques.

80. Bebbington (2009: 19) identifies five types in staking out positions in debates over environment and economic development: conservationist environmentalism, deep ecology, environmental justice, environmentalism of the poor, and resource-nationalist environmentalism.

81. Interview SMA 42 (2013).

82. Bebbington et al. (2008a: 897) note that the global share of investment in mining increased in Latin America from 12 percent in 1990 to 33 percent in 2000 and this has led to conflict throughout the region. The new law encouraged foreign companies to explore for reserves and increased the state's share of revenues. This law was and is incredibly controversial.

83. Dosh and Kligerman (2009: 22–23).

84. Santacruz (2008).

85. Dosh and Kligerman (2009: 23).

86. Under Rich Earth (2008).

87. See https://www.salvalaselva.org for online petition to Correa, "No a la minería en Intag Ecuador #LibertadparaJavierRamirez," and Carlos Zorrilla (2014), "Illegal Arrest and Illegitimate Mining in Intag Valley." Accessed February 5, 2015. http://www.ejolt.org/2014/04/illegal-arrest-and-illegitimate-mining-in-intag-valley-ecuador/. Another high profile case was the arrest of indigenous leader and anti-mining activist Pepe Acacho. He was arrested in January 2011 on charges of terrorism (Arsel and Angel 2012: 212) and sentenced to twelve years in prison ("Legislador Pepe Acacho es sentenciado a 12 años de prisión." Accessed February 5, 2015. http://www.eluniverso.com/noticias/2013/08/12/nota/1278231/legislador-pepe-acacho-sentenciado-12-anos-prision).

88. De la Torre (2013: 45).

89. Acción Ecológica (February 2014) has produced a report warning of the new dependency on China. "Chinese Mining in Ecuador: New Dependency." http://www.accionecologica.org/component/content/article/1741.

90. There were numerous reasons for the march. One was to resist the signing of the agreement with Ecuacorriente. According to an article on the website of Amazon Watch, an INGO dedicated to protect the rainforest, including the indigenous people who live there, "Thousands of indigenous peoples led by CONAIE (Confederation of Indigenous Nationalities of Ecuador) converged on Quito ... culminating a fifteen-day march demanding a new water law, land reform, and an end to open-pit mining and new oil concessions. The march, timed to arrive with World Water Day, was the first major indigenous mobilization in recent years, and it was an indictment of President Rafael Correa's environmental and social policies that the left-wing leader has touted as hallmarks of his 'Citizens Revolution'" (Becker 2012).

91. This would not have been the first time the rights of nature were invoked in court cases. In March 2011 there was the first successful case defending the rights of nature: Wheeler versus the Provincial government protected the Vilcabamba River against construction debris that caused flooding and destruction of the riverside. A second case with the Ministry of the Interior versus illegal gold miners also won in that same year (Daly 2012).

92. "Ecuador indigenous leader found dead days before planned Lima protest." 2014 (December 6) The Guardian. Accessed January 23, 2015. http://www.theguardian.com/world/2014/dec/06/ecuador-indigenous-leader-found-dead-lima-climate-talks?utm_content=bufferd7380&utm_medium=social&utm_source=facebook.com&utm_campaign=buffer.

93. Domingo Ankuash (2014), "Death of a Shuar leader resisting Ecuador's Mirador mine." http://www.ejolt.org/2014/12/death-shuar-leader-resisting-ecuadors-mirador -mine/.

94. Interview SMA 41 (2013).

95. Interview SMA 41 (2013).

96. Acosta (2013b: 73).

97. Denvir (2009).

98. ICNL (2012). In Ecuador, the laws ruling NGOs are governed by Executive Decrees.

99. ICNL (2012).

100. Alternet (2011).

101. Interview former NGO/government 43 (2013).

102. NGO Law Monitor: Ecuador. Accessed February 5, 2015. http://www.icnl.org/ research/monitor/ecuador.html.

103. Interview NGO 38 (2013).

104. CEDENMA, June 27, 2013. "Posición de CEDENMA ante el Decreto Presidencial No. 16: Relamento para el Funcionamiento del Sistema Unificado de Información de las Organizaciones Sociales y Ciudadanas. Quito. Accessed February 5, 2015. http://cedenma.org/start/wp-content/uploads/2013/07/Decreto -16-CEDENMA1.pdf.

105. Interview INGO 40 (2013).

106. Interview SMA 42 (2013).

107. Interview SMA 41 (2013).

108. Interview INGO 40 (2013).

109. Interview INGO 40 (2013).

110. Interview SMA 41 (2013). Despite the repression and fear, many ecosisters remain outspoken critics of the state. For instance, one whom I had just met said to me, "The government has lied to the people saying that they are going to eliminate extreme poverty .... It is the same thing that FAO and the World Bank said. Governments in general say this, whether of the right or of the left" (Interview SMA 42, 2013).

111. Dosh and Kligerman (2009: 243).

112. De la Torre (2013: 45).

113. Acosta (2013b: 77).

114. Interview SMA 42 (2013).

115. Interview SMA 43 (2013).

116. There is a conflict between what the state says it will do to protect nature in the constitution and what actions it has actually taken on the ground. Murat Arsel (2012: 161) notes: "… within the context of nature–society relationships there have been hugely significant attempts to reach a post-neoliberal order but these have given birth to uneven results …. [T]he constitution of Ecuador has indeed paved the way for the state to take the driving seat in the economy, especially in nature and natural resource management …. [But the state] has so far remained loyal to a notion of development that sees a material basis to societal well-being …. [T]he increase in state revenues from extraction has been used not only to finance stronger social security mechanisms, but also the construction of classic imprints of modern development, including schools, hospitals, bridges and power plans. Thus, instead of displacing the prevailing notion of development, the notion of *buen vivir* as a national goal has broadened it to include a harmonious co-existence of nature and society."

117. Acosta (2013b: 80).

Chapter 8

1. World Bank (2014).

2. Using what Keck and Sikkink (1998: 16) call information politics and accountability politics.

3. See also Lewis (2000) and Pellow (2007).

4. However, if the state's model is developmentalist, it too can be a limiting agent to radical, social independent environmentalists.

5. See Schnaiberg (1980: ch. 9). In line with the original formulation, Schnaiberg (2007) later argues that production contraction would make the most difference on transforming the treadmill of production. The non-use of goods is the most eco-efficient and has the greatest effect on the treadmill, while by comparison the recycling of goods has a lower level ecological value and moderate effects on the treadmill (table 9.2, p. 429).

6. Schnaiberg (1980: 431). The socioenvironmental policy program that he lays out to do this uses managed scarcity policies plus other plans. It "consciously redirect[s] social surplus towards more labor-intensive production and presumably away from higher levels of ecosystem withdrawals and additions …. The major intent of the

program is to maximize social welfare in economic growth, within the context of limited biospheric resources" (1980: 431).

7. Schnaiberg (1980: 432).

8. Schnaiberg and Gould (2000), Gould et al. (2008), and Pellow (2007).

9. Gould et al (2008: 101).

10. Ecuador's 2008 Constitution prohibits the use of genetically modified seeds and crops in the nation. They can only be introduced if (like oil drilling), it is in the "national interest." In 2012, President Correa said he regretted that the GMO ban was in the constitution. When in the United States we have been mostly unwitting guinea pigs to the environmental and health effects of GMOs, it gives me hope that there are individuals and nations observing the precautionary principal and resisting the corporate control of food.

11. Gould et al. (2008: 105).

12. Gould et al (2008: 110).

13. Kauffman and Martin (2014) argue that the approach to the development of watershed management associated with FONAG in Tungurahua, Ecuador is a way that the concept of *buen vivir* can be scaled up.

14. Fabricant and Gustafson (2014/15: 45).

15. See the collection *Beyond Development: Alternative Visions from Latin America,* edited by M. Lang and D. Mokrani, especially the chapter by Eduardo Gudynas, "Transitions to Post-Extractivism: Directions, Options, Areas of Action."

16. Gudynas (2011) compares and contrasts the Ecuadorian and Bolivian conceptions of *buen vivir*. There is a rich and growing literature on this topic. See also Kepa Artaraz and Melania Calestani (2014), "Suma qamaña in Bolivia: Indigenous Understandings of Well-being and Contribution to a Post-Neoliberal Paradigm." *Latin American Perspectives* (published online August 20, 2014).

17. Grugel and Riggirozzi (2011); Gregory Wilpert (February 2, 2011), "An Assessment of Venezuela's Bolivarian Revolution at Twelve Years." *Upside Down World.* http://upsidedownworld.org/main/venezuela-archives-35/2889-an-assessment-of-venezuelas-bolivarian-revolution-at-twelve-years.

18. Raúl Zibech (December 10, 2014.), "Developmentalism and Social Movements in Bolivia." *Upside Down World.* http://upsidedownworld.org/main/bolivia-archives-31/5147-developmentalism-and-social-movements-in-bolivia.

19. Quincy Saul and Hugo Blanco (May 19, 2015), "From Indigenous Struggle to Ecosocialism." *Counterpunch.* http://www.counterpunch.org/2015/05/19/from-indigenous-struggle-to-ecosocialism/; Emily Achtenberg (August 12, 2011), "Bolivia: Indigenous Groups to March Against TIPNES Highway." *NACLA.*

20. Devin Beaulieu and Nancy Postero (November 1, 2013), "Bolivia: The Politics of Extractivism." *Upside Down World.* http://upsidedownworld.org/main/bolivia -archives-31/4536-bolivia-the-politics-of-extractivism.

21. Alexandra Ellerbeck and Benjamin Soloway (May 22, 2015), "Red Tape or Repression? NGOs Fight for a Place in the New Bolivia They Helped Evo Morales Create." http://news.mongabay.com/2015/0522-sri-ellerbeck-soloway-bolivia-morales.html ?tw!ttr=yes.

22. Gould (1999) elaborates on this idea in terms of the trade-offs between ecotourism and rainforest development.

References

Abramovitz, J. M. 1994. *Trends in Biodiversity Investments: U.S.-Based Funding for Research and Conservation in Developing Countries, 1987–1991*. Washington, DC: World Resources Institute.

Acción Ecológica. nd. Historia. http://www.accionecologica.org/iquienes-somos/nuestra-historia. Accessed December 3, 2012.

Acción Ecológica. nd. Petroléo. http://www.accionecologica.org/petroleo. Accessed December 3, 2012.

Acción Ecológica (Ecuador). 1996. La Defensa Del Manglar "Tración a la Patria." *Ecología Política* 11:163–165.

Acción Ecológica. 2014. Chinese mining in Ecuador: New dependency. http://www.accionecologica.org/component/content/article/1741.

Achtenberg, Emily. 2011. Bolivia: Indigenous groups to march against TIPNES Highway. *NACLA: Report on the Americas.* August 12.

Acosta, Alberto. 2013a. Ecuador: Building a good life—*Sumak Kawsay*. Translation by Christina Hewitt. January 24. http://upsidedownworld.org/main/ecuador-archives-49/4087-ecuador-building-a-good-life-sumak-kawsay .

Acosta, Alberto. 2013b. Extractivism and neoextractivism: Two sides of the same curse. In *Beyond Development,* M. Lang and D. Mokrani, (eds.), 61–86. Amsterdam: Permanent Working Group on Alternatives to Development/Transnational Institute.

Acosta, Alberto, Eduardo Gudynas, Esperanza Martínez, and Joseph H. Vogel. 2009. Leaving the oil underground. A political, economic, and ecological initiative from Ecuador. August 13. http://www.sosyasuni.org/en/index.php?option=com_content&view=article&id=134:leaving-the-oil-underground-a-political-economic-and-ecological-initiative-from-ecuador&catid=1:news&Itemid=34. Accessed July 4, 2011.

Adams, Guy. 2011. Chevron's dirty fight in Ecuador. February 16. *The Independent.* http://www.independent.co.uk/environment/nature/chevrons-dirty-fight-in -ecuador-2216168.html. Accessed July 4, 2011.

Alternet. 2011. Ecuador shuts down foreign NGO operations. August 19. http:// www.trust.org/alertnet/news/ecuador-shuts-down-foreign-ngo-operations has been redirected to http://www.trust.org/item/?map=ecuador-shuts-down-foreign-ngo -operations. Accessed November 14, 2011.

Alvarez, Sonia E. 1998. Latin American feminisms "go global": Trends of the 1990s and Challenges for the new millenium. In *Cultures of Politics/Politics of Cultures: Re-visioning Latin American Social Movements,* Sonia E. Alvarez, Evelina Dagnino, and Arturo Escobar (eds.). Boulder: Westview.

Alvarez, Sonia E. 1999. The Latin American feminist NGO "boom." *International Feminist Journal of Politics* 1 (2): 181–209.

Alvarez, Sonia E. 2009. Beyond NGO-ization: Reflections from Latin America. *Development* 52 (2): 175–84.

Anderson, Joan B. 1990. *Economic Policy Alternatives for the Latin American Crisis.* New York: Taylor and Francis.

Andolina, Robert. 2003. The sovereign and its shadow: Constituent assembly and indigenous movement in Ecuador. *Journal of Latin American Studies* 35 (4): 721–50.

Ankuash, Domingo. 2014. Death of a Shuar leader resisting Ecuador's Mirador mine. http://www.ejolt.org/2014/12/death-shuar-leader-resisting-ecuadors-mirador-mine/.

Armbruster-Sandoval, Ralph. 2005. *Globalization and Cross-Border Labor Solidarity in the Americas: The Anti-Sweatshop Movement and the Struggle for Social Justice.* London: Routledge.

Arsel, Murat. 2012. Between "Marx and markets"? The state, the "Left turn" and nature in Ecuador. *Journal of Economic and Social Geography* 103 (2): 150–63.

Arsel, Murat, and Natalia Avila Angel. 2012. "Stating" nature's role in Ecuadorian development: Civil society and the Yasuní-ITT Initiative. *Journal of Developing Societies* 28: 203–27.

Artaraz, Kepa, and Melania Calestani. 2014. *Suma qamaña* in Bolivia: Indigenous understandings of well-being and contribution to a post-neoliberal paradigm. *Latin American Perspectives.*

Asamblea Nacional de Ambiental. 2005. Declaratoria. May 20. https://docs.google. com/viewer?a=v&q=cache:ENbcBKfkMIsJ:www.redmanglar.org/imagesFTP/1787. DECLARATORIA_ANA.doc+asamblea+nacional+ambiental+ecuador+2005&hl=en&g l=us&pid=bl&srcid=ADGEESh6FKj5uwQ2UHTlCXoQymbTBbH6R7bJXjgWPfIK672d ZLvsj-_v5Lzx8IHS0HZj8tJyVJaaiw5K0PtYIiEwTdexsdPu97cAL4vSJJViq5U1kdEtrTd

5fn-mWNry6anV1SdyDlI_&sig=AHIEtbRMgGnlvMZ2lvK7ukrdXAAL2HJ75g. Accessed July 5, 2011.

Asamblea Nacional Ambiental. 2008. Hacia Una Sociedad Equitativa Y Sostenible. http://www.ccondem.org.ec/imagesFTP/2905.libro_ana.pdf. Accessed December 2, 2010.

Banco Central de Ecuador. 2013. Boletín Anuario No. 35, tables 2.1, 3.2.2, 3.2.3. http://www.bce.fin.ec/index.php/component/k2/item/327-ver-bolet%C3%ADn-anuario-por-años. Accessed January 29, 2015.

Banco Central de Ecuador. 2014. Boletín Anuario No. 36, tables 2.1, 3.2.2, 3.2.3. http://www.bce.fin.ec/index.php/component/k2/item/327-ver-bolet%C3%ADn-anuario-por-años. Accessed January 29, 2015.

Bandy, Joe, and Jackie Smith, eds. 2005. *Coalitions across Borders: Transnational Protest in a Neoliberal Era*. Lanham, MD: Rowman and Littlefield.

Beaulieu, Devin, and Nancy Postero. 2013. Bolivia: The politics of extractivism. *Upside Down World*. http://upsidedownworld.org/main/bolivia-archives-31/4536-bolivia-the-politics-of-extractivism.

Bebbington, Anthony. 2009. The new extraction: Rewriting the political ecology of the Andes? *NACLA Report on the Americas* 42 (September/October): 12–20.

Bebbington, Anthony, Leonith Hinojosa, Denise Humphreys Bebbington, Maria Luisa Burneo, and Ximena Warnaars. 2008a. Contention and ambiguity: Mining and the possibilities of development. *Development and Change* 39 (6): 887–914.

Bebbington, Anthony, Denise Humphreys Bebbington, Jeffrey Bury, Jeannet Lingan, Juan Pablo Muñoz, and Martin Scurrah. 2008b. Mining and social movements: Struggles over livelihood and rural territorial development in the Andes. *World Development* 36 (12): 2888–2905.

Becker, Marc. 2011. *Pachakutik: Indigenous Movements and Electoral Politics in Ecuador*. Lanham, MD: Rowman and Littlefield.

Becker, Marc. 2012. Ecuador: Plurinational march for life, water, and dignity. April 24. http://upsidedownworld.org/main/ecuador-archives-49/3592-ecuador-plurinational-march-for-life-water-and-dignity. Accessed November 14, 2012.

Becker, Marc. 2013. The stormy relations between Rafael Correa and social movements in Ecuador. *Latin American Perspectives* 40 (3): 43–62.

Beitl, Christine M. 2012. Shifting policies, access, and the tragedy of enclosures in Ecuadorian mangrove fisheries: Towards a political ecology of the commons. *Journal of Political Ecology* 19: 94–113.

Boli, John, and George N. Thomas. 1999. *Constructing World Culture: International Non-governmental Organizations since 1875*. Stanford: Stanford University Press.

Bräutigam, Deborah A., and Monique Segarra. 2007. Difficult partnerships: The World Bank, states, and NGOs. *Latin American Politics and Society* 49 (4) (Winter): 149–81.

Brechin, Steven R., and Willett Kempton. 1994. Global environmentalism: A challenge to the postmaterialism thesis? *Social Science Quarterly* 75: 245–69.

Brechin, Steven R., Peter R. Wilshusen, Crystal L. Fortwangler, and Patrick C. West. 2003. *Contested Nature: Promoting International Biodiversity with Social Justice in the 21st Century*. Albany: SUNY Press.

Brooks, T. M., R. A. Mittermeier, G. A. B. da Fonseca, J. Gerlach, M. Hoffmann, J. F. Lamoreux, C. G. Mittermeier, J. D. Pilgrim, and A. S. L. Rodrigues. 2006. Global biodiversity conservation priorities. *Science* 313 (5783): 58–61.

Brulle, Robert J. 2000. *Agency, Democracy, and Nature: The U.S. Environmental Movement from a Critical Theory Perspective*. Cambridge: MIT Press.

Brysk, Alison. 1993. From above and below: Social movements, the international system, and human rights in Argentina. *Comparative Political Studies* 26 (3): 259–85.

Brysk, Allison. 1996. Turning weakness into strength: The internationalization of Indian rights. *Latin American Perspectives* 23 (2): 38–57.

Burbach, Roger, Michael Fox, and Federico Fuentes. 2013. *Latin America's Turbulent Transitions: The Future of Twenty-First Century Socialism*. London: Zed Books.

Buttel, Frederick H. 2003. Environmental sociology and the explanation of environmental reform. *Organization & Environment* 16: 306–44.

CAAM. 1995. *Informe de Actividades*. September 22, 1993–April 22, 1995.

CAAM. N.d. Propuesta de Políticas y Estrategias Ambientales. Republica del Ecuador.

California Department of Fish and Game. 2003. "Plants" entry by Roxanne Bittman in *Atlas of the Biodiversity of California*. Sacramento, California. http://www.dfg.ca.gov/biogeodata/atlas/pdf/Plant_24b.pdf. Assessed April 4, 2014.

Cardoso, F. H., and E. Faletto. 1979. *Dependency and Development in Latin America*. Berkeley: University of California Press.

Carmin, JoAnn, and Barbara Hicks. 2002. International triggering events, transnational networks, and the development of the Czech and Polish environmental movements. *Mobilization* 7(3): 305–24.

Carruthers, David V., ed. 2008. *Environmental Justice in Latin America: Problems, Promise and Practice*. Cambridge: MIT Press.

Castro, G., and I. Locker. with V. Russell, L. Cornwell, and E. Fajer. 2000. *Mapping Conservation Investments: An Assessment of Biodiversity Funding in Latin America and the Caribbean.* Washington, DC: Biodiversity Support Program/World Resources Institute.

C-CONDEM. 2011. Website home page. http://www.ccondem.org.ec/tempccon. php?c=43. Accessed July 5, 2011.

CEDENMA. 1995a. El Primer Y Segundo Congresos del Medio Ambiente: Sociedad Civil, Estado y Medio Ambiente en el Ecuador entre 1987 y 1995. II Congreso Nacional Ecuatoriano del Medio Ambiente. April.

CEDENMA. 1995b. Propuesta de Politicas Ambientales Nacionales del Comite Ecuatoriano para la Defensea de la Naturaleza y el Medio Ambiente. II Congreso Nacional Ecuatoriano del Medio Ambiente. April.

CEDENMA. 2013. Posición de CEDENMA ante el Decreto Presidencial No. 16: Relamento para el Funcionamiento del Sistema Unificado de Información de las Organizaciones Sociales y Ciudadanas. Quito. http://cedenma.org/start/wp -content/uploads/2013/07/Decreto-16-CEDENMA1.pdf.

Central Intelligence Agency (CIA). Multiple years. The World Factbook. Ecuador. www.cia.gov/library/publications/the-world-factbook/geos/ec.html.

CETUR (Corporación Ecuatoriana de Turismo). nd. *Ecuador. Bulletin de Estadiscticas Turisticas 1988–1992. Ministerio de Información y Turismo.*

Christen, Catherine, Selene Herculano, Kathryn Hochstetler, Renae Prell, Marie Price, and J. Timmons Roberts. 1998. Latin American environmentalism: Comparative views. *Studies in Comparative International Development* 33 (2): 58–87.

CLIRSEN-PMRC. 2007. *Actualización del Estudio Multitemporal de Manglares, Camaroneras y Áreas Salinas en la Costa Continental Ecuatoriana al año 2006.* Guayaquil, Ecuador: Centro de Levantamientos Integrados de Recursos Naturales por Sensores Remotos & la Programa de Manejo de Recursos Costeros.

Collinson, Helen, ed. 1996. *Green Guerillas.* London: Latin American Bureau.

Conaghan, Catherine M. 2008. Ecuador: Correa's plebiscitary presidency. *Journal of Democracy* 19 (2): 46–60.

CONAIE. 2015. "The Plurinational State." www.conaie.org/.

Conservation International. 2011. Hotspot science. http://www.biodiversityhot-spots.org/xp/hotspots/hotspotsscience/Pages/impact_of_hotspots.aspx.

Conservation International. 2014. Economic incentives to protect Ecuador's forests. http://www.conservation.org/projects/Pages/Economic-Incentives-to-Protect -Ecuadors-Forests-socio-bosque.aspx.

Corkill, David, and David Cubitt. 1988. *Ecuador: Fragile Democracy.* London: Latin American Bureau (Research and Action).

Daly, Erin. 2012. The Ecuadorian exemplar: The first ever vindications of constitutional rights of Nature. *Review of European Community & International Environmental Law* 21 (1): 63–66.

Davalos, Pablo. 2009. Reflections on *sumak kawsay* (good living) and theories of development. Latin America in Movement. http://www.alainet.org/en/active/33609. Accessed July 4, 2011.

De Konig, Free, Marcela Aguiñaga, Manuel Bravo, Marco Chiu, Max Lascano, Tannya Lozada, and Luis Suarez. 2011. Bridging the gap between forest conservation and poverty alleviation: The Ecuadorian Socio Bosque program. *Environmental Science & Policy* 14: 531–42.

De la Barra, Ximena, and Richard A. Dello Buono. 2009. *Latin America after the Neoliberal Debacle: Another Region Is Possible.* Lanham, MD: Rowman and Littlefield.

De la Torre, Carlos. 2013. Technocratic Populism in Ecuador. *Journal of Democracy* 24 (3): 33–46.

Della Porta, Donatella, and Sidney Tarrow, eds. 2005. *Transnational Protest and Global Activism.* Lanham, MD: Rowman and Littlefield.

Democracy Now. 2009. Keep the oil in the soil. Amy Goodman interviewing Ivonne Yanez. December 9. http://www.democracynow.org/2009/12/11/ecuadorian_activist _heads_to_cop15_with. Accessed November 7, 2012.

Denvir, Daniel. 2009. Ecuadorian government shuts down leading environmental group. March 16. http://www.grist.org/article/ecuadorian-government-shuts-down -leading. Accessed July 4, 2011.

Derber, Charles. 2008. *Corporation Nation* New York: St. Martin's Press.

Didia, Dal. 2001. Debt-for-nature swaps, Market imperfections, and policy failures as determinant of sustainable development and environmental quality. *Journal of Economic Issues* 35(2) (June): 477–86.

Díez, Jordi. 2008. The rise and fall of Mexico's green movement. *European Review of Latin American & Caribbean Studies* 85: 81–99.

Dosh, Paul, and Nicole Kligerman. 2009. Correa vs. social movements: Showdown in Ecuador. *NACLA Report on the Americas* (September/October): 21–24.

Dowie, Mark. 1995. *Losing Ground.* Cambridge: MIT Press.

Doyle, Timothy. 2005. *Environmental Movements in Majority and Minority Worlds: A Global Perspective.* New Brunswick: Rutgers University Press.

Dunlap, Riley E., and Richard York. 2008. The globalization of environmental concern and the limits of the postmaterialist values explanation: Evidence from four multinational surveys. *Sociological Quarterly* 49: 529–63.

Economist Intelligence Unit (EIU). 1993. *Country Profile: Ecuador, 1993/4.* United Kingdom: Economist Intelligence Unit.

Ecuador designated 2015 as the year of touristic quality. March 31, 2015. Accessed at http://www.andes.info.ec/en/news/ecuador-designated-2015-year-touristic-quality.html.

Ecuador indigenous leader found dead days before planned Lima protest. 2014. *The Guardian.* http://www.theguardian.com/world/2014/dec/06/ecuador-indigenous -leader-found-dead-lima-climate-talks?utm_content=bufferd7380&utm_medium =social&utm_source=facebook.com&utm_campaign=buffer. Accessed January 23, 2015.

Ecuador oks protections for Galapagos Islands. 1998. CNN. Accessed July 7, 2014. http://www.cnn.com/EARTH/9803/12/galapagos/.

Ecuador set to leave OPEC. 1992. *New York Times.* Accessed July 1, 2014. http://www .nytimes.com/1992/09/18/business/ecuador-set-to-leave-opec.html.

Ecuadorian Environmental Organization Survey. 2007. Conducted by Tammy Lewis, Muhlenberg College.

Ellerbeck, Alexandra, and Benjamin Soloway. 2015. Red tape or repression? NGOs fight for a place in the new Bolivia they helped Evo Morales create. http://news. mongabay.com/2015/0522-sri-ellerbeck-soloway-bolivia-morales.html?tw!ttr=yes.

Ellner, Steve. 2012. The distinguishing features of Latin America's new Left in power: The Chávez, Morales, and Correa governments. *Latin American Perspectives* 182 (39): 96–114.

Escobar, Arturo. 1995. *Encountering Development: The Making and Unmaking of the Third World.* Princeton: Princeton University Press.

Escobar, Arturo. 1998. Whose knowledge, whose nature? Biodiversity, conservation, and the political ecology of social movements. *Journal of Political Ecology* 5: 53–82.

Escobar, Arturo. 2010. Latin America at a crossroads: Alternative modernizations, post-liberalism, or post-development. *Cultural Studies* 24 (1): 1–65.

Escobar, Arturo, and Sonia Alvarez. 1992. *The Making of Social Movements in Latin America: Identity, Strategy, and Democracy.* Boulder: Westview.

Escribano, Gonzalo. 2012. Ecuador's energy policy mix: Development, conservation and nationalism with Chinese loans. Real Instituto Elcano. July 17. http://www. realinstitutoelcano.org/wps/portal/web/rielcano_en/contenido?WCM_GLOBAL _CONTEXT=/elcano/Elcano_in/Zonas_in/ARI26-2012#.VeTDsTqChUQ.

Fabricant, Nicole, and Bret Gustafson. 2014/2015. Moving beyond the extractivism debate, imagining new social economies. *NACLA Report on the Americas,* 40–45.

Faust, Jorg, Florian Arneth, Nicolaus von der Goltz, Imke Harbers, Judith Illerhues, and Michael Schloms. 2008. *Political Fragmentation, Decentralization and Development Cooperation: Ecuador in the Latin American Context.* Bonn: German Development Institute.

Finer, Matt, Carsha Vijay, Fernando Ponce, Clinton N. Jenkins, and Ted R. Kahn. 2009. Ecuador's Yasuní biosphere reserve: A brief modern history and conservation challenges. *Environmental Research Letters* 4: 1–15.

Food and Agriculture Organization of the United Nations. 1995. Follow-up report on forests.

Food and Agriculture Organization of the United Nations. 2014. Intergovernmental group on bananas and tropical fruits. *Banana Market Review and Banana Statistics, 2012–2013.* Rome. http://www.fao.org/docrep/019/i3627e/i3627e.pdf.

Frank, David John, Ann Hironaka, and Evan Schofer. 2000. The nation-state and the natural environment over the twentieth century. *American Sociological Review* 65: 96–116.

Freedom House. 2014. Freedom in the World 2014. https://freedomhouse.org/report-types/freedom-world#. Accessed April 4, 2014.

Fundación Maquipicuna. nd.a. Maquipucuna, de la mano con la conservación.

Fundación Maquipicuna. nd.b. Proyectos y Logros de Fundación Maquipucuna.

Fundación Maquipicuna. nd.c. *Institutional CV.*

Fundación Natura. nd, c. 1993. *Proyectos en Marcha: Areas Protegidas.* Quito, Ecuador.

Fundación Natura. 1991. *Acciones de Desarrollo en Zonas de Influencia de Areas Protegidas.* Fundación Natura.

Fundación Natura. 1993. *Ponencias del Ecuador Presentadas en el IV Congreso de Parques Nacionales y Areas Protegidas, Caracas, Febrero 1992.* Fundación Natura.

Gedicks, Al. 1993. *The New Resource Wars: Native and Environmental Struggles against Multinational Corporations.* Cambridge, MA: South End Press.

Gedicks, Al. 2001. *Resource Rebels: Native Challenges to Mining and Oil Corporations.* Cambridge, MA: South End Press.

Goldman, Michael. 2005. *Imperial Nature: The World Bank and Struggles for Social Justice in the Age of Globalization.* New Haven: Yale University Press.

Gould, Kenneth A. 1999. Tactical tourism: A comparative analysis of rainforest development in Ecuador and Belize. *Organization and Environment* 12 (3): 245–62.

Gould, Kenneth A., and Tammy L. Lewis. 2010. Transnational social movements. In *International Studies Encyclopedia*. Oxford: Blackwell.

Gould, Kenneth A., and Tammy L. Lewis. 2015. The paradoxes of sustainable development: Focus on ecotourism. In *Twenty Lessons in Environmental Sociology*, 2nd ed., K. Gould and T. Lewis (eds.), 330–51. New York: Oxford University Press.

Gould, Kenneth A., David N. Pellow, and Allan Schnaiberg. 2004. Interrogating the treadmill of production: Everything you wanted to know about the treadmill but were afraid to ask. *Organization & Environment* 17 (3): 296–316.

Gould, Kenneth A., David N. Pellow, and Allan Schnaiberg. 2008. *The Treadmill of Production: Injustice and Unsustainability in the Global Economy*. Boulder, CO: Paradigm.

Gould, Kenneth A., Allan Schnaiberg, and Adam Weinberg. 1996. *Local Environmental Struggles: Citizen Activism in the Treadmill of Production*. New York: Cambridge University Press.

Grugel, Jean, and Pía Riggirozzi. 2012. Post-neoliberalism in Latin America: Rebuilding and reclaiming the state after crisis. *Development & Change* 43 (1): 1–21.

Gudynas, Eduardo. 2011. *Buen vivir*: Today's tomorrow. *Development* 54 (4): 441–47.

Gudynas, Eduardo. 2013. Debates on development and its alternatives in Latin America: A brief heterodox guide. In *Beyond Development*, ed. M. Lang and D. Mokrani. Amsterdam: Permanent Working Group on Alternatives to Development/ Transnational Institute.

Guha, Ramachandra. 2000. *Environmentalism: A Global History*. New York: Longman.

Guha, Ramachandra, and Juan Martinez-Alier. 1997. *Varieties of Environmentalism: Essays North and South*. London: Earthscan.

Hayes, Monte. 2006. Ecuador leader eyes wealth distribution. Associated Press. http://www.washingtonpost.com/wp-dyn/content/article/2006/12/02/ AR2006120200590_pf.html.

Hey, Jeanne A. K. 1993. Foreign policy options under dependence: A theoretical evaluation with evidence from Ecuador. *Journal of Latin American Studies* 25: 543–574.

Hey, Jeanne A. K., and Thomas Klak. 1999. From protectionism toward neoliberalism: Ecuador across four administrations (1981–1996). *Studies in Comparative International Development* 34 (3): 66–97.

Hicks, Barbara. 2004. Setting agendas and shaping activism: EU Influence on Central and Eastern European environmental movements. *Environmental Politics* 13 (1): 216–33.

Hicks, Robert L., Bradley C. Parks, J. Timmons Roberts, and Michael J. Tierney. 2008. *Greening Aid: Understanding the Environmental Impact of Development Assistance.* Oxford: Oxford University Press.

Hipsher, Patricia L. 1998. Democratic transitions as protest cycles: Social movement dynamics in democratizing Latin America. In *The Social Movement Society: Contentious Politics for a New Century,* ed. David S. Meyer and Sidney Tarrow, 153–72. Lanham, MD: Rowman and Littlefield.

Hochstetler, Kathryn, and Margaret E. Keck. 2007. *Greening Brazil: Environmental Activism in State and Society.* Durham: Duke University Press.

Humphrey, Craig R., Tammy L. Lewis, and Frederick H. Buttel. 2002. *Environment, Energy and Society: A New Synthesis.* Belmont, CA: Wadsworth.

Humphreys, Macartan, Jeffrey D. Sachs, and Joseph E. Stiglitz, eds. 2007. *Escaping the Resource Curse (Initiative for Policy Dialogue).* New York: Columbia University Press.

International Center for Not-for-Profit Law. 2012. NGO Law Monitor: Ecuador. http://www.icnl.org/research/monitor/ecuador.html. Accessed November 14, 2012.

International Center for Not-for-Profit Law. 2015. NGO Law Monitor: Ecuador. http://www.icnl.org/research/monitor/ecuador.html. Accessed February 5, 2015.

International Tropical Timber Organization (ITTO). 2011. *Status of Tropical Forest Management, Technical Series 38, June.* Yokohama, Japan.

International Union for the Conservation of Nature. 2011. Invasive species. https://www.iucn.org/about/union/secretariat/offices/iucnmed/iucn_med_programme/species/invasive_species/.

Interview with Alberto Acosta. The "Citizen Revolution," the extractive model and the Left critiques. 2013. *Upside Down World.* http://upsidedownworld.org/main/news-briefs-archives-68/4139-interview-with-alberto-acosta-the-qcitizen-revolutionq-the-extractive-model-and-the-left-critiques.

Jakobeit, Cord. 1996. Nonstate actors leading the way: Debt-for-nature swaps. In *Institutions for Environmental Aid,* Robert O. Keohane and Marc A. Levy (eds.), 127–66. Cambridge: MIT Press.

Jenkins, J. Craig, and Craig M. Eckert. 1986. Channeling Black insurgency: Elite patronage and professional social movement organizations in the development of the Black movement. *American Sociological Review* 42: 249–68.

Jenkins, J. Craig, and Abigail Halcli. 1999. Grassrooting the system? The development and impact of social movement philanthropy, 1953–1990. In *Philanthropic Foundations: New Scholarship, New Possibilities,* Ellen Condliffe Lagemann (ed.), 229–56. Bloomington: Indiana University Press.

Jiménez, Agustin Grijalva. 1994. *Datos Básicos de la Realidad Nacional.* Quito: Corporación Editora Nacional.

Jochnick, Chris, Roger Normand, and Sarah Zaidi. 1994. *Violaciones de Derechos en la Amazonia Ecuatoriana: Las Consecuencias Humanas del Desarrollo Petrolero.* Quito, Ecuador: Ediciones Abya-Yala.

Johnston, Hank, and Paul Almeida, eds. 2006. *Latin American Social Movements: Globalization, Democratization, and Transnational Networks.* Lanham, MD: Rowman and Littlefield.

Kane, Joe. 1995. *Savages.* New York: Vintage.

Karl, Terry Lynn. 1997. *The Paradox of Plenty: Oil Booms and Petro-States.* Berkeley: University of California Press.

Kaufmann, Craig M. 2014. Financing watershed conservation: Lessons from Ecuador's evolving water trust funds. *Agricultural Water Management* 145: 39–49.

Kaufmann, Craig M., and Pamela L. Martin. 2014. Scaling up *buen vivir*: Globalizing local environmental governance from Ecuador. *Global Environmental Politics* 14 (1): 40–58.

Kauneckis, Derek, and Krister Andersson. 2009. Making decentralization work: A cross-national examination of local governments and natural resource governance in Latin America. *Studies in Comparative International Development* 44: 23–46.

Kaup, Brent Z. 2013. *Market Justice: Political Economic Struggle in Bolivia.* New York: Cambridge University Press.

Keck, Margaret E., and Kathryn Sikkink. 1998. *Activists beyond Borders: Advocacy Networks in International Politics.* Ithaca: Cornell University Press.

"Keeping the Oil in the Soil": Ecuador seeks money to keep untapped oil resources underground. 2007. http://www.sosyasuni.org/en/index.php?option=com_content&view=article&id=136%3Akeep-the-oil-in-the-soil-ecuador-seeks-money-to-keep-untapped-oil-resources-underground&catid=15%3Acampaign&Itemid=27. Accessed 16 June 2013.

Keese, James R., and Marco Freire Argudo. 2006. Decentralisation and NGO-municipal government collaboration in Ecuador. *Development in Practice* 16 (2): 114–27.

Kennemore, Amy, and Gregory Weeks. 2011. Twenty-first century socialism? The elusive search for a post-neoliberal development model in Bolivia and Ecuador. *Bulletin of Latin American Research* 30 (3): 267–81.

Khagram, Sanjeev, James V. Riker, and Kathryn Sikkink. 2002. *Restructuring World Politics: Transnational Social Movements, Networks, and Norms.* Minneapolis: University of Minnesota Press.

Kimerling, Judith. 1991. *Amazon Crude*. Natural Resources Defense Council.

Kitschelt, H. P. 1986. Political opportunity structures and political protest: Anti-nuclear movements in four democracies. *British Journal of Political Science* 16: 57–85.

Kuecker, Glen David. 2007. Fighting for the forests: Grassroots resistance to mining in northern Ecuador. *Latin American Perspectives* 34 (2): 94–107.

Land, M., and D. Mokrani. 2013. *Beyond Development: Alternative Visions from Latin America*. Amsterdam: Permanent Working Group on Alternatives to Development/ Transnational Institute.

Larrea, Carlos, and Liisa L. North. 1997. Ecuador: Adjustment policy impacts on truncated development and democratisation. *Third World Quarterly* 18 (5): 913–34.

Larrea Maldonado, Ana María. 2012. *Modo de Desarrollo, Organización Territorial y Cambio Constituyente en el Ecuador*. Quito: Secretaría Nacional de Planificación y Desarrollo.

Legislador Pepe Acacho es sentenciado a 12 años de prisión. 2013. http://www .eluniverso.com/noticias/2013/08/12/nota/1278231/legislador-pepe-acacho -sentenciado-12-anos-prision. Accessed February 5, 2015.

Lewis, Tammy L. 1996. The land protection strategy of conserving global biodiversity: Northern influence on southern sustainability. PhD dissertation. University of California, Davis.

Lewis, Tammy L. 2000. Transnational conservation movement organizations: Shaping the protected area systems of less developed countries. *Mobilization: An International Quarterly* 5 (1): 105–23.

Lewis, Tammy L. 2003. Environmental aid: Driven by recipient need or donor interests? *Social Science Quarterly* 84 (1): 144–61.

Lewis, Tammy L. 2011a. Global civil society and the distribution of environmental goods: Funding for environmental NGOs in Ecuador. In *Environmental Inequalities beyond Borders: Local Perspectives on Global Inequities*, Julian Agyeman and JoAnn Carmin (eds.), 87–104. Cambridge: MIT Press.

Lewis, Tammy L. 2011b. Thick conservation networks and thin pollution networks in Ecuador's environmental organizations. *Journal of Natural Resources Policy Research* 3 (3): 315–27.

Lewis, Tammy L. 2014. How biodiversity science shaped Ecuadorian environmental organizations. In *Experts and Campaigners: Scientific Information and Collective Action in Socio-ecological Conflicts*, ed. Mercedes Martinez-Iglesias, 71–86. Valencia, Spain: Universitat de Valéncia.

Mahony, Rhona. 1992. Debt-for-nature swaps: Who really benefits. *Ecologist* 22 (3): 97–103.

Manosalvas, Rossana, Jorge Mariaca, and Jaime Estrella. 2002. Guia metodologica para el acceso de recursos genericos. In *La biodiversidad del Ecuador: Informe 2002*, Carmen Josse (ed.), 60–78. Quito: Ministerio del Medio Ambiente, UICN.

Martin, Pamela L. 2003. *The Globalization of Contentious Politics: The Amazonian Indigenous Rights Movement*. New York: Routledge.

Martin, Pamela L. 2011. *Oil in the Soil: The Politics of Paying to Preserve the Amazon*. Lanham, MD: Rowman and Littlefield.

Martínez, Esperanza. 2000. Los estándares: Garantizan la sustentabilidad. *Ecología Política* 19: 111–13.

Martinez-Alier, Joan. 2002. *The Environmentalism of the Poor*. Cheltenham, UK: Elgar.

McAdam, Doug. 1982. *Political Process and the Development of Black Insurgency, 1930–1970*. Chicago: University of Chigaco Press.

McAdam, Doug. 1996. Conceptual origins, current problems, future directions. In *Comparative Perspectives on Social Movements*, Doug McAdam, John McCarthy, and Mayer Zald (eds.), 23–41. Cambridge: Cambridge University Press.

McCarthy, John D., David W. Britt, and Mark Wolfson. 1991. The institutional channeling of social movements by the state in the United States. *Research in Social Movements, Conflicts and Change* 13: 45–76.

McCarthy, John D., and Mayer N. Zald. 1977. Resource mobilization and social movements: A partial theory. *American Journal of Sociology* 82 (6): 1212–41.

McMichael, Philip, ed. 2010. *Contesting Development: Critical Struggles for Social Change*. New York: Taylor and Francis.

McMichael, Philip. 2012. *Development and Social Change: A Global Perspective*, 5th ed. Thousand Oaks, CA: Sage.

McNeely, Jeffrey A. 1991. Bio-diversity: The economics of conservation and management. In *Development Research: The Environmental Challenge*, ed. J. T. Winpenny, 145–155. London: Overseas Development Institute.

Megadiverse countries. http://www.biodiversitya-z.org/content/megadiverse -countries. Last updated November 2014.

Meyer, Carrie. A. 1993. Environmental NGOs in Ecuador: An economic analysis of institutional change. *Journal of Developing Areas* 27: 191–210.

Miller, Daniel, C., Arun Agrawal, and J. Timmons Roberts. 2012. Biodiversity, governance, and the allocation of international aid for conservation. *Conservation Letters* 6: 12–20.

Mills, C. Wright. 1959. *The Sociological Imagination*. New York: Oxford University Press.

Ministerio del Ambiente. 2014. Resultados de Socio Bosque. http://sociobosque. ambiente.gob.ec/node/44. Accessed January 27, 2015.

Ministerio de Relaciones Exteriores del Ecuador. 1993. *La Gestion Ambiental en el Ecuador*.

Minkoff, Debra C. 2002. Macro-organizational analysis. In *Methods of Social Movement Research*, Bert Klandermans and Suzanne Staggenborg (eds.), 260–85 Minneapolis: University of Minnesota Press.

Mitchell, Robert C., Angela G. Mertig, and Riley E. Dunlap. 1992. Twenty years of environmental mobilization: Trends among national environmental organizations. In *American Environmentalism: The U.S. Environmental Movement, 1970–1990*, ed. R. E. Dunlap and A. G. Mertig, 12–26. New York: Taylor and Francis.

Mittermeier, Russell A. 1988. Primate diversity and the tropical forest: Case studies from Brazil and Madagascar and the importance of the megadiversity countries. In *Biodiversity*, ed. E. O. Wilson, 145–154. Washington, DC: National Academy Press.

Movimiento Alianza PAIS. http://www.alianzapais.com.ec.

Multi Partner Trust Fund. Nd. Ecuador Yasuní ITT Trust Fund—Fact Sheet. http:// mptf.undp.org/yasuni. Accessed July 30, 2013.

Murphy, Gillian. 2005. Coalitions and the development of the global environmental movement: A double-edged sword. *Mobilization: An International Quarterly* 10 (2): 235–50.

Myers, Norman. 1988. Threatened biotas: "Hot spots" in tropical forests. *Environmentalist* 8 (3): 187–208.

Naples, Nancy A., and Manisha Desai, eds. 2002. *Women's Activism and Globalization: Linking Local Struggles and Transnational Politics*. New York: Routledge.

Narváez, Iván, Massimo De Marchi, and Salvatore Eugenio Pappalardo, eds. 2013. *Yasuní zona de sacrificio: Análisis de la Iniciativa ITT y los derechos colectivos indígenas*. Quito: FLACSO Sede Ecuador.

National Environmental Coalition on Invasive Species. 2011. http://www.necis.net/ intro-to-invasive-species/what-we-know/.

National Plan for Good Living. 2009. Change of paradigm: From development to good living. http://plan2009.senplades.gob.ec/web/en/change-of-paradigm.

National Plan for Good Living. 2009. Presentation. http://plan2009.senplades.gob .ec/web/en/presentation.

New York Flora Association. Nd. New York Flora Atlas. http://newyork.plantatlas.usf
.edu. Accessed on April 4, 2014.

O'Connor, James. 1973. *The Fiscal Crisis of the State.* New York: St. Martin's.

OPEC Annual Statistical Bulletin. 2013. http://www.opec.org/opec_web/static_files
_project/media/downloads/publications/ASB2013.pdf. Accessed November 15,
2013.

Parks in Peril. 2008. http://expomaquinarias.com. Accessed April 15, 2014.

Pearce, Stephanie. 2013. Chávez in the Americas: Increasing autonomy in Latin
America and the Caribbean. *NACLA Report on the Americas.* Summer, 41–44.

Pellow, David. 2007. *Resisting Global Toxics: Transnational Movements for Environmental Justice.* Cambridge: MIT Press.

Petras, James. 1997. Imperialism and NGOs in Latin America. *Monthly Review.*
December 1. http://monthlyreview.org/1997/12/01/imperialism-and-ngos-in-latin-
america Accessed July 1, 2014.

Pfaff, Alexander, Paulo Barelli, and Shubham Chaudhuri. 2004. Aid, economic
growth and environmental sustainability: Rich–poor interactions and environmental choices in developing countries. *International Journal of Global Environmental Issues* 4 (1–3): 139–59.

Pfeffer, J., and G. R. Salancik. 1978. *The External Control of Organizations.* New York:
Harper and Row.

Radcliff, Sarah A. 2012. Development for a postneoliberal era? *Sumak kawsay,* living
well and the limits to decolonisation in Ecuador. *Geoforum* 43: 240–49.

Rathke, Wade, and Marcos Gomez. 2013. Progressive victory, power consolidation,
or both? *Social Policy* (Spring): 18–23.

Redclift, Michael, and Colin Sage. 1998. Global environmental change and global
inequality: North/South perspectives. *International Sociology* 13 (4): 499–516.

REDMANGLAR. 2012. Acerca de Nosotros. http://redmanglar.org/sitio/index.php
?option=com_content&view=article&id=46&Itemid=27. Accessed October 27, 2014.

Republic of Ecuador. Constitution of 2008. Last updated January 31, 2011. http://
pdba.georgetown.edu/Constitutions/Ecuador/english08.html.

Rival, Laura. 1997. Oil and sustainable development in the Latin American humid
tropics. *Anthropology Today* 13 (6): 1–3.

Roberts, J. Timmons, and Amy Hite, eds. 2000. *From Modernization to Globalization:
Perspectives on Development and Social Change.* Oxford: Blackwell.

Rochlin, James. 2011. Development, the environment and Ecuador's oil patch: The context and nuances of the case against Texaco. *Journal of Third World Studies* 28 (2): 11–39.

Rodrigues, Maria Guadalupe Moog. 2004. *Global Environmentalism and Local Politics: Transnational Advocacy Networks in Brazil, Ecuador, and India.* Albany: State University of New York Press.

Rosen, Fred. 2013. What was created? What remains? *NACLA Report on the Americas.* Summer, 23–24.

Rudel, Thomas K. 2000. Organizing for sustainable development: Conservation organizations and the struggle to protect tropical rain forests in Esmeraldas, Ecuador. *Ambio* 29 (2): 78–82.

Rudel, Thomas K. with B. Horowitz. 1993. *Tropical Deforestation: Small Farmers and Land Clearing in the Ecuadorian Amazon.* New York: Columbia University Press.

Santacruz, Silvia. 2008. Correa confirms WFT, condemns eco-extremists. *Ecuador Mining News.* October 13.

Saul, Quincy, and Hugo Blanco. 2015. From indigenous struggle to ecosocialism. *Counterpunch.* http://www.counterpunch.org/2015/05/19/from-indigenous-struggle -to-ecosocialism/.

Sawers, Larry. 2005. Nontraditional or new traditional exports: Ecuador's flower boom. *Latin American Research Review* 40 (3): 40–67.

Sawyer, Suzana. 2004. *Crude Chronicles: Indigenous Politics, Multinational Oil, and Neo-liberalism in Ecuador.* Durham: Duke University Press.

Schnaiberg, Allan. 1980. *The Environment: From Surplus to Scarcity.* New York: Oxford University Press.

Schnaiberg, Allan. 2007. Draft for the second edition of the *Handbook of Economic Sociology.* Chapter 31: The economy and the environment. http://www .sociology.northwestern.edu/people/faculty/documents/schnaiberg/22 .ECONOMYYENVIRONMENT.pdf.

Schnaiberg, Allan, and Kenneth A. Gould. 1994. *Environment and Society: The Enduring Conflict.* New York: St. Martin's.

Schneyer, Joshua, and Medina Mora Perez Nicolas. 2013. Special report: How China took control of an OPEC country's oil. Reuters. November 26. http:// www.reuters.com/article/2013/11/26/us-china-ecuador-oil-special-report -idUSBRE9AP0HX20131126. Accessed March 28, 2014.

Seligson, M. A. 2003. *Democracy Audit 2001. Nashville: Vanderbilt University Latin American Public Opinion Project.*

Shandra, John M., Thomas K. Rudel, Michael Restivo, and Bruce London. 2010. Nongovernmental organizations and protected land areas: A cross-national analysis. *International Sociology* 40 (2): 85–99.

Smith, Jackie. 1995. Characteristics of the modern transnational social movement sector. In *Transnational Social Movements and Global Politics*, J. Smith, C. Chatfield, and R. Pagnucco (eds.), 42–58. Syracuse: Syracuse University Press.

Smith, Jackie, Charles Chatfield, and Ron Pagnucco, eds. 1997. *Transnational Social Movements and Global Politics*. Syracuse: Syracuse University Press.

Smith, Jackie, and Hank Johnston, eds. 2002. *Globalization and Resistance: Transnational Dimensions of Social Movements*. Lanham, MD: Rowan and Littlefield.

Smith, Jackie. 2008. *Social Movements for Global Democracy*. Baltimore: Johns Hopkins University Press.

Southgate, Douglas, Kenneth Frederick, Josn Strasma, Allen White, Lori Lach, John Kellenberg, and Patricia Kelly. 1995. *An Assessment of Urban Environmental Problems in Ecuador*. Columbus, OH: EPAT.

Staggenborg, Suzanne. 1998. The consequences of professionalization and formalization in the Pro-Choice movement. *American Sociological Review* 53 (4): 585–605.

Stahler-Sholk, Richard, Harry E. Vanden and Marc Becker. 2014. *Rethinking Latin American Social Movements: Radical Action from Below*. Lanham, MD: Rowman and Littlefield.

Stahler-Sholk, Richard, Harry E. Vanden and Glen David Keucker. 2008. *Latin American Social Movements in the Twenty-First Century: Resistance, Power and Democracy*. Lanham, MD: Rowman and Littlefield.

Tamayo, Eduardo. 1996. *La Riqueza de la Diversidad*. Agencia Latinamericana de Información. América Latina en Movimiento. http://www.alainet.org/es/active/43485. Accessed October 1, 2012.

Tamayo, Eduardo. 2011. Conservation International can no longer operate in Ecuador. América Latina en Movimiento. September 28. http://www.alainet.org/en/active/49758. Accessed October 2, 2012.

Tarrow, Sidney. 2005. *The New Transnational Activism: Movements, States, and International Institutions*. New York: Cambridge University Press.

Taylor, Bron, ed. 1995. *Ecological Resistance Movements*. Albany: State University of New York Press.

Taylor, Bron, Heidi Hadsell, Lois Lorentzen, and Rik Scarce. 1993. Grass-roots resistance: The emergence of popular environmental movements in less affluent countries. In *Environmental Politics in the International Arena,* Sheldon Kamieniecki (ed.), 69–89. Albany: State University of New York Press.

Taylor, Dorceta. 2009. *The Environment and the People in American Cities, 1600s–1900s.* Durham: Duke University Press.

"Teddy bear" carnivore emerges from the mists of Ecuador. 2014. http://www.theguardian.com/science/2013/aug/15/teddy-bear-olinguito-ecuador-carnivore. Accessed on November 5, 2014.

The Nature Conservancy. "Our History." 2014. http://www.nature.org/about-us/vision-mission/history/.

The Pachamama Alliance. 2012. *Sumak kawsay*: Ancient teaching of indigenous peoples. http://www.pachamama.org/sumak-kawsay. Accessed November 14, 2012.

United Nations. 1992. Earth Summit press release. Department of Public Information. New York.

United Nations Development Programme. 2013a. Extractive industries for sustainable *development.* http://www.undp.org/content/undp/en/home/ourwork/povertyreduction/focus_areas/extractive-industries/#. Accessed September 19, 2013.

United Nations Development Programme. 2013b. Human Development Report. http://hdr.undp.org/sites/default/files/reports/14/hdr2013_en_complete.pdf.

UN-REDD Programme. 2014. http://www.un-redd.org/aboutredd/tabid/102614/default.aspx. Accessed April 14, 2014.

USAID. 1993. Project completion report. EDUNAT III. http://pdf.usaid.gov/pdf_docs/PDABH424.pdf. Accessed September 26, 2012.

USAID. 1994. *Biodiversity Conservation and Sustainable Use: USAID Program Overview.* Washington, DC: Environment and Natural Resources Information Center.

USAID. 2003. 60 Years of cooperation. USAID/Ecuador. Quito, Ecuador.

USAID. 2006. Decentralization and Democratic Local Governance Project (DDLGP). Final report, vol. I, prepared by ARD, Inc. http://pdf.usaid.gov/pdf_docs/PDACI435.pdf. Accessed April 18, 2007.

USAID. 2010. Ecuador environment summary. http://transition.usaid.gov/locations/latin_america_caribbean/environment/country/ecuador.html. Accessed December 3, 2012.

USAID's days counted in Ecuador. 2014. AP Exclusive. http://www.nytimes.com/aponline/2014/05/09/world/americas/ap-lt-ecuador-usaid.html.

US Energy Information Administration. 2014. Ecuador. Last updated January 16, 2014. http://www.eia.gov/beta/international/analysis_includes/countries_long/Ecuador/Ecuador.pdf.

Varea, Anamaría, Ana María Maldonado, and Carmen Barrera. 1993. *Directorio Verde: Organismos ambientalistas en Ecuador.* Quito: Comité Ecuménico de Proyectos y Alemania: Central Evangélica de Ayuda al Desarrollo (EZE).

Varea, Anamaría, Carmen Barrera, Ana María Maldonado, Lourdes Endara, Byron Real, Victoria Reyes, and Guillermo Robalino. 1997. *Desarrollo Eco-ilógico.* Quito: CEDEP and Abya Yala.

Varea, Anamaría, Carmen Barrera, Ana María Maldonado, Lourdes Endara, and Byron Real. 1997. *Ecologismo Ecuatorial.* Quito: CEDEP and Abya Yala.

Walker, Jack L. 1991. *Mobilizing Interest Groups in America: Patrons, Pressions, and Social Movements.* Ann Arbor: University of Michigan Press.

Walton, John, and Charles Ragin. 1994. *Free Markets and Food Riots: The Politics of Global Adjustment.* Hoboken, NJ: Wiley-Blackwell.

Wapner, Paul. 1996. *Environmental Activism and World Civic Politics.* Albany: State University of New York Press.

Waterman, Peter. 2001. *Globalization, Social Movements and the New Internationalisms.* New York: Continuum.

Widener, Patricia. 2011. *Oil Injustice: Resisting and Conceding a Pipeline in Ecuador.* New York: Rowman and Littlefield.

Wills, Eliza, Christopher da C.B. Garman, and Stephan Haggard. 1999. The politics of decentralization in Latin America. *Latin American Research Review* 34 (1): 7–56.

Wilpert, Gregory. 2011. An assessment of Venezuela's Bolivarian revolution at twelve years. *Upside Down World.* http://upsidedownworld.org/main/venezuela -archives-35/2889-an-assessment-of-venezuelas-bolivarian-revolution-at-twelve -years.

World Bank. 1994. Biodiversity Protection (GEF). Ecuador-Biodiversity Protection Project. http://www.worldbank.org/projects/P007029/biodiversity-protection-gef ?lang=en. Accessed July 4, 2014.

World Bank. 2004. Environment at a glance: 2004 Ecuador. http://siteresources. worldbank.org/INTEEI/Data/20806987/Ecuador.pdf.

World Bank. 2006. Little Green Data Book. https://openknowledge.worldbank.org/ bitstream/handle/10986/14396/9780821398142.pdf.

World Bank. 2013. The Little Green Data Book. https://openknowledge.worldbank. org/bitstream/handle/10986/14396/9780821398142.pdf.

World Bank. 2014. Ecuador Overview. Last update November 5, 2014. http://www .worldbank.org/en/country/ecuador/overview.

270   References

World Bank. 2015a. Ecuador Data Profile and Latin America and Caribbean Data Profile. data.worldbank.org/country/Ecuador. Accessed August 20, 2015.

World Bank. 2015b. GINI Index. http://data.worldbank.org/indicator/SI.POV.GINI/. Accessed March 19, 2015.

World Bank. 2015c. World DataBank, Poverty and Inequality Database. http://databank.worldbank.org/data. Accessed March 19, 2015.

World Commission on Environment and Development. 1987. *Our Common Future (The Bruntland Report)*. Oxford: Oxford University Press.

World Resources Institute (WRI). 1994. *World Resources, 1994/95: A Guide to the Global Environment*. Oxford: Oxford University Press.

World Tourism Organization. 2013. Tourism highlights. http://www.e-unwto.org/doi/pdf/10.18111/9789284415427.

World Wildlife Fund (WWF), Center for Conservation Finance. 2003. Commercial debt for nature swaps. http://www.cbd.int/doc/external/wwf/wwf-commercial-swaps-en.pdf.

YASunidos. 2014. Buscará Respuesta de la CIDH a Dos Solicitudes. *El Universo*. http://www.eluniverso.com/noticias/2014/12/29/nota/4385116/yasunidos-buscara-respuesta-cidh-dos-solicitudes.

YASunidos. 2015. http://sitio.yasunidos.org/en/. Accessed January 29, 2015.

Zald, Mayer N., and Roberta Ash. 1966. Social movement organizations: Growth, decay and change. *Social Forces* 44 (3): 327–41.

Zibech, Raúl. 2014. Developmentalism and social movements in Bolivia. *Upside Down World*. http://upsidedownworld.org/main/bolivia-archives-31/5147-developmentalism-and-social-movements-in-bolivia.

Zorrilla, Carlos. 2011. Large-scale mining to test rights of nature in Ecuador. July 1. http://upsidedownworld.org/main/ecuador-archives-49/3105-large-scale-mining-to-test-rights-of-nature-in-ecuador. Accessed July 4, 2011.

Zorrilla, Carlos. 2014. Illegal arrest and illegitimate mining in Intag Valley. http://www.ejolt.org/2014/04/illegal-arrest-and-illegitimate-mining-in-intag-valley-ecuador. Accessed February 5, 2015.

Index